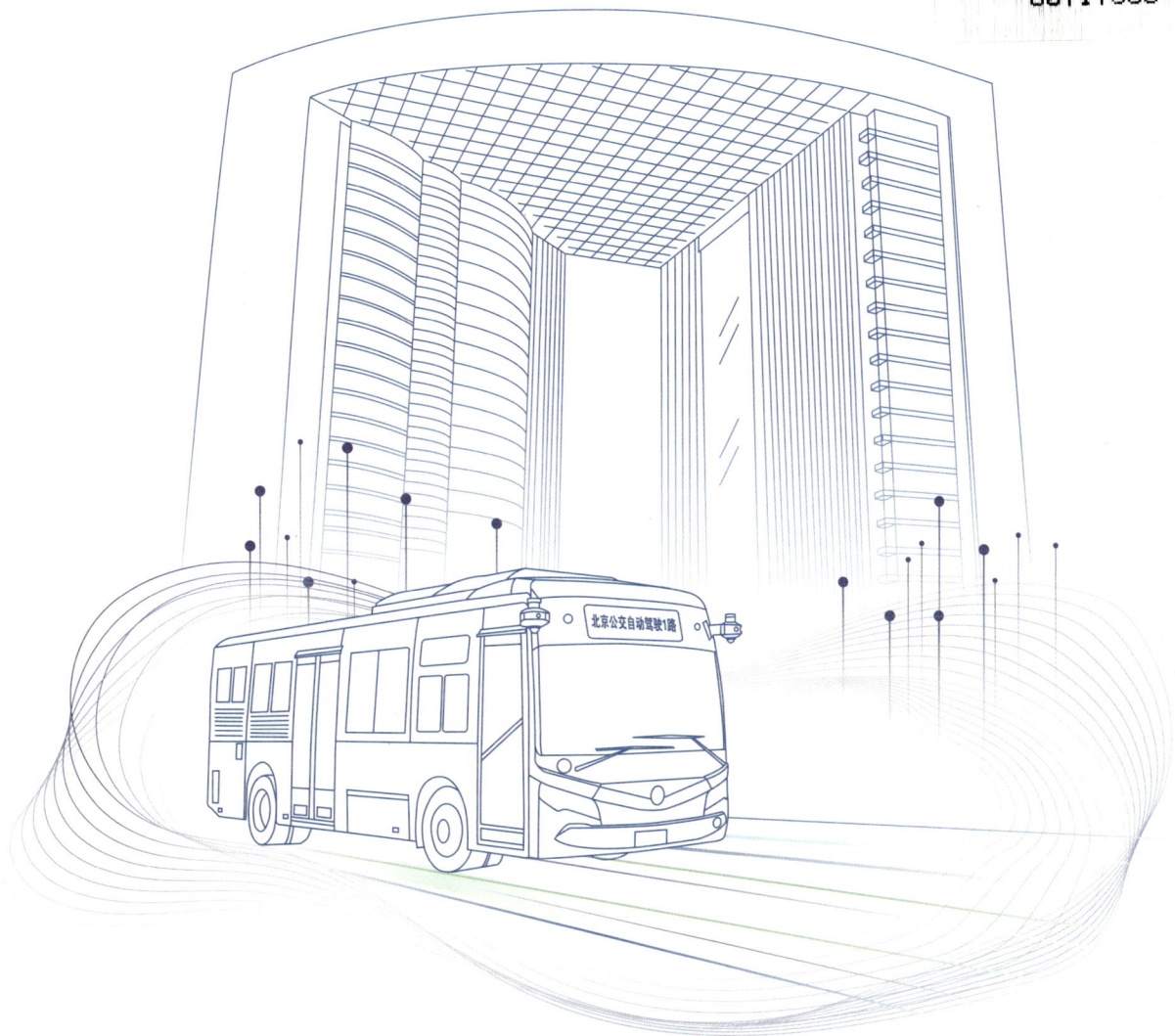

服务乘客是贯穿北京公交发展始终的主旋律，是北京公交人心中永恒的牵挂。精神有源，情怀有根。"一心为乘客"的口号出现于北京公交在新中国成立初期激情岁月里掀起的服务热潮。以此，为人民群众提供优质的公交出行服务蔚然成风，服务质量不断提升，劳模先进辈出，为北京公交增添了无上荣光，"一心为乘客，服务最光荣"的首都公交行业精神应运而生。与时代偕行，共促首都发展，北京公交人"一心为乘客，服务最光荣"的思想共识和文化情怀不变，新时代北京公交人赓续为民服务基因，在各自岗位上诠释责任精神，用真诚细致的服务和勇往无前的担当，为更多人提供更高品质的公共出行服务，让"一心为乘客，服务最光荣，真情献社会，责任勇担当"的企业精神历久弥新、熠熠生辉。

本报告设立初心传承、畅享出行、挺膺担当、相伴共享、未来可期五大篇章。初心传承篇章为今年创新设计的责任专题板块，前置突出2023年亮点工作；畅享出行篇聚焦运营服务主责主业；挺膺担当篇围绕重大活动、重要时刻运输服务保障；相伴共享篇关注社会公益与慈善；未来可期篇着眼前沿领域创新发展成果。

目录 CONTENTS

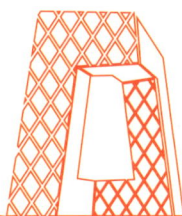

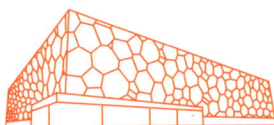

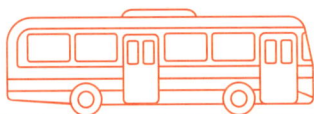

孩子们坐上通学公交，在安全与欢乐中放飞梦想

冬日的星夜间

夜班线公交车穿梭在街头巷尾

转角处，公交便民驿站为疲惫归家的人留了灯……

北京公交人的服务

是民有所需、我有所应的守候

北京公交人的光荣

是让更多人享受更好出行服务的坚持

向着未来

向着新的更大的光荣

北京公交将初心如一，一往无前

持续推动公交服务向高品质和多样化升级

用一流设施、一流技术、一流管理、一流服务

陪伴每一位乘客的出行和生活

奉献首都城市发展的日新与月异

让人民见证、让首都见证

新时代的公交精神，

依旧生生不息、光芒永续

卷首语

公交姓公，公交为民

北京公交为民服务的基因
内化为「一心为乘客，服务最光荣，
真情献社会，责任勇担当」的企业精神
从20世纪50年代的首次提出
到2023年的矢志不移，

驶过六十余载光阴
北京公交人的赤诚之心光芒未减
365个「一心为乘客，服务最光荣」的平凡日常
组成了不平凡的2023年

春日的和风里
「万人真情大调研」
用脚步丈量首都每一寸土地，聆听民意心声
夏日的大雨中
闻令而动、使命必达
「逆行」驰援京冀两地，与受灾群众同舟共济
秋日的朝阳下
一抹新绿装点求学路

我们的问候

一心为乘客，服务最光荣

1959年，北京公交首次提出了"一心为乘客，体贴乘客心"的企业精神。在企业精神的引领下，北京公交人积极开展业务练兵，大力提升服务质量，全国级、市级荣誉车组和先进个人不断涌现，北京公交成为劳模先进的摇篮，"服务"为北京公交增添了无限荣光。1988年，"一心为乘客，服务最光荣"被确立为首都公交的行业精神，从此激励着一代代公交人践行初心使命，投身到为人民群众提供优质公交服务的奋斗中去。

时代的发展日新月异，但北京公交为乘客服务的精神始终如一。伴随着首都城市建设的脚步，北京公交不断创新变革、转型升级，"一心为乘客，服务最光荣"的内涵日益充实。从"人跟线走"转向"线跟人走"，从"拉钩站牌"升级为"智能电子站牌"，从"扇子、白开水、小人书"的车厢服务延伸到"便民驿栈、超级充电站、共享停车场"的社会化服务。进入新时代，现代公交建设持续高位发展，优质公交服务产品分类多样，北京公交人一次次向乘客证明，"公交姓公，公交为民"的情怀分毫未变，"一心为乘客，服务最光荣"这最质朴又深厚的价值理念，具有最蓬勃不息的奋进力量。

东风浩荡疾驰远，大潮奔涌奋楫先

2023年，是全面落实党的二十大精神的开局之年，是全面建设社会主义现代化国家新征程的起步之年。这一年，我们牢固树立以乘客为中心的服务理念，打造高品质、多元化公交服务产品，引领公众出行方式，提升城市生活品质。这一年，我们全面贯彻新发展理念，坚持以新时代首都发展为统领，以创新驱动企业改革和高质量发展，主动融入新发展格局。这一年，我们挺膺国企责任担当，聚焦"七有""五性"，与利益相关方一道，携手绘就民生幸福画卷，共同谱写推动新时代首都发展的公交新篇章。

坚持乘客为本，我们用真情做优服务。扎实开展学习贯彻习近平新时代中国特色社会主义思想主题教育，"万人真情大调研"，深入社区、乡村和站台，用心倾听民需民意民声，积极推动调研成果转化落地；持续优化公交线网布局，增加线网覆盖134.2公里，方便313个居民小区出行；立足乘客多样化出行需求，累计推出品牌线路107条，丰富公交出行新体验；稳步扩大定制公交规模，新开定制公交428条（区位），共有定制公交660条（区位），新开多样化公交专线19条，共有多样化公交专线139条；精准回应乘客高频共性诉求，新开通医、通游专线，开行通学公交

> 深入践行'公交姓公'的政治属性和'公交为民'的服务宗旨,坚持'构建以轨道交通为骨干、地面公交为支撑、多种出行方式为补充,结构合理、衔接顺畅、便捷有序的综合交通体系'的发展方向,继续发挥好北京公交在首都交通运输保障工作中的骨干作用,持续擦亮北京公交金字服务品牌。

线路48条,服务学校21所,日出车达到100辆,日均运送学生4600余人次;贯彻落实京津冀协同发展战略,运营跨京冀线路38条,运营雄安新区常规公交线路20条、定制公交线路7条,着力构建京津冀交通一体化格局。

坚持守正创新,我们用改革推动发展。主动服务首都功能优化提升,创新延伸惠民服务,在行业内首创公交场站资源对外共享,开放公交便民驿栈30处,建成超级充电站18处,开放21处共享场站,提供366个错时共享停车位,初步形成规模化效应;探索发展公交行业新质生产力,超常规举措推进公交自动驾驶,取得首张大型普通客车自动驾驶路测牌照,2辆自动驾驶大型客车累计行驶里程突破4000公里;坚持人才强企战略,多措并举开展员工职业教育和人才培养,北京市公共交通技师学院获批成立,培育交通行业"大国工匠";积极推进博士后工作站建设工作,在站博士后来自清华大学、中国人民大学等院校,与对外经济贸易大学、北京交通大学达成联合培养博士后协议,建设走在世界前列的新型公交智库;持续深化国际交流,多渠道、多场景参与国际公共交通行业交流与合作,在世界舞台传播北京公交好声音。

坚持服务大局,我们用担当诠释忠诚。面对历史罕见的"23•7"特大暴雨洪涝灾害,北京公交闻令而动、使命必达,举全集团之力打赢防汛救灾攻坚战,全力保障受灾群众生命财产安全;秉持高度政治使命感,圆满完成第三届"一带一路"国际合作高峰论坛、夏季达沃斯论坛、全国两会等重大活动交通运输服务保障任务;深入开展内蒙古、西藏、新疆等地的支援合作工作,完成三个集体经济薄弱村年度"消薄"帮扶任务,巩固脱贫攻坚成果;打造交邮合作示范线,提高乡村物流运输效率,增强农村群众用邮幸福感,服务首都乡村振兴;贯彻落实绿色发展理念,加速老旧公交车辆淘汰,清洁能源和新能源公交车占比达94.7%,推进绿色低碳装备更新,加强充电桩、加氢站等配套设施建设,积极开展碳排放交易,共交易2.01万吨,实现净收益234.35万元,以低碳公交建设担当绿色发展使命,守护绿水青山。

接续奋斗,塑造新时代首都公交

2024年是落实党的二十大精神的重要之年,是中华人民共和国成立75周年,也是实现"十四五"规划目标任务的关键一年。奋斗是最好的传承,北京公交"一心为乘客,服务最光荣"的道不变、志不改,一以贯之、同心同力、苦干实干、接续奋斗,秉持"公交姓公"的政治属性,锚定"公交为民"的服务宗旨,坚决落实北京市委、市政府的重大决策部署,以轨道交通为骨干、地面公交为支撑、多种出行方式为补充,在服务新时代首都发展中勇挑重担,凝聚高质量发展的磅礴力量,努力打造国内领先、世界一流的现代城市客运出行综合服务商,在大潮滂滂的新时代争取新的更大的光荣。

北京公交集团党委书记、董事长

走进北京公交

关于我们

北京公共交通控股(集团)有限公司是以经营地面公共交通客运业务为依托,多元化投资,多种经济类型并存,集客运、汽车修理、旅游、汽车租赁、广告等为一体的国有独资大型公交企业集团。2020年4月,北京市委明确了北京公交"城市客运出行综合服务商"的战略定位。"十四五"时期,北京公交聚焦发展定位,确定了城市客运出行综合服务、汽车服务与贸易两大主业。

截至2023年底,北京公交资产总额665.77亿元,净资产457.22亿元,共有员工78936人,公共电汽车23385辆。常规公交线路1285条,运营西郊线和亦庄线2条现代有轨电车线路,定制公交和多样化公交专线799条[定制公交线路660条(区位),多样化公交专线139条],通学公交运营线路48条。共有二级企事业单位25个,其中,公益性企业14个,市场化企业9个,直属事业单位2个。2023年公共电汽车行驶里程11.51亿公里,年客运量20.87亿人次,承担着北京地面公交的主体任务。

报告期内,北京公交在社会、环境和治理(ESG)方面拥有良好的绩效表现。在治理(Governance)维度,拥有董事7人,女性董事占比28.57%,开展反腐败培训595场次,反腐败培训覆盖21837人次。在环境(Environmental)维度,开展碳交易2.01万吨,净收益234.35万元。在社会(Social)维度,安全生产投入22.98亿元,女性管理者占比41%,员工培训时长超1576688小时,开展志愿服务4.9万次。

企业文化

使命

让更多的人享受更好的公共出行服务

愿景

引领公众出行方式,提升城市生活品质,成为国际知名的现代城市客运出行综合服务集团

核心价值观

以人为本 乘客至上 创新发展 追求卓越

企业精神

一心为乘客 服务最光荣
真情献社会 责任勇担当

组织机构

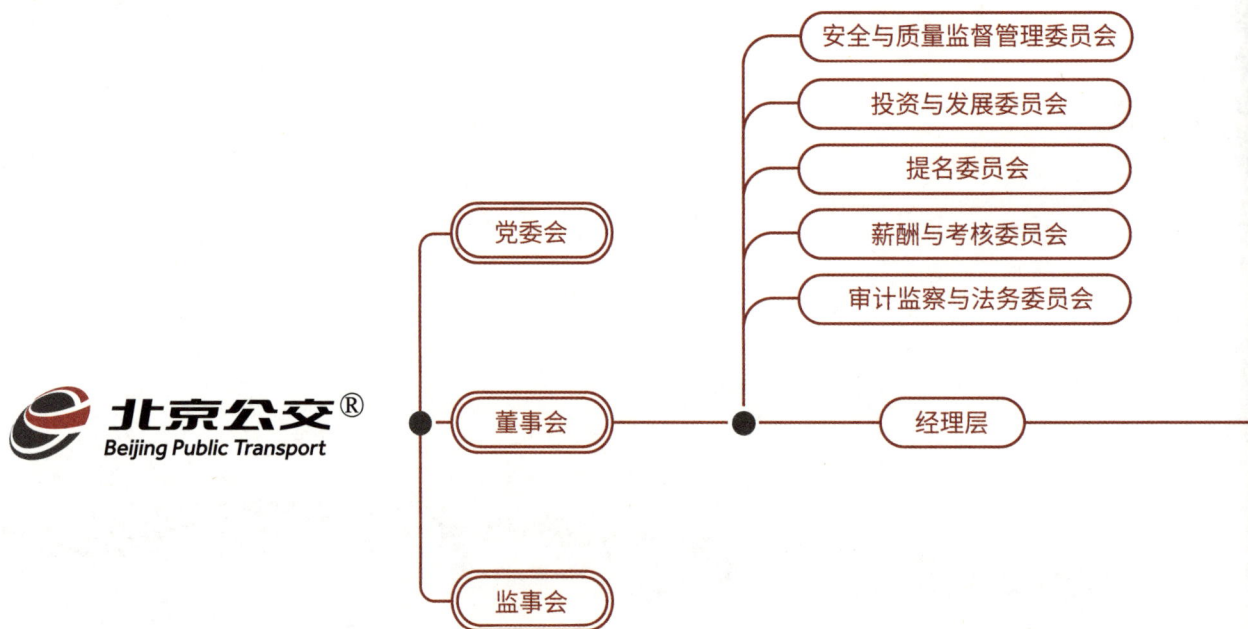

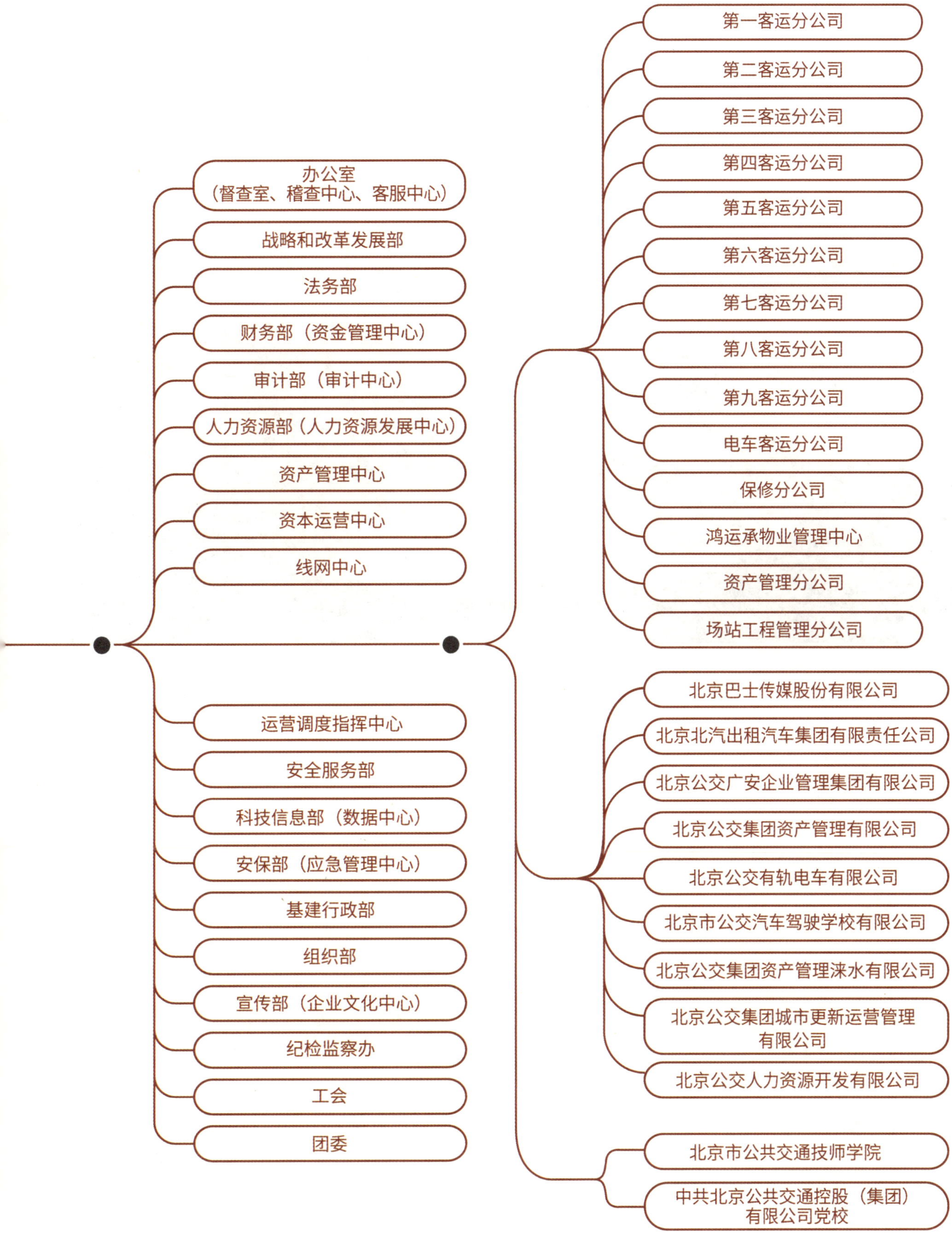

第一客运分公司

第二客运分公司

第三客运分公司

第四客运分公司

第五客运分公司

第六客运分公司

第七客运分公司

第八客运分公司

第九客运分公司

电车客运分公司

保修分公司

鸿运承物业管理中心

资产管理分公司

场站工程管理分公司

北京巴士传媒股份有限公司

北京北汽出租汽车集团有限责任公司

北京公交广安企业管理集团有限公司

北京公交集团资产管理有限公司

北京公交有轨电车有限公司

北京市公交汽车驾驶学校有限公司

北京公交集团资产管理涞水有限公司

北京公交集团城市更新运营管理有限公司

北京公交人力资源开发有限公司

北京市公共交通技师学院

中共北京公共交通控股（集团）有限公司党校

办公室（督查室、稽查中心、客服中心）

战略和改革发展部

法务部

财务部（资金管理中心）

审计部（审计中心）

人力资源部（人力资源发展中心）

资产管理中心

资本运营中心

线网中心

运营调度指挥中心

安全服务部

科技信息部（数据中心）

安保部（应急管理中心）

基建行政部

组织部

宣传部（企业文化中心）

纪检监察办

工会

团委

公司治理

北京公交坚持党的领导和完善公司治理机制有机统一,持续完善中国特色现代企业制度,构建先进的企业治理结构,不断提升企业治理体系和治理能力现代化水平,以战略思维谋划、推动企业高质量可持续发展。

党建领航

党委理论学习中心组开展集中学习

2023

- 召开党委常委会
  30次
- 研究议题
  236项
- 党员
  12903人
- 党支部
  369个
- 开展党建活动
  4428次
- 党建培训时长
  1223小时

坚持党的领导、加强党的建设,是国有企业的光荣传统,是国有企业的"根"和"魂",是国有企业的独特优势。北京公交深刻理解和把握新时代党的建设总要求,以坚定政治信仰为基石,持续深入学习宣传贯彻党的二十大精神,加强党建与生产经营管理深度融合,不断把国有企业政治优势转化为发展优势,推动党的二十大精神在北京公交形成生动实践。

我们深入学习贯彻习近平总书记关于党的自我革命的重要思想,把严的基调、严的措施、严的氛围贯彻到企业改革发展全过程。持续深化正风肃纪反腐,坚决惩治群众身边的腐败和作风问题。紧盯"一把手"和关键少数,围绕城市副中心线网优化、安全生产等重点任务强化监督,健全完善企业监督体系。锲而不舍落实中央八项规定及其实施细则精神,推进作风建设常态化、长效化。加强新时代廉洁文化建设,引导广大党员干部职工筑牢拒腐防变的政治自觉、思想自觉、行动自觉。

主题教育走深走实

北京公交坚持以习近平新时代中国特色社会主义思想为指导,以高度政治自觉和责任担当扎实开展主题教育,牢牢把握主题教育"学思想、强党性、重实践、建新功"总要求,深刻领会开展主题教育的重大意义,突出公交特色,制订工作方案,搭建形成"56741"工作任务,即学习教育体现"五个面向",调查研究做到"六个聚焦",高质量发展上突出"七个强化",检视整改围绕"四个方面",建立形成"一批"长效机制。同时,结合实际形成23项工作举措,制定领导班子主题教育周计划,细化主题教育任务清单,明确52项重点任务,形成了"总方案""周计划"和"任务单",一体推进理论学习、调查研究、推动发展、检视整改,确保主题教育取得实实在在的成效。

主题教育宣讲会

2023

主题教育期间召开党委理论学习中心组学习
167次

主题教育期间各基层党支部共组织党员学习
5211次

"万人真情大调研"活动解决意见建议
2756条

"万人真情大调研"活动推出惠民举措
460余项

治理机制

北京公交不断推进形成权责法定、权责透明、协调运转、有效制衡的公司治理机制,巩固提升法人治理水平。我们制定《北京公共交通控股(集团)有限公司董事会决策重点事项清单》和《北京公共交通控股(集团)有限公司董事会决策重点事项权限流程表》。严格执行"三重一大"决策制度,积极推进北京市国资委"三重一大"管控平台建设。印发《公交集团公司关于印发对标一流管理提升行动实施方案的通知》,全系统法人治理工作稳步推进,各级子企业董事会建设趋于完善,形成推动高质量、健康可持续发展的强大合力。

2023

召开董事会
11次

董事会讨论议题
69项

专委会研究议题
63项

召开经理办公会
26次

经理办公会讨论议题
202项

全面深化改革

北京公交坚持在改革中创新、在创新中发展，主动向前，积极谋划部署新一阶段改革任务，加快推进全面深化改革五年行动重点工作。同时，深入梳理总结国企改革三年行动以来的工作完成情况和工作经验，形成《北京公交集团关于国企改革三年行动完成情况和新一轮国企改革深化提升行动思路的报告》，以适应新的发展形势、政策要求和市场变化，形成全面深化改革工作合力，为建设国内领先、世界一流的现代城市客运出行综合服务商做出新的贡献。

法治公交建设

北京公交坚持以习近平法治思想为指导，持续深化法治公交和合规管理体系建设，不断提升依法合规经营管理水平和风险防范能力。我们印发《北京公交集团法治建设考核评价指标体系（2023年版）》，切实发挥关键少数作用，有效推动各单位法治建设第一责任人亲自协调、亲自督办法治建设的制度化和常态化。围绕"国家宪法日"等重点节点广泛深入开展法治宣传教育活动，践行普法责任，传递法治力量，积极打造法治公交文化，营造良好法治氛围。

我们进一步明确合规管理方针和"人人合规、事事合规、时时合规、处处合规"的合规理念，印发《北京公共交通控股（集团）有限公司合规行为准则》，组建北京公交集团合规管理员（合规联络员）队伍，推进合规管理"三张清单"编制与完善工作，召开"北京公交集团第一次合规联席（扩大）会议暨合规管理体系建设评估工作动员会"，顺利通过北京市国资委合规管理体系建设现场评估，全面推进集团公司合规管理体系建设。同时，积极推进标准化建设工作，制定《北京公交集团标准化工作三年提升计划（2023-2025年）》，开展世界标准日系列宣传活动，提高集团公司标准化水平。

合规管理员暨合规联络员大会

合规行为准则承诺书

"法治相伴"宣传线

2023

发布企业标准
12项

参与行业、团体标准
制修订
4项

发布法治动态
58篇

新获授权发明专利
4件

累计授权专利
75件

累计实用新型专利
60件

审计监督

北京公交充分发挥审计监督保障作用,为企业改革深化提升行动和高质量发展提供有力保障。我们全面落实企业内控监督评价"三年全覆盖"任务目标,切实加大监督评价检查覆盖力度。围绕企业中心和重点改革举措、经营管理和降本增效任务目标、重点基建项目和重大资金等,精准高效全面推进审计计划和工作落实。同时,加大审计制度法规宣传教育力度,落实技能知识培训,共组织专业线上业务知识培训12次,有效加强审计政策法规、上级指示精神相关工作信息的普及与传导。2023年,完成年度68项、166项次的审计计划任务,审计单位96家,出具审计报告167份,提出建议412条,为规范企业经营管理,促进企业内控体系建设和规范运行提供了有力保障。

社会责任管理

城市公共交通是重大的民生工程,是保证城市正常运转的"血脉"。百年公交,为公为民,始终坚定公益性服务,将社会责任理念融入企业发展战略和运营管理,建立健全社会责任管理体系,不断推动社会责任理念在公司内外落地生根,为经济、社会、环境等发展提供思路、贡献力量,以责任和担当铸就北京公交引领可持续发展的典范。

责任理念

在新的时代背景下,可持续发展已成为主流共识,联合国可持续发展目标(SDGs)旨在"为所有人实现更美好、更可持续的未来蓝图",北京公交始终胸怀"国之大者",不断在可持续交通领域创新实践、积极贡献,秉承"安全、方便、快捷、舒适"的责任理念,全心全意为乘客服务,让更多的人享受更好的公共出行服务。

北京公交责任理念与贡献的SDGs目标

责任管理

北京公交积极践行可持续发展理念,将环境、社会和治理(ESG)标准融入公司管理和生产经营,构建形成科学、专业的社会责任管理体系和清晰、透明的治理架构,社会责任工作更加体系化。同时,不断丰富社会责任信息的披露形式,精益求精提升社会责任信息的披露质量,传递北京公交的社会责任价值。

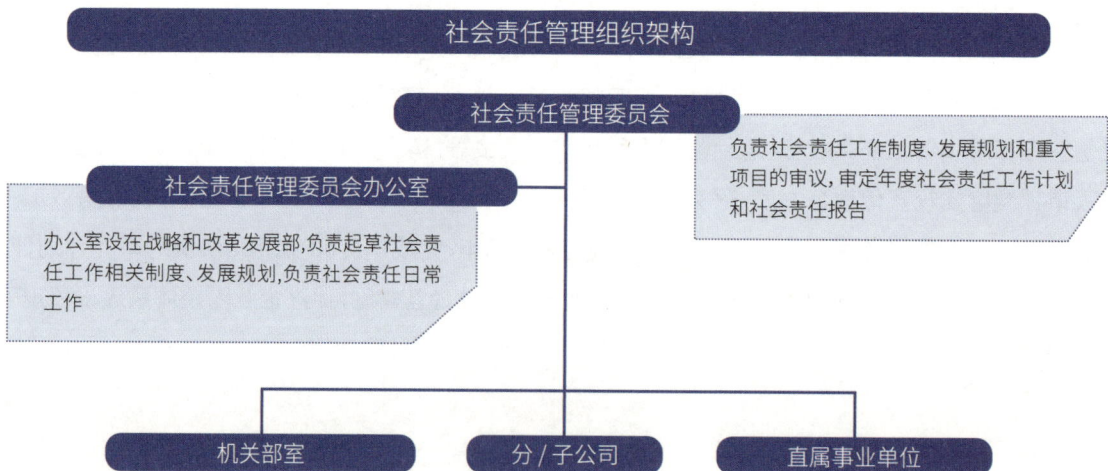

社会责任管理组织架构

社会责任管理委员会
负责社会责任工作制度、发展规划和重大项目的审议,审定年度社会责任工作计划和社会责任报告

社会责任管理委员会办公室
办公室设在战略和改革发展部,负责起草社会责任工作相关制度、发展规划,负责社会责任日常工作

机关部室　　分 / 子公司　　直属事业单位

责任沟通

责任沟通,创造价值。北京公交深知责任沟通已经成为各利益相关方对企业的一种期望,也是各方携手建立共识、创造多样价值的重要桥梁。我们通过实质性议题调研、"北京交通开放日"活动、新媒体渠道等,与利益相关方实现协同联动,并以社会责任报告全面呈现传递北京公交的责任担当和企业价值。

实质性议题

实质性议题体现组织对经济、社会和环境的重大影响。我们结合2023年行业发展环境和重要战略方向,对标国内外社会责任指南和标准,从"经济、环境和社会影响的重要性"和"对利益相关方评估和决策的影响"两个维度,识别出对集团公司和利益相关方都重要的实质性议题,并绘制实质性议题矩阵,为提升报告透明度和可持续发展管理水平提供了重要参考。

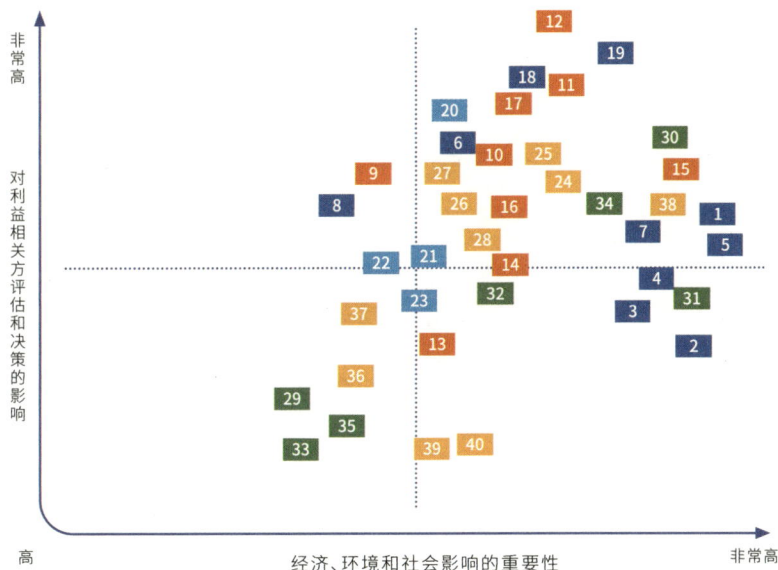

实质性议题矩阵

1.完善公司治理	11.公交服务便利性	21.提升应急管理能力	31.碳中和
2.加强党建	12.乘客满意度	22.强化安全管理	32.节能减排
3.依法治企	13.服务京津冀一体化	23.科技创安	33.绿色办公
4.贯彻宏观政策	14.科技创新	24.员工权益保护	34.应对气候变化
5.深化国企改革	15.数字化转型	25.平等雇佣	35.绿色环保公益
6.责任管理	16.重大活动和重要时期保障	26.职业健康管理	36.促进就业
7.党建引领	17.服务首都发展	27.员工培训与发展	37.乡村振兴
8.引领行业发展	18.保障乘客安全	28.员工关爱	38.应急救援
9.个性化服务	19.加强公共安全	29.倡导绿色出行	39.倡导文明出行
10.无障碍服务	20.培育安全文化	30.优化能源结构	40.志愿服务

注:2023年社会责任议题审核中,基于行业发展趋势和集团公司战略规划,我们提升了议题8"引领行业发展"、议题9"个性化服务"、议题12"乘客满意度"的重要等级。

利益相关方沟通

我们高度重视与利益相关方的沟通和合作,持续关注利益相关方的期望和核心诉求,通过多种形式的沟通渠道,积极主动回应各方的热切关注,为可持续发展管理注入源源不断的智慧与力量,与利益相关方一道共赴美好未来。

利益相关方	期望和诉求	回应方式
政府	守法合规 落实政府交通规划 服务区域经济发展 带动就业	合规运营与风险控制 依法纳税 主动接受政府监督 服务京津冀协同发展
乘客	优质贴心服务 保障出行安全	提供多样化出行服务 促进无障碍服务 乘客满意度调查 接诉即办 驾驶员行车安全培训 安全应急管理
员工	员工权益保障 员工成长发展 关爱员工生活	完善薪酬福利体系 工会、职工代表大会 职业健康与安全管理 开展员工培训 困难员工帮扶
行业/合作伙伴	遵守商业道德 促进行业共建	负责任采购 反不正当竞争 推进科技创新 与合作伙伴开展战略合作 组织开展行业交流
社区	加强社区共建 助力公益慈善	开展志愿服务 助力乡村振兴 促进社会就业 倡导文明出行
环境	遵守环境法律法规 保护环境	节能减排 推广新能源车辆 垃圾分类和"光盘行动" 倡导绿色出行 绿色公益

与首都机场集团签署战略合作协议

开展"万人真情大调研"活动

开展"小小公交驾驶员"职业体验活动

交邮合作运营服务

焦点·2023

1月
完成元旦、春节期间交通运输服务保障

王佐公交保养场完成生产布局调整并投入使用

2月
召开2023年党政工作会,对重点工作进行全面总结和安排部署

召开第三届职工代表大会第六次全体会议

以春季开学季为契机,持续开展"文明驾车 礼让行人"活动

3月
举办品牌线路建设暨T115路"创品牌线路 展巾帼风采"启动仪式,城市副中心首条女驾驶员专线T115路亮相

完成全国两会期间运输服务保障工作

承办第二届全国城市公交行业职业技能竞赛大客车驾驶员决赛

首次开通职工心理健康咨询热线,持续保障员工心理健康

与北京汽车集团有限公司签署《战略合作框架协议补充协议》,双方充分发挥各自优势,拓展合作内容,实现协同发展

柳芳公交便民驿栈投入运营

9月
试点开通通学公交线路

北京市公共交通技师学院获批设立

完成2023年服贸会交通运输服务保障工作

怀柔区H16路、H31路开展交邮运力合作

取得北京市第一张大型普通客车自动驾驶路测牌照,长8.5米、宽2.4米,配备19个座位的纯电动L4级高级别自动驾驶公交车开展公开道路测试

8月
支援定点帮扶村特大暴雨灾后恢复重建工作,公交技校为抗洪救灾驻守大堤的武警官兵提供后勤保障

首批100辆通学公交车交付使用

举办"大手牵小手 公交伴成长"暑期职工亲子体验活动

与北京金融控股集团有限公司签订战略合作框架协议,深化生态圈共同发展战略,以期实现优势互补、合作共赢

4月

房山区F82路、门头沟区929路作为第一批试点线路开展交邮运力合作

开展"4·26"世界知识产权日宣传教育活动

客九分公司、公交驾校、北汽出租集团等7家子企业参与"京企直卖——国企消费季"活动

举行第八届职工运动会、第五届职工文化节开幕式暨千人赏春健步走活动

5月

启动"万人真情大调研"活动

举办第二届"职工创新成果大赛",全力推进创新成果转化应用

作为国内公共交通服务领域数字化转型的典型代表参加2023年中关村论坛

纪录电影《一路幸福》全国上映

马官营公交便民驿栈投入运营

7月

"1921智享空间"新风街项目荣获西城区数字经济产业园区称号

举办2023年驾驶员"金、银方向盘奖"颁奖仪式

"北京地面公共交通运营服务标准化试点"项目获得首都标准化战略补助资金

有效组织"23•7"强降雨期间公交运营工作,全力以赴开展防汛救灾工作

《张家湾设计小镇公交服务提升实施方案(2022—2035年)》发布

6月

开展定制公交体验推广月活动

开展"润心送健康 助力乡村振兴"义诊活动

开放首批11处资源共享公交场站

与内蒙古巴林左旗签订防返贫基金协议,并捐款用于开展吸纳就业、公益岗位设置等帮扶事项

《地面公交运营调度指挥与车辆技术保障数字化转型应用实践》入选"2023全国企业数字化转型十佳案例"

首座超级充电站——木樨园超级充电站投入使用

召开第三届职工代表大会第七次全体会议

10月

与北京一轻控股有限责任公司签订战略合作框架协议,双方加大业务融合发展及资源共享,进一步扩大品牌联动的影响力,提高首都服务保障民生的能力和水平

北汽出租集团完成第三届"一带一路"国际合作高峰论坛交通运输服务保障工作

承办"轨道上的京津冀"职工职业技能竞赛决赛客运车辆驾驶员赛项

通过北京市碳排放管理平台上缴900741吨排放量,顺利完成年度碳排放履约工作

11月

延庆区Y16路开展交邮运力合作

完成通州全域公交站杆站牌更换工作

《北京公共交通控股(集团)有限公司"十四五"发展规划和2035年远景目标纲要》中期评估报告经北京公交集团第八次董事会审议通过,并报北京市国资委备案

12月

北京公交馆对公众开放试运行

与首都机场集团有限公司签署战略合作协议,共同探索打造"陆空"综合交通系统新框架

责任荣誉

北京公交集团、所属单位部分荣誉和奖项

北京公交区域智能调度改革项目荣获UITP大奖之特别荣誉奖

集团公司荣获国务院国资委主办的"国企数字场景创新专业赛"一等奖

集团公司绿色低碳发展实践入选国家生态环境部"2022年全国绿色低碳典型案例"（企业类）

集团公司入选全球数字经济大会第二届全国企业数字化转型高峰论坛"2023全国企业数字化转型十佳案例"

集团公司入选2023中国国际数字经济博览会首届全国企业数字化应用生态大会"全国企业数字化应用典型场景"

集团公司荣获"2022—2023年度全国企业文化优秀成果二等奖"

集团公司荣获"全国安全文化建设示范企业"称号

集团公司荣获中国设备管理协会授予的"2023年度碳达峰碳中和标杆企业"称号

集团公司荣获中国城市公共交通协会授予的"2022—2023年度城市交通低碳榜样单位"称号

集团公司荣获北京社会企业质量协会、北京能源学会、北京环境科学学会联合授予的"绿色创建活动推进单位"称号

集团公司《北京地面公共交通运营服务标准化"双体系"构建与运行的创新管理实践》等2项成果荣获第三十七届北京市企业管理现代化创新成果一等奖

集团公司《坚定政治方向 服务职工群众 奋力谱写北京公交工会工作新篇章——北京公交集团公司工会建设"五型"工会成果》荣获中国企业文化促进会颁发的"职工文化建设优秀成果一等奖"

客一分公司《品牌、管理、服务"三位一体"打造"细微真情"企业文化》荣获2022—2023年度全国企业文化优秀成果二等奖

客二分公司荣获中华全国总工会授予的"全国五一劳动奖状"

客三分公司"男子汉精神"文化品牌荣获全国交通运输"十佳文化品牌"称号

客三分公司第十八车队党支部入选"第二届交通运输行业基层党建创新案例企业类十佳案例"

客八分公司877路荣获"北京市青年安全生产示范岗榜样集体"称号

客八分公司防汛救灾青年突击队荣获"北京市青年突击队"称号

有轨电车公司西郊线荣获"第21届全国青年文明号"称号

北巴传媒公司参加城市交通媒体（广告）高峰论坛并荣获"最具影响力企业"称号

员工部分荣誉和奖项

客一分公司王昆荣获"首都最美志愿者"称号

客三分公司驾驶员崔志勇荣获"全国五一劳动奖章"

客三分公司陈萌、刘然，客四分公司郭森，客五分公司樊路彬荣获"首都最美志愿服务家庭"

客五分公司调度员崔嫚荣获"全国巾帼建功标兵"称号

客五分公司安保部郑达荣获"2023年第三届平安交通奋斗者·北京榜样"个人优秀奖

客六分公司驾驶员粘志宽荣获第三十五届"北京青年五四奖章"

电车分公司何少花荣获2023年度"全国五一巾帼标兵"、"国企楷模·北京榜样"敬业楷模、"强国复兴有我"首都国企职工宣讲比赛第一名

保修分公司一车间职工李跃华被交通运输部办公厅授予"全国交通技术能手"荣誉称号

客一分公司项硕、客二分公司章征、客三分公司李雪杰、客四分公司刘硕、客五分公司沈雪松、客六分公司赵昂、保修分公司董茁、物业管理中心郭志强、有轨电车公司张陈、公交党校顾惜荣获第五届"北京公交新时代青年榜样"称号

北汽出租集团敬清波、赵志国、李国庆、谢红革、李亮五名驾驶员荣获2022年度"北京榜样·京城的哥"称号

集团公司宣传部王超、张轩、李天赐报送的新闻专栏《一路同行》栏目，荣获2022年度北京市专业报刊一等奖

集团公司组织部张帅荣获"北京市组织系统优秀信息员"称号

HONOR

初心传承
续写新的荣光

响应联合国可持续发展目标

| 4 优质教育 | 9 产业、创新和基础设施 | 11 可持续城市和社区 | 12 负责任消费和生产 |

"一心为乘客、服务最光荣"，是责任、是担当、更是情怀。它穿越历史巷道而来，在一代又一代北京公交人的传承中生生不息，不断展现着源远流长的活力，流淌在一条条公交线路上，续写着北京公交人的一路荣光。北京，16个区，16419平方公里，北京公交的每次出发都与这座城市有关，与这座城市里千千万万的人们有关。民之所想，行之所向，赴之以往，我们用一份份真诚的心意，在纵横阡陌、昼夜穿梭中不断筑就北京公交为民"连心桥"。新时代的漫漫征程上，奉献的荣耀与奋斗的足迹依然会铺满前方的路，我们会一直以炙热的情怀与赤诚的服务守护人们日复一日的可贵日常，绘就为民服务的幸福画卷。

北京公交馆

BEIJING PUBLIC TRANSPORT HALL

一路同行, 服务您的每时每刻

光阴流转, 为民情怀不变; 行程万里, 服务初心如一。从晨光熹微到灯火阑珊, 从华灯初上到东方既白, 北京公交步履不停, 塑造着首都发展热土上的"纵横骨骼", 将声声民意浓缩进十米车厢, 用真情服务与您恒守相伴。

05:00

晨光熹微, 首班车驾驶员开始发车前的准备工作, 早班车出场唤醒城市生活

09:00

晴空万里, 定制公交随时出发, 朝着向往的方向, 去您想去的地方

12:00

正午阳光, 转角处的超级充电站让您出行无忧, 从容轻松

07:00

旭日东升, 通学公交准时等候, 护航学生平安到校, 在车水马龙中增添一抹绿意

10:00

艳阳高照, 北京公交馆里的驻足, 是一起见证, 一起回忆, 也是携手向前

15:00

风和日丽, 花开的季节, 邀您乘坐有轨电车, 沿着"最美西郊线"踏青赏花

17:00 ----------------------

日渐西斜,家门口的公交便民驿栈让您的生活所需,步行可及

21:00 ----------------------

夜幕深垂,错时共享停车位让下班回家的您不再"转圈圈"

03:00 ----------------------

长夜漫漫,深夜满负行囊的您,仍会听到一句"乘客您好"

19:00 ----------------------

暮色渐浓,晚高峰的智能调度中心,是城市公交幕后的"指挥家",虽不与您相见,但心系您的出行

01:00 ----------------------

灯光璀璨,夜班车为您带来另一种陪伴,悄然行驶中送您安全回家

07:00 日出破晓的期待

通学公交护航，温暖一路"童"行

迎着清晨的第一缕阳光，学生们带着新一天的雀跃，从四面八方齐聚通学公交的候车地。学生出行，往往牵动社会之心，汇聚社会关怀，也体现城市的公共服务水平，映射城市公共服务的人文温度。"构建首都中小学通学公共交通运营管理体系"是首都进入新发展阶段、解决特有问题的创新之举，是增进民生福祉的实事工程、暖心工程、惠民工程。民有所需，必有所为，北京公交充分利用自身资源和优势，担任通学公交的运营方并积极推进试点任务，助推首都通学公共交通运营体系高质量构建与运行，打造全国通学公交服务示范工程，建立"中国标准、首都特色"，让儿童友好与城市美好共成长。

2023年9月1日，我们在朝阳、海淀、丰台和西城4个区13所试点学校高质量开行通学公交试点线路，一人一座一带（安全带）、专线快速直达、各环节"手递手"衔接……通学公交的开通与运营让越来越多的学生和家长有了更加绿色、安全、便捷的通学新选择，有效缓解了学校周边交通拥堵问题。

试运行规模

试点校
13所

线路
25条

车辆
47辆

日均运送
1599人次

逐步扩大

试点校
21所

线路
48条

车辆
100辆

日均运送
4600人次

线路量身定制，精准对接每一位学生的需求

我们按照"一区一策""一校一策""一线一方案"的原则，开展乘车需求摸底、线路规划与站点设计，根据校方提供的到校、离校时间需求，综合考虑道路通行条件、安全行车要求、各站预订乘车人数等因素制定站间行驶时长和单程点，并通过"京通"小程序向乘车人公示每站发车时间，确保车辆准时准点到达。同时，针对不同道路与学生需求情况，推出8米和12米两款不同车型，在实际运行中，因地制宜进行选配，以提高资源利用率和通行效率。

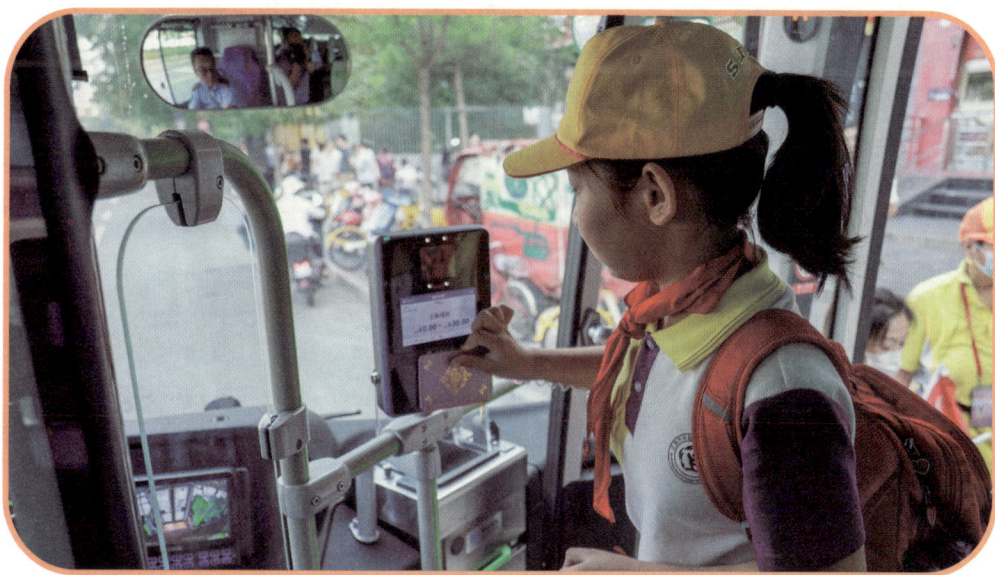

学生乘坐通学公交

安全至高无上,用心守护每一次到达

通学公交的开通运营,安全是第一要义。在通学公交设计之初,我们就将安全置于核心地位,确保每一个细节都充分体现出对安全的重视。在车辆选型方面优先选择具备卓越稳定性和精准操控性的车型,并在安全防护装置上作出充分的考量,不仅为车辆配备全面先进的安全应急预警系统,还采取整车内饰软化的处理方式,努力为小乘客们提供安全、舒适的乘车环境。

外观颜色

"春辰绿"为标志性配色,取自《阳春赋》中的"龙星正乎春辰",象征青春和希望

内饰设计

圆角化设计,无螺钉外露
阻燃材料防火防爆

车窗设置

上半部设推拉窗,防止学生将头、手伸出窗外

车门设置

"低地板、少台阶"的形式,上下车更安全便捷

行车安全

360度全景环绕摄像头、搭载侧向BSD盲区预警:彻底消除视角盲区

驾驶辅助预警系统:防止车道偏离、车距监测预警、限速识别

应急装置

防火安全舱设计:可构建起整车结构防火墙

安全应急开关:实现一键应急

自动开门断电:车内启动应急照明

座椅

全软包处理,配两点式安全带,有效防止碰撞

实时监测

防遗忘摄像头:如遇学生遗留车内会自动报警

巡检按钮:驾驶员巡视车辆确保无学生遗留

异常行为监测系统:对驾驶员疲劳驾驶等进行预警

完善应急预案

制定《通学公交车突发情况应急处置预案》，充分考虑学生乘客群体的特殊性，制定"8+1"种通学公交车可能发生突发情况的应对流程

健全管理制度

建立涵盖线路设置、运输管理、行车安全、应急运输、人员管理、车辆维保、信息化运维等方面共计26项相关制度

全程实时监测

智能化的技术实现实时定位，身份识别刷卡系统可以实现刷卡上下车数据比较，对学校和家长实现信息透明，并发挥运行监测平台的功能作用，确保各个环节服务人员做到"手递手"衔接

驾乘人员选拔

从内部择优选拔责任意识强、业务能力强、处置能力强、心理素质强的"精兵强将"

多措并举保障学生出行

同时，在试点开通前，我们逐一在线路、场站进行多次运输及应急演练，全面模拟学生上学、放学和应急转运等运输情景。我们的演练涵盖驾驶员、乘务员、调度员、学生、同乘家长、志愿者、学校老师等全角色，涉及运营车辆、调度平台、抢修救援等全要素，并着重在行车安全、服务流程、乘车组织、站台登降、手递手交接、应急处置等环节开展实操演练。针对车辆故障、应急疏散、倒乘转运和车辆救援等应急情况，我们遵循各关键岗位操作规程逐一演练，全面确保每一处细节精确到位。

开学季做好通学公交车安全检查工作

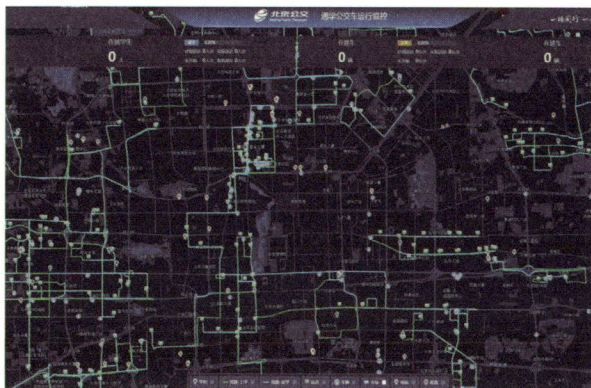

通学公交车运行监控

服务细致入微，只为通学之路更舒心

为给小乘客提供更细致入微的周到服务，我们选派具有亲和力的女乘务员随车，并专门进行理论实操培训，包括中小学生心理教育及沟通技巧，伤口包扎、海姆立克急救法等常见急救知识。同时，我们结合中小学生的学习特点和文化需求，不断增强广大中小学生乘车过程中的文化体验，配合试点学校围绕安全常识、国学文化、德育故事、传统节日、诗词歌赋五个主题对通学公交车进行车厢文化布置，让通学车成为流动的微课堂，实现寓教于行、融学于途。

舒适温馨的通学车厢

通学公交作为一项重要民生举措，试点以来在安全性、舒适性、便利性、准时性以及解决通学痛点、缓解学校周边交通拥堵等方面受到社会各界好评。中央巡回指导组、北京市委市政府、各相关委办局对通学公交工作都表示肯定，学校、家长为通学车服务点赞。

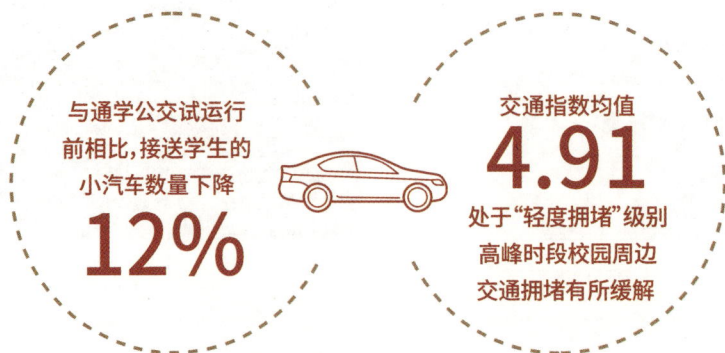

与通学公交试运行前相比，接送学生的小汽车数量下降

12%

交通指数均值

4.91

处于"轻度拥堵"级别
高峰时段校园周边
交通拥堵有所缓解

资料来源：北京市交通委

"北京公交在前期的线路踏勘、站点设置、配套设施优化、线上运行平台等方面全力配合推进,确保9月1日通学公交的顺利运行。通学公交运行以来,无论是家长还是学校,对北京公交的运行管理和服务都极为满意,给出了高度的肯定和认可。北京公交作为市属国有企业来运营通学公交,就象征着更加的规范和安全。同时,北京公交的乘务员和驾驶员都受过严格细致的培训,他们的服务态度和专业性给家长留下了深刻的印象,孩子们上下学路上很开心,大家也都很放心。"

——朝阳区教委通学公交专班负责人

"当走进多条线路跟车体验后,我通过所见所闻发现了通学公交的'魔力',孩子们都很爱乘坐,甚至还会'治'好孩子赖床的问题。此外,遵守规则、自我管理等能力的锻炼都发生在这小小的通学车厢里,很多孩子从这里迈出了独立出行的第一步。"

——北京日报记者手记

"刚开始我们没有选择乘坐通学公交,因为会有一些安全等方面的顾虑,后来小孩想坐我们就试了试,发现无论是便捷度、安全性还是费用等方面都挺好的,之前的顾虑也没有了,整体还是挺满意的。"

——首师大附属朝阳小学 学生家长

"我和周围的同学都特别喜欢乘坐通学公交,车上会有乘务员阿姨点名检查、帮我们系安全带,平时路上我们会在车上聊天、看书,很开心。"

——首师大附属朝阳小学 学生

10:00 感受岁月的馈赠

方寸之间的时光记忆

艳阳当空,驻足聆听,一眼便是百年。北京公交馆是约5000平方米的浓缩展厅,《一路百年》是公共交通与城市发展的对话融合,《一路幸福》是95分钟的光影记录,它们都珍藏着因出行服务、百年公交创造的城市集体记忆,映衬着北京公交人始终不变的为民初心。

时光守印记,旧物藏初心

北京公交馆

走进北京公交馆,感受百年奋进点滴印记,与人们一起见证岁月的力量,倾诉传承的意义,是新时代北京公交人与乘客建立连接的新方式。在这里,您可以踩响铛铛车,聆听百年前回荡在北京城的车铃响;也可以体验拉钩站牌,感受上世纪我们与乘客的"约定";您也可以通过科技加持,在光影变换间,见证公交线路如何从一条线编织成一张网,闪耀整座北京城……

我们沿着社会发展的主脉络,运用"人、车、线、票、站、事"六个载体,呈现百年领航、百年积淀、百年变迁、百年光耀、百年回忆、百年演进、百年铭刻、百年印记八个主题板块,全景展示北京公交与时代和城市共同成长进步的辉煌历程。同时,我们的北京公交馆是北京首家以地面公共交通为主题,集展示、收藏、研究、教育、互动于一体的综合性中型行业博物馆,将为北京建设"博物馆之城"提供有力支持。

在这里,6000余件馆藏物品,16辆主力车型,10余个互动区域,有声、有影、有物、有故事,通过全场景沉浸式交互、实物触感体验、数字化云游虚拟现实技术,将属于人民的记忆一一具象呈现。截至2023年12月31日,北京公交馆累计接待参观453场次,19651人次。

荣誉

荣获全国交通运输
"十佳文博馆"和"人气文博馆"

北京公交馆六个载体

案例：会"说话"的公交站牌

20世纪50年代，科技信息不发达，大部分乘客都没有手表，为了让乘客准确掌握首末车通过时间、避免空等，北京公交设置了"拉钩站牌"——站杆顶端有个圆形铁牌，双层铁牌中间夹有铁质弯箭头，红底白字写着"末班车已过"。晚上的末班车每到一站，售票员都会下车把铁钩拉出，次日头班车经过时，售票员会把这些拉钩再挑回，开始一天的正常运营。由此，老百姓有一句比较通俗的话形容叫"有钩没车，没钩有车"。一枚小小的拉钩，体现了北京公交人乘客至上、如约而至的价值情怀。如今，拥有电子显示屏的智慧站牌越来越多地出现在人们身边，站牌标识的信息也日益丰富，给乘客候车带来了极大方便。

拉钩站牌

首批参观市民在北京公交馆"打卡"留念

"我小时候最主要的交通工具是公交车，也很好奇第一代公交车是什么样子的，同时也很想看看北京公交这么多年的发展，所以就提前预约来参观。另外，我是从小听着李素丽的故事长大的，虽然没有坐过她的车，但是现在在北京公交馆看到她曾经工作的公交车，可以站在上边回想当年的场景，是一件很特别也挺不容易的事情。"

——首位参观北京公交馆的市民

一路百年，抒写城市记忆

回眸百年公交变迁，车轮滚滚见证着人民幸福生活，也触动着城市发展的集体记忆。2023年2月20日，纪录片《一路百年》在中央广播电视总台央视纪录频道（CCTV-9）开播，作为首个登陆央视的"北京大视听"110部重点文艺精品项目，以纪实影像的魅力尽显北京公交历史风采、见证城市发展变化，陪伴几代北京人成长的"大一路"第一次成为纪录片主角。影像透过"1路"公交车这个可视可知的窗口，顺着一个多世纪的时间绵延，从《初声醒故都》《旧城换新颜》《春光洒一路》《同住地球村》《一起向未来》，循序渐进讲述北京公交百余年的发展历史，在追寻集体记忆的同时见证时代变迁，让"历史的车轮"勾连古今，呈现北京这座古老而充满活力的国际化大都市的民生图景。

步履不停，道路一直向前，新时代北京城市故事和公交故事仍在继续，向着美好、向着未来。

《一路百年》纪录片

历经百年变迁，收获一路幸福

《一路幸福》电影主题海报

百年光影流转，北京公交一路同行，陪你长大，陪您变老，一起收获《一路幸福》，这是坚守在平凡岗位上的北京公交人不断进取、无私奉献、为民服务的初心故事。

2023年5月29日，纪录电影《一路幸福》在全国电影院线上映，影片通过独特的记录形式，真情倾诉，展现了一代代公交人为人民幸福出行奋斗的系列感人事件。随着影像的流动，我们会看到无数北京公交人的身影，无论寒暑、不分昼夜，用坚守和责任唤起了北京公交人时代发展的记忆共鸣，细数着美好出行幸福景象的来之不易，传递公交精神薪火相传的重要意义。电影公映以来，引起全国各地公交同行以及社会各界市民百姓的关注、认可和高度评价，票房累计580余万元。同时，被《"十四五"文化发展规划》重大文化工程项目国家影像典藏工程永久收藏，着力展示了北京公交现代企业形象。

荣誉

- 第九届中国嘉峪关国际短片电影展优秀纪录片
- 2023年第十九届中美电影节"金天使奖""年度最佳纪录电影"
- 第二十届中国（广州）国际纪录片节金红棉优秀纪录片复评（纪录长片部分）
- 第二届华语纪录电影大会文化历史类推荐作品、特别推荐剪辑奖

♥ 北京公交人的服务心声

"开公交车,是值得一辈子骄傲的事情"

——第一代无轨电车女司机 宋淑慧

幸福之路需要一心摆渡、全心守护,遥望历史巷道,幸福已在回响。北京公交的发展始于电车,如今为数不多的电车线路已成为不可替代的城市文化符号,对于城市和人民有着特殊纪念意义和价值。那么有轨电车是如何运行的?第一代无轨电车女司机是谁?那个年代的公交车是什么样的?为乘客服务需要注意哪些……这些问题,开了30年公交车如今已经90岁的宋淑慧老人都可以解答。

无轨电车"胡兰组"女司机宋淑慧

1951年,宋淑慧进入电车公司,并很快成长为一名让乘客喜爱的优秀售票员,对于当时的工作场景,老人仍然记忆犹新:"把乘客当亲友,乘客上车如到家,见面笑哈哈。'请您劳驾'在嘴边,介绍线路说快板。车上搁一碗水,起站落站,这碗水不能洒,要保持车子平稳,等等。"

无轨电车"胡兰组"女司机(后排左一为宋淑慧)

经过几年售票员的工作,由于表现出色,1954年,宋淑慧被推荐到驾驶班学习有轨电车驾驶,经过系统训练后,成为一名有轨电车司机。"有轨电车有轨道,遇到情况它只能慢慢减速停下,它没有方向盘,当时那车四面透风,车门是推拉的。它的车铃在脚底下,脚一踩'铛铛'响,所以才叫铛铛车呢。虽然它行驶速度慢,但驾驶起来没那么容易,由于够不到操纵杆,我干脆就站着开,一天下来两条腿都麻了。那个时候多艰苦啊,但我们热爱这份公交事业,内心很知足。到'五一''十一'时候,经过东单、西单、天安门,观礼台摆灯、摆花,站那儿开车特自豪、特高兴。"老人激动地说。

1958年,北京市政府发出了有轨电车无轨化的号召,无轨电车蓬勃发展。同年,中国工人在自力更生的精神鼓舞下,用一年时间手工打造出了中国第一辆无轨电车,驾驶国产第一批"京一型"无轨电车的十二姐妹的事迹被很多媒体报道,她们被分成两组,每6人一组,宋淑慧所在的组自己起名为"胡兰组",激励每个人克服困难,学习刘胡兰顽强不屈的精神。

"今天的一切都来之不易,新一代年轻的公交人要珍惜,好好练就本领,全心全意为乘客做好服务。公交车是城市的脸面,作为一名公交车司机值得骄傲和自豪。"老人坚定地说。在此,我们仿佛看到代代公交人挥洒激情与汗水,一路奋进砥砺前行的身影。

17:00 斜阳余晖下的港湾

便民服务,为美好生活"加码"

落日黄昏,一天的疲累即将结束,余晖笼罩下的城市重新热闹起来,市民的美好生活也正从公交场站不断向外延伸。始终把人民对美好生活的向往作为奋斗目标,在发展中保障和改善民生,积极构建有效的超大城市治理体系,努力让发展成果更多更公平惠及全体人民,是北京作为首都的特殊地位在社会治理工作方面的更高要求。北京公交以新时代首都发展为统领,找准定位、服务大局,高质量服务首都"四个中心"功能建设,着力提高"四个服务"水平,探索从"城市公共交通提供者"向"城市公共服务提供者"多元化转型,在打造"出行+生活"高品质公交出行服务的基础上,聚焦"七有""五性"民生所望,拓展公交资源的社会服务功能,更好满足人民群众对美好生活的需要。

我们坚持多谋民生之利、多解民生之忧,深入挖潜公交场站资源价值,践行公益资源为公众服务的理念,有序推进场站资源共享,在具备条件的公交场站开设公交便民驿栈,提供新能源车快速充电、私家车错时共享停车等便民服务,解决市民出行生活中"急难愁盼"问题,用心提供民生服务需求、持续补齐城市功能,实现为民生加码、为生活加温。

开设公交便民驿栈 **30** 处,客单量 **64.41** 万余人次

建成首批超级充电站,累计投运木樨园、柳村等 **18** 处场站
累计产生充电量 **259.82** 万度,累计订单数 **10.52** 万次

开放 **21** 处共享场站,提供 **366** 个错时共享停车位

公交便民驿栈，是风景也是人间烟火

北京公交积极响应首都一刻钟便民生活圈的建设需求，不断延伸服务触角，利用公交场站边角资源补齐社区便民服务短板。2023年3月31日，柳芳公交便民果蔬车项目启动试营业，标志着公交便民驿栈项目正式开始为市民提供服务。

我们组织专班统筹谋划，以社区居民的需求为出发点，周密考量、细致规划，遵循"建一处、成一处、稳一处、发展一处"原则，联合政府部门、社区等协同开展驿栈选址考察，在确保场站运营不受影响的情况下，选择社区集中、交通便利、便民服务相对缺失的地方，利用场站边角空间进行建设，以"缺什么补什么"为原则规划各类便民业态，让有限的空间发挥最大便民服务价值。同时，为了最大程度照顾到每位早出晚归市民的采买需求，我们将公交便民驿栈运营时间设置为早7点到晚10点，让更多的市民都能在公交便民驿栈感受到烟火气里的温暖与小确幸。

卖的是低价蔬果，算的是民生大账，体现的是责任与担当。未来，我们将持续探索便民服务的可持续发展路径，更多做到就地取材挖掘现有空间潜力，以社区居民需求为导向，不断丰富便民服务业态，努力把居民的"需求清单"转化为"满意清单"，通过贴近百姓"生活圈"，放大民生"幸福圈"，让更多市民享有更便利、更宜居的城市生活。

马官营公交便民驿栈

超级充电站成为车主的港湾

随着新能源汽车的逐渐普及，充电桩作为重要的配套设施，也越来越多地出现在我们的生活中。然而，使用新能源汽车，难免会遇到充电桩数量少、充电等待时间过长等各类"充电焦虑"问题。

为缓解市民的"充电焦虑"，2023年6月底，我们在木樨园公交场站投运的首座超级充电站正式对社会开放。我们充分利用场站的电力资源，向周边居民提供24小时小客车充电服务，切实解决周边社区居民电动汽车充电桩距离远、数量少的难题，让充电也可以像加油一样快捷方便，真正实现"充电一刻钟、畅行800里"。此外，我们还在每个充电桩上都配备了二维码，当前时段电价、服务费等信息一扫即现，充电桩屏幕上还会实时显示充电量、充电费用、充电电流、剩余时间等信息，一目了然，车主可以轻松完成自助充电。

除了为车主提供全天候的充电服务，我们还在超级充电站内搭建车主服务中心，并配备空调、座椅、微波炉、充电宝等服务设施，让每一个温暖的"细节"给车主带去"用心、暖心、贴心"的服务，让超级充电站真正成为车主的幸福港湾，为更多市民的绿色出行保驾护航。

木樨园隆瑞三优超级充电站

"这里确实挺方便的，不收停车费，半个多小时就能充满电，这个时间正好可以把午饭问题解决了，累了还能去车主服务中心歇会儿，有座椅、空调，还能接热水。"

——出租车驾驶员赵师傅

扫一扫，观看北京公交超级充电站向市民开放实时报道

错时共享停车，让停车不再"转圈圈"

夜已深，海淀田村半壁店公交场站相比白天安静了不少。这里，除了停放运营的公交车，还"挤出"20个小汽车车位，错时共享给周边居民，让社会车辆也可以"夜停晨走"，将公共资源"反哺"给社会，真正实现公共资源的惠民化。

我们以保障公交车辆安全运营为前提，开放公交场站内无法停放大型公交车辆的边角狭窄区域，于晚上停放周边居民的私家车，实现错时停车、共享共用，缓解停车供需矛盾，促进停车资源良性互动循环。同时，为保证错时共享停车的科学、有序管理，我们运用先进的数字化技术，提升停车设施的智能化水平，建立车辆信息、车位信息、支付信息等多种数据共享机制，精准对接停车供需双方，实现了由"人人管理"向"人机管理"的转变，并协调组织停车需求方、停车管理方、属地街道社区等各方共同签订《错时共享停车协议》，确保停车环境安全稳定，共谱错时共享停车"协奏曲"。

田村半壁店公交场站错时共享停车

"以前下班回家，要围着小区周边道路转圈寻找停车位。车停不下来，心就放不下来。现在，我在小区附近公交场站租了一个错时共享车位，开车回来再也不愁没地方停车了。"

——市民林先生

23:00 星夜归途的陪伴

深夜暖心线,守护夜归人

超大城市的夜晚依旧繁忙,有人带着憧憬出发,有人背着行囊归来。当首都北京在夜幕下继续着繁华与灵动,当这个城市中生活的人们在夜色里步履匆匆,北京公交用一路守护、一路服务,让每一份期盼都能到达,让首都的夜有了流动的光。

启程织梦,与你同行

1958年,为满足夜班工人上下班需求,我们开通两条夜班线路,北京成为全国第一座公交通宵运营的城市。20世纪90年代,夜班线继续扩充后达到15条。2014年起,我们重新规划建立了由37条"夜"字头线路组成的夜班线网,形成网状棋盘型格局。此后,夜班线路继续延伸,乘客在深夜的北京也可以实现自由方便的出行。如今,夜间出行承载的意义不断丰富,我们倾情打造"深夜摆渡"暖心线,让"一心为乘客,服务最光荣"的光辉本色在夜行的路上持续闪耀。

所念恰逢其时,美好如期而至

为了深夜里的等待不再漫长,我们统筹夜班线网规划,精准了解、悉心总结夜行乘客的出行与换乘需求,精益求精制定夜班时刻表,并加强信息化支撑,让乘客及时掌握车辆运营动态。严格选拔技术过硬、驾驶经验丰富的驾驶员,以责任和担当握紧手中的方向盘,并通过车辆驾驶员异常行为判别系统监测实况,让晚归的路踏实平安。同时,于细微处给予贴心服务,营造温馨的乘车环境,精心布置"温情暖公交""温暖回家路"等主题车厢文化,让乘客感受到北京公交的满腔热情和满心牵挂。

夜7路"深夜摆渡"暖心线

"温情暖公交"车厢文化

♡ 北京公交人的服务心声

夜色里的微光守护者
——夜7路驾驶员 吕振安

夜班驾驶员如同晚归路上的一盏灯，始终坚守在岗位上，用微光陪伴着都市夜归人。作为一名拥有多年夜班线路行车经验的公交驾驶员，吕振安见证了北京的发展和变迁，也目睹了这座城市夜幕中仍在奔波的深夜工作者的百态人生。

二十二载栉风沐雨，七十万里路和月。2001年，吕振安开始公交驾驶员生涯，2014年9月夜班车调整前夕，吕振安为了白天能够照顾瘫痪在床的父亲，主动申请开夜班车，就这样开始了他9年多的夜班车工作生涯，其间没有请过一天假、缺过一次班，坚持每日21:00前必到车队接班，做好发车前一切准备工作，直到23:20发车的那一刻。

常年行驶在两广大街上，吕振安的脑海里已经形成了这样一幅乘客图鉴："乘坐夜班车的有代驾司机、各大火车站换乘枢纽的乘客、去医院挂号就医的乘客、晚上喝酒的人、环卫工人、晨练人员以及来京游客等，我们会针对不同的乘客提供相应的贴心服务，比如对喝酒睡觉的乘客会进行到站提醒，随时观察乘客的状态及时提供所需等。"为了给乘客提供更加舒心、安心、暖心的乘车体验，吕振安所在的夜7路班组提炼形成了"三心三勤工作法""一个标准、二乐于、三看、四对待、五好操作"等工作理念和准则，大家都以细致入微的服务守护着每一个晚归的人。

"让乘客满意是我们夜班线驾驶员的目标，大家也是这么做的。"在北京公交，还有很多像吕师傅这样的夜班线驾驶员，他们每一次细微的服务都宛若夜空中的繁星，汇聚成了北京公交服务初心的璀璨星河，照亮了晚归的人们回家的路，温暖了城市的每一个角落。

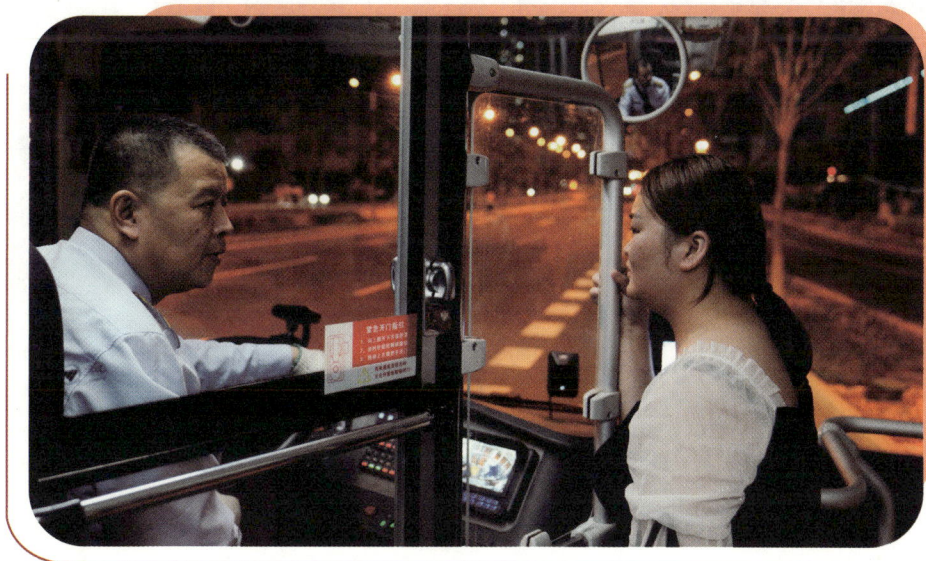

吕振安热心回复乘客问题

畅享出行

让生活更多选择

响应联合国可持续发展目标

| 9 产业、创新和基础设施 | 10 减少不平等 | 11 可持续城市和社区 | 12 负责任消费和生产 |

为了让每一次等待都有方向，为了让每一段路程都有陪伴，为了让人们的生活因出行而有更多选择，北京公交满载人民期许，始终与乘客同心同行，步履不停驰行在路上，求新求变推动转型与发展，用心用情追求卓越与品质，倾情守护每一个晨曦与日暮，在时光流转中谱写出为民服务的诗行，让用心服务落在千家万户的日常，让人们的生活因出行服务而更美好。

全面深化改革
全面建设社会主义现代化国家

全面从严治党
全面依法治国

北京城市副中心

XJ 011

咫尺繁华，举步通达

我们始终铭记"让更多的人享受更好的公共出行服务"的使命，用更多更优的出行选择，串联起城市里的每一个幸福站点，用不断升级的出行服务，让公共出行更有温度和质感。一路前行中，百年公交"老字号"焕发新颜，一条条高品质的品牌线路在新时代赓续城市文脉，让城市专属记忆与温情随着公交线网不断蔓延。

2023

○ 常规公交线路开调延
144条

○ 增加线网覆盖
134.2公里

○ 高峰车次兑现率
99.07%

织密城市出行"幸福网"

我们以提升乘客出行体验为根本，致力于构建地面公交优质线网，提升重点区域公交服务能力，推动与轨道协同发展，提高公交出行的可达性，让线网优化不断拉伸城市脉络、扩大人们生活圈。

—— 线网优化重点任务 ——

加强轨道接驳
- 微调390路接驳地铁14号线大井站，解决程庄路沿线就近接驳地铁
- 增设62路"莲花桥"公交站，实现轨道交通与地面公交高效接驳"无缝换乘"
- 通过新开、调整线路，增设站位等措施，实现轨道车站出入口换乘距离小于50米的公交站点占比达86%

优化微循环线路
- 新开专125路，解决郭公庄地区新建小区基础出行需求
- 新开S102路，方便马坡新城各小区居民日常生活需求
- 调整专155路、专189路线路走向，提升公交吸引力

有序推进准点工程
- 完善准发监控技术保障，完成680处场站、1105条线路站点新围栏的施划，提升车辆准发精准识别度
- 持续推动中途区段点管理，利用运营报表系统数据统计功能，对符合条件的线路全部设置中途控制站
- 加强定点班线表定正点管理，利用运营准点报表，实现对全日定点班线进行表定正点的管理和讲评

2021—2023年运营指标统计表

	指标	2021年	2022年	2023年
运营线路	运营线路总数（条）	1225	1299	1293
	常规公交线路条数（条）	1217	1291	1285
	常规公交线路长度（公里）	28579.7	30173.9	29738.5
	线网长度（公里）	7771.3	8180.6	8314.8
	站位数（个）	19262	20469	20792
优化线网	优化线路总数（条）	151	100	144
	减少重复线路长度（公里）	384.6	276	1069
	削减重复设站（个）	941	700	2099
	解决有路无车里程（公里）	142.7	82.5	134.2
	方便小区出行（个）	186	118	313

如约而至的专属出行

为满足乘客更多美好出行愿望,我们时刻关注当下的热点需求,持续创新发展定制公交,为乘客定制差异化、多样化出行服务。同时,创新数字化管理手段,联动多种新媒体渠道开展定制公交体验推广月活动,提升定制公交品牌认知度和用户参与度,实现通勤、旅游、日常休闲、短途接驳等不同场景全覆盖,让乘客体验"可以预约的公交",随时随地,随心出行。

开展定制公交体验推广月活动

2023

新开定制公交
428条(区位)

共有定制公交
660条(区位)

新开多样化公交专线
19条

共有多样化公交专线
139条

行驶中的定制公交

案例:打辆公交逛北京

旅游旺季核心区打车难、等车排队时间长是很多游客的感受,北京公交以提高核心区旅游客流保障能力为目标,打造横向协调配合机制,依托核心区巡游定制公交的业务赋能,以"错位式"发展为原则,进一步提升核心区出行服务保障能力和水平。2023年6月,客九分公司针对故宫景区神武门站位的团体出行游客,采取"导游+"的预约模式,推出核心区"动态优享"公交服务,游客可以乘坐巡游定制公交前往故宫及周边地区。巡游定制公交已覆盖28个大小区域,不少游客都选择"打公交"出行,旅游幸福感不断提升。

畅享品质出行

时光更迭，使命随行，持续提升服务是我们不变的初心。我们聚焦乘客多元化、高品质、交互式美好出行新向往，从满怀温度的巧思设计，到有规划有体系地倾情倾力打造品牌线路，已基本建立"标杆线路+品质线路+特色线路"的畅享公交品牌线路体系框架。未来，我们将打造完备的"10+100+N"畅享公交品牌线路体系，推出10条标杆线路、100条品质线路和N条特色线路，让公交线路成为流动的宣传站、移动的博物馆、运动的大讲堂，让乘客的每一次出行都成为美好的体验。

北京公交品牌线路体系

标杆线路
公交典型服务的代表，是公交服务的"代表队"，高品质服务的"领头羊"，包括"神州一路"领先线、"首善同行"示范线2个主题

品质线路
公交优质服务的代表，在服务、安全、运营某一方面具有突出优势，社会影响较大，是公交服务的中坚力量，包括"优质服务"真情线、"文明礼让"安全线、"敬老助残"爱心线、"便捷通勤"惠民线4个主题

特色线路
公交增值服务的代表，包括"守望中轴"文化线、"古都记忆"京味线、"远山呼唤"为民线、"深夜摆渡"暖心线、"法治相伴"宣传线、"巾帼建功"贴心线等15个主题

2023

累计推出品牌线路
107条

其中，1路、563路、141路、夜7路、5路、淼水线
荣获"全国优秀品牌线路"称号

案例：23路公交车全新涂装成为亮丽风景线

北京公交23路于1949年开线，是一条与新中国同龄、京味儿十足、文化深厚的老公交线路。2023年，北京公交对23路公交车的整体车身涂装穆桂英、赵云的京剧扮相及沿线北京历史风貌老照片，涂装后的车身颜色艳丽、绘画精美，行驶在道路上给人们带来十足的惊艳与震撼。如今，23路公交车已成为内外兼修的传统文化"流动展厅"。

全新涂装后的23路公交车

"神州一路"领先线

"远山呼唤"为民线

"古都记忆"京味线

"砥砺初心"教育线

"巾帼建功"贴心线

"守望中轴"文化线

案例：乘107路，寻古都记忆

北京公交以穿行于古都文化遗存、京味文化浓郁的107路为重点，打造"古都记忆"京味线，线路自西向东，穿过北京最有代表性的地标景点，钻进京味儿十足的胡同，融进繁华时髦的都市街景，串联起古城经典文脉。乘坐107路，一幅古都北京的画卷便会徐徐展开。如今，107路也已成为北京标志性打卡线路之一。

107路"古都记忆"无轨电车

乘客所需,事事有回音

倾听民之所需,笃行民之所盼。我们用矢志不渝的真诚坚守给予乘客温暖,全面启动"万人真情大调研"活动,用心用情用力解决乘客的"急愁难盼",持续深化"接诉即办",让每一个期盼都有回应,将优质、温馨的服务落到每一个平凡细微处,用为民服务的光辉本色照亮人们的出行之路。

万人奔赴,真情调研

行之力则知愈进,知之深则行愈达。2023年5月,我们以"用情访一线、用心听意见、用功解民需"为主题,精心设计"一图一表一卷一册一单"工作机制,以近1.3万名党员为依托,从繁忙场站走到偏僻站台,从大型社区延伸至边远山村,倾听乘客的烦恼与呼唤,聆听人民的殷切期盼。同时,我们依据调研实际对症施策,推出一系列惠民举措,畅通了市民出行"最后一公里",增强了广大市民乘客的获得感、幸福感和安全感。

2023

近**1.3**万名党员

走进村庄 **50**个

走进企业 **220**家

走进社区 **212**个

走进学校 **107**所

走进医院 **33**家

走进各级政府机构 **43**个

走进基层单位和站台 **333**个

召开座谈会 **620**场次

发放调研问卷 **3.2**万张

解决意见建议 **2756**条

━━ "万人真情大调研"工作机制 ━━

一幅"划片图",科学定调研
采取分区域包片负责制确定调研范围,按照街道、区域、性质等分级分层规划管理

一份"计划表",均衡定布局
近370个党支部覆盖近千个调研点位,既走入繁华市井街区,又延伸到最远山村、艰苦场站和偏僻站台,关照到更大范围的市民和乘客

一套"问卷题",真情察民意
编制对内对外不同需求的调研问卷,对外聚焦开调延线路、提升服务、建设驿栈等内容,对内突出关心员工、解决困难等内容

一本"清单册",用心解民忧
采取实地察看、现场发放调研问卷、线上调研、随机访谈、座谈交流等方式,充分吸收社会期盼、群众智慧和基层经验,形成调研"清单册"

一张"转化单",求实又问效
在"清单册"的基础上,逐条研究制定成果转化方案,上下联动,同题共答,推动调研形成闭环,确保取得实效和成果

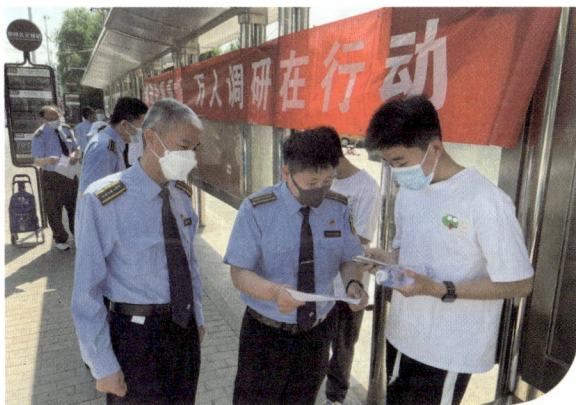

走进站台调研市民需求

走进社区主动问需

走进学校调研后增设校门口站位

倾听民需调整公交首末站

案例：调研搭建真情路·架起服务彩虹桥

2023年5月17日，电车分公司机关第四党支部在东城区东交民巷小学开展调研活动，通过深入了解倾听，在校师生希望增设103路台基厂站，从而减少学生上下学步行距离，节约出行时间。电车分公司通过实地踏勘，引入学生喜闻乐见的设计形式，6月9日，两处独具特色的彩虹站现身103路台基厂站，方便了学校师生的通行。看似一个简单的站位，架起了北京公交服务百姓的"桥梁"，打通了服务民生的"最后一公里"。

103路新设的"彩虹站"

"接诉即办"，细听每声期盼

坚守为民初心，真情温暖民心。我们竭力满足市民对美好出行品质的追求，深化"接诉即办"标尺作用，通过制定专项工作方案，落实联系服务群众制度，完善考核激励机制等，不断助力服务人员提升理论水平和业务能力。同时，深入分析诉求背后问题和乘客意愿，联动各方合力"解题"，做到接诉有响应、解决有举措、结果有把握，不断推动"接诉即办"向"未诉先办"转变。

北京公交客服中心

2023

乘客满意率
94.04%

投诉办结率
100%

"接诉即办"三率综合
99.83分

客户沟通（热线、信箱等）
263706次

畅通渠道，察情问需

我们坚守在出行的最前沿，作为乘客出行的贴心向导，为乘客提供准确、及时的信息，确保每一次出行都畅通无阻。我们以"每月一题"为重要抓手，深化上站台、进车厢等活动，深入一线听取并有效回应乘客诉求。健全7x24小时全时接听机制，即时解答乘客咨询，确保每一个来电都能得到及时、满意的回应。丰富新媒体平台矩阵，通过官方微博、微信服务号、微信员工号、抖音、微视等多种渠道，与乘客实时互动。邀请网络"大V"、抖音达人等实地探访，共同见证北京公交在设施改造、服务升级等方面的努力与成果，感受市民出行之便。

2023

接听96166热线来电
848265个

"进社区、上站台"工作调研，累计走访市民
1220次

倾心服务，温暖"美程"

为让更多人都能享受到更好的公共出行服务，我们持续提升整体服务质量，深入开展七项服务规范宣贯落实，积极开展站台秩序维护，大力开展车厢日常清洁工作，不断优化适老化出行的"软服务"和"硬设施"，以"有爱"助"无碍"，让每一次出行都充满关怀与温度，提高出行幸福指数，增亮民生幸福底色。

乘务人员清理车厢环境

帮扶老年乘客上车

2023

○ 组织
2.1万余人次

○ 集中清理车辆
9.6万余车次

○ 布置车厢文化线路
120条

○ 布置车厢文化车辆
3500辆

○ 收到拾金不昧表扬
11158件

○ 收到敬老助残表扬
4000余件

○ 帮扶老年人、残障乘客安全乘车
5.3万余人次

细微处见真情

精神绵亘，积淀文化

"一心为乘客、服务最光荣、真情献社会、责任勇担当"的公交精神，在一代代北京公交人的薪火相传中，形成了一套独特的企业文化体系，滋养着公交人锐意进取、阔步向前。客一分公司在百年公交精神和北京公交"同行"文化的指引下，提炼萃取出独有的"细微真情"品牌文化，倡导"人人讲精细，处处见真情"，这是新时代践行"一心为乘客，服务最光荣"的客一答案。

细微真情
XI WEI ZHEN QING

客一分公司细微真情文化品牌标识

致广大而尽精微

客一分公司从真情出发，精细设计线网优化的每一个环节，"以米丈量"确定站位地理坐标，竭诚为乘客排忧解难，当好乘客的向导和"活地图"，精益求精所有细节确保安全行车"零事故"。同时，不断深化员工对"细微真情"服务理念的认同感，推动企业文化"外化于行、内化于心、固化于制"，使"细微真情"文化内涵转化为员工的自我认同和行动实践，共同追求实现"真情客一、精细客一、品质客一"。

数智赋能,出行有"数"

我们主动拥抱数字化浪潮,加快数字化发展步伐,始终以乘客出行为核心,创新升级区域智能调度指挥和监控水平,构建数字化支撑体系,持续推动全面数字化转型,为乘客出行带来更智能的服务体验。

"智慧大脑"实现精准调度

我们通过信息化建设与运营管理的深度融合,持续深化区域智能调度的升级与转变,全方位提升智能调度水平,实现资源与效率更高效,运力与运量更匹配,满载与舒适更平衡,让出行脚步更顺畅,出行工具更智能,出行体验更美好。

提升区域智能调度水平

建立时刻表评价体系,完善行车计划辅助编制系统功能,提高区域调度模式下行车计划的编制质量

开发日常运营报表、实时监控报表等32张综合报表,通过数据报表高效分析及监控日常运营数据等信息

制定综合使用运力相关规则和流程,推进100组167条线路综合使用运力

缩减整合12处区域调度中心,不断提高调度集成化水平

加强运营讲评提示,强化对基层管理指导力度,全年组织开展20余次调度会,发布41期运营讲评、18期调度提示

不断升级优化智能调度系统,进一步适配区域智能调度模式下的多线路发车、多线路指挥和远距离监控场景

北京公交调度应急指挥中心

数字化转型踏浪前行

我们持续在智慧公交领域深耕细作,推动数字化建设提质升级,运用各类信息化技术手段监测预警网络安全态势,以数字化转型释放的强大势能,为乘客提供高效、安全的出行体验,切实提升人们出行的获得感、幸福感、安全感。

荣誉

- ★《地面公交运营调度指挥与车辆技术保障数字化转型应用实践》入选"2023全国企业数字化转型十佳案例"
- ★《基于数据中台的公交车辆资源使用仿真平台》入选2023年中国国际数字经济博览会首届全国企业数字化应用生态大会"全国企业数字化应用典型场景"
- ★"城市公交运营调度指挥和车辆技术保障数字化应用赋能"应用场景创新项目荣获"国企数字场景创新专业赛"一等奖

数字化转型不断升级

打造数字化业务中台,启动业务全面数字化建设

通学公交运行监测平台顺利上线,为本市中小学生提供高效、便民通学服务

建设智慧加燃管理平台,推动能源管理与结算的数字化转型

推进企业在线管控平台、人力资源系统、站杆站牌管理、大型活动指挥平台建设,数字化转型更加深入

完善发布数据安全管理办法,监测预警网络安全态势,预警并通报漏洞,封禁恶意IP 50余次,聘请网络安全专家推进网络安全及信息化培训

安全,我们比您更关心

作为公共交通的生命线,安全不仅是每一位乘客出行的最基本需求,更是公交系统稳定运行的基石,也是每一位公交从业者必须坚守的底线。北京公交坚持将安全理念深深植入运营的每一个环节,渗透至服务的每一个细节,携手各方共同构筑起安全、和谐的公共出行空间。

让乘客坐上放心车、安全车

我们深知每一次出行都承载着乘客的信任与期待,因此,我们始终坚守"生命至上、安全第一"的理念,以严格的标准和高度的责任心融入每一次驾驶、每一次检查、每一次维护,确保车辆处于最佳运行状态,让乘客在每一次出行中都能感受到我们提供的安全保障和殷切关怀。

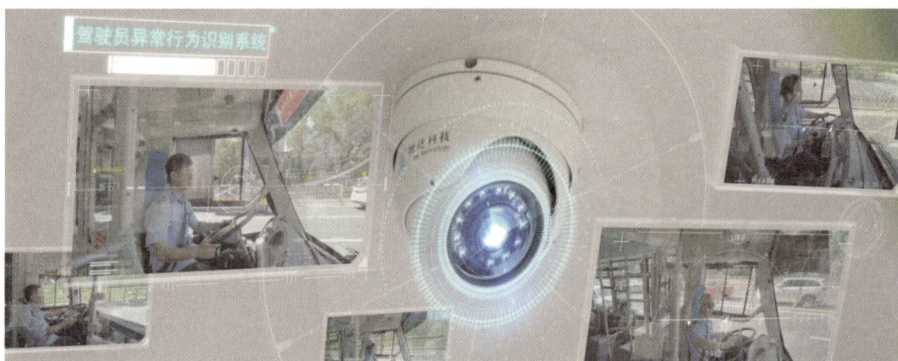

驾驶员异常行为识别系统

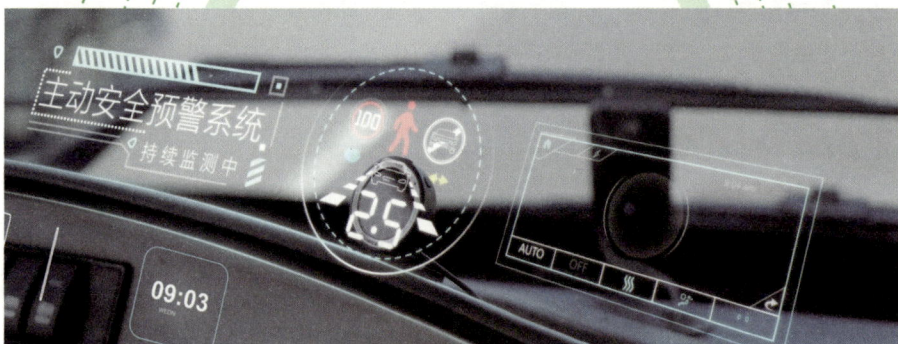

主动安全预警系统

智能语音安全提示系统

2023

○ 累计安装主动安全预警系统的车辆达到
1.1万辆

○ 安装驾驶员异常行为识别系统的车辆达到
1.3万辆

○ 累计为双层车、长单机等重点车辆安装A柱盲区透视预警系统
563台

○ 妥善处置运营车辆上的各类突发事件共
3762起

○ 涉及人员
4147人次

全方位强化行车安全预防管理 ///////////

- 根据公交专用道调整变化情况,总结线路途径道路通行规律,对新发现的风险点制定有效措施,及时修订行车安全作业指导书
- 强化行车安全预防管理,快速启动预案,主动应对低温寒潮、降雪天气对行车安全的影响
- 根据不同节日交通特点,开展季节转换、严格执行节日安全行车措施的教育,提高驾驶员特殊时期安全意识和适应能力

维车保运,车辆出行安全平稳 ///////////

- 开展"零中途"(指杜绝在线路运营途中发生故障坏车)活动,通过故障排查、消除安全隐患、树立一批"零中途"线路、班组、车组,提高基层车辆管控水平
- 优化完善保养制度、补充检查工具、出台隐患排查与故障诊断等相关培训教材,确保制度规范完善,杜绝机电安全事故
- 结合季节变化,针对不同时期开展季节性车辆保障,提高车质,为乘客提供更加舒适、安全的乘车环境

科技创安,推进行车安全转型 ///////////

- 推进技防系统用车改造和新车标配工作,为车辆安装主动安全预警系统、驾驶员异常行为识别系统
- 建立驾驶员多体征情绪感知设备定期通报机制,在176条干线安装安全智能语音提示系统
- 首创驾驶员行车安全数字画像,立足安全意识、身心健康、驾驶技能等五个维度近百项指标,科学精准识别驾驶员风险等级

科技赋能数智安防

"平安公交"装在心间

安全不仅是公交企业的责任,更是对乘客的庄重承诺。我们坚定不移地执行最严格的安全标准,深化各类隐患排查治理与应急演练活动,系统开展安全培训教育,培养员工高度的安全意识和专业的应对能力,同心齐力守护平安公交。

2023

安全隐患整改率达到 **100**%

修订二级单位突发事件应急预案 **438**个

开展各类应急演练 **6212**次

参与人数 **86232**人次

安全教育培训参与人数 **26.5**万人次

2021—2023年人防、物防、技防统计表

	项 目	2021年	2022年	2023年
人防 物防 技防	乘务管理员（名）	36679	31630	35803
	封闭电子围栏（处）	500	500	500
	一键报警系统（辆）	17271	21500	21354
	自动识别系统（套）	17249	24043	14500

稳固安全基础

- 修订《安全生产责任制规定》,落实新安全生产法,建立全员安全生产责任制工作要求
- 开展内部安全审计工作,强化安全生产事中、事后监管,全面提升全系统安全管理水平
- 完善场站安全管理,组织开展公交场站标志标线施划工作

隐患排查治理

- 修订《生产安全事故隐患排查治理管理办法》等制度,强化隐患排查管理
- 以安全生产和火灾隐患大排查大整治专项行动为抓手,全面消除各类火灾事故隐患
- 强化隐患排查系统,使用"企安安"填报解决各类隐患问题

加强应急管理

- 规范突发事件信息报送流程和内容
- 做好重点时期、汛期应急保障工作,完成"两会""一带一路"应急值守
- 开展火灾应急疏散、火情应急处置演练和"119"消防安全宣传培训体验活动

丰富安全培训

- 组织开展警企培训班,聘请外部专家等为安保管理人员授课,提升处置突发事件水平
- 组织开展年度安保专业管理人员培训班,依托"一个中心,两个基地",开展乘务管理员入职培训、能力提升培训

厚植安全文化土壤

安全文化源自于日常规范的养成、源自于一点一滴的坚持、源自于内心不可动摇的责任。我们持之以恒加强安全文化建设,多维度加强安全教育,常态化开展"金、银方向盘奖"表彰、"全国交通安全日"主题宣传教育、安全生产月等各类活动,营造良好的安全宣传氛围。同时,大力开展全国安全文化建设示范企业创建,有效提升企业安全文化水平,推动安全文化与企业生产运营的深度融合。

消防宣传月活动

案例:平安公交同心同向,鎏金十年致敬时代

2023年7月28日,北京公交隆重举行2023年驾驶员"金、银方向盘奖"十周年颁奖仪式。大会主题为"鎏金十年 致敬时代",十年来,共有1293名驾驶员获得"金方向盘奖",展现了北京公交安全管理锐意改革的十年,也是安全文化启智润心的十年。

"鎏金十年 致敬时代"2023年驾驶员"金、银方向盘奖"颁奖仪式

2023

全系统获得北京市安全文化示范企业荣誉称号的单位增至 **10**家

获得安全行车最高荣誉"金方向盘奖"的驾驶员 **168**名

获得"银方向盘奖"的驾驶员 **1055**名

安全生产知识竞赛活动员工参与人数达 **51096**人

2023

安全生产月系列活动共设置宣传站 **24**处

咨询台 **375**个

发放安全生产知识手册 **65443**册

接受乘客咨询 **21156**次

十年京津冀,协同共发展

京津冀协同发展战略实施以来,北京公交积极响应,落实京津冀交通协同政策,主动融入京津冀城市群建设,在公共交通出行领域先行先试,引领带动三地公共交通产业发展,努力建设与首都城市战略定位和京津冀协同发展相适应的地面公交发展新格局。"十四五"以来,北京公交确定"立足首都,服务京津冀,努力打造国内领先、世界一流的现代公共交通综合服务企业"的企业定位,十年蝶变,2500余公里跨市域公交线让京津冀联系更紧密,京津冀交通一体化从蓝图一步步变为现实。

服务京津冀交通一体化举措

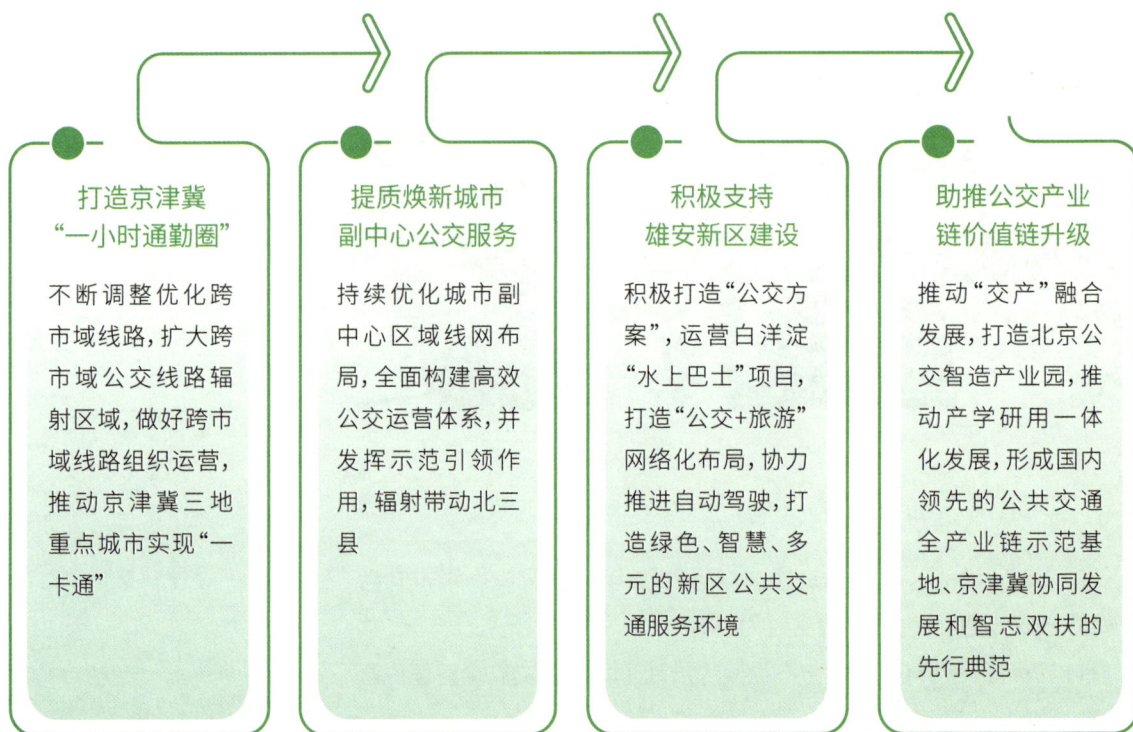

打造京津冀"一小时通勤圈"	提质焕新城市副中心公交服务	积极支持雄安新区建设	助推公交产业链价值链升级
不断调整优化跨市域线路,扩大跨市域公交线路辐射区域,做好跨市域线路组织运营,推动京津冀三地重点城市实现"一卡通"	持续优化城市副中心区域线网布局,全面构建高效公交运营体系,并发挥示范引领作用,辐射带动北三县	积极打造"公交方案",运营白洋淀"水上巴士"项目,打造"公交+旅游"网络化布局,协力推进自动驾驶,打造绿色、智慧、多元的新区公共交通服务环境	推动"交产"融合发展,打造北京公交智造产业园,推动产学研用一体化发展,形成国内领先的公共交通全产业链示范基地、京津冀协同发展和智志双扶的先行典范

案例:"水上巴士"带你畅游白洋淀

为大力支持京津冀协同发展战略,北京公交积极参与雄安新区建设,开展白洋淀水上交通项目,专门定制打造100艘LPG(液化石油气)画舫船、200艘生态木船。同时,成立白洋淀水上巴士调度指挥中心,搭建船舶安全保障集中监控管理平台,并配备应急船及安全员,提升白洋淀水上交通出行服务水平。如今的白洋淀水清淀蓝,乘坐更清洁的"水上巴士"畅游白洋淀已成为一种全新的旅游方式,在这里可以尽享人与自然的和谐之美。

运营雄安地面公交线路

2023

○ 跨市域公交线路
38条

○ 线路长度
2500余公里

○ 城市副中心全域运营
公交线路
178条

○ 雄安新区运营常规公
交线路
20条

○ 雄安新区运营定制公
交线路
7条

白洋淀"水上巴士"

北京公交
Beijing Public Transport
8130847
准乘84人

挺膺担当
我们风雨同舟

响应联合国可持续发展目标

3 良好
健康与福祉

11 可持续
城市和社区

大道之行也，天下为公。始终胸怀"国之大者"，担当使命任务，与各方守望相助、同舟共济，是北京公交的责任基因。作为这座城市的重要公共交通系统，北京公交始终承载着城市的脉搏，与首都同呼吸、共风雨，带着使命的呼唤出发，载着对承诺的坚守抵达。在每一个重要时刻，都以专业的素养和优质的服务，认真践行每一份职责，用心诠释大国公交的责任与担当。

无畏风雨，倾情守护

携手同行，才能无畏风雨。面对罕见强降雨，北京公交上下闻令而动，周密部署，沉着应对，全力做好降雨应对保障工作和乘客平安出行服务。在这场洪流之中，北京公交人用"逆行"而上的坚守，化身为守护城市的砥柱，成为这场暴雨之下最暖心的风景。经风历雨，终见彩虹。

吹响防汛救灾"集结号"

面对突如其来的极端强降雨天气，我们提早研判、提早部署，启动红色Ⅰ级汛情预警应急响应，以"时时放心不下"的高度责任感和更加科学、精准、有力的举措，统筹协调全系统高效应对，汇聚多方力量，充分发挥基层党支部战斗堡垒作用和党员先锋模范作用，全体员工拧成"一股绳"冲锋在前，坚决打赢防汛救灾的抢险攻坚战。

系统布置汛情应对

强化组织，健全机制

成立防汛指挥部，统筹协调三级指挥体系，严格落实领导带班制度。制定《公交集团公司2023年防汛工作方案》，指导全系统有效应对汛情

决策会商，多方联动

组织多部门、跨专业联合决策会商，协调市防汛办、市消防救援总队等专业力量开展专业抢险救援工作

加强调度，快速响应

加强线路监控和调度指挥，及时决策，果断处理紧急情况，采取停驶、区间、等停等措施，加大隐患排查整治力度，保障线路安全运营

集中力量，重点保障

提前构筑防汛保障力量，储备机动运力200余辆，合理布局130支（共354人）技术服务保障小分队，对116个重点场站、重点区域车辆进行强检回修，抢修救援中心调整救援布局，将救援力量向西部地区集中。系统摸排并储备充足的防汛物资

2023

出动防汛应急运输公交车
200 余辆

抢险车
50 余辆

应急抢修人员
1000 余名

坚守待命的各级管理人员
2000 余名

成立"党员先锋队、突击队、志愿服务队"
425 个

针对
466 条公交线路

采取临时调度措施
744 次

累计转移受困群众
2 万余人

在洪峰中勇当"逆行者"

越是风急浪高,越见中流砥柱。我们全力以赴防汛救灾,党员干部冲锋在前,勇当抢险救灾的"主力军",广大员工挺身而出,同心同力做好应急运输、车辆抢修、场站抢险、紧急转运等工作。"以人为尺"用脚丈量积水深度,冒雨逆行抢修救援涉水车辆,与风雨赛跑转运被困群众……北京公交人用自己的实际行动筑起了一道坚固的生命防线。

雨中救援被困群众

降雨险情下行驶的公交车辆

📄 **案例:"一个不能少,一个不能伤"**

2023年7月29日,以雨为令,北京公交进入应急状态,北京公交人冲在应急救援最前线。7月31日洪峰突然来袭,客四分公司第十一车队队长李洁一行4人被洪流拦在路边,焦急地等待还没回来的公交车。洪水仍在继续上涨,形势愈加危急,还有20辆车在路上,李洁心急如焚。有人想把没打伞的李洁拽进屋,她甩开手说,"所有车全部回来,我才能放心。员工一个不能少,乘客一个不能伤。"8月1日凌晨4点,当最后一辆公交车归队,李洁的眼泪哗地流了下来。

客四分公司第十一车队队长李洁指挥公交车驶进场站

齐心协力绘就"同心圆"

风雨无情人有情。我们按下生产"复原键"，全力以赴保障市民平安出行，力保线路快速通车，完成紧急转运任务，积极投身于抢险救灾工作，帮助受灾单位做好灾后重建工作，凝心聚力，攻坚克难，吹响复工复产冲锋号。

开展灾后恢复重建工作

转移受灾群众
紧急转运河北省涿州市码头镇码头村及北芦小区居民6000余人，转移K396次列车第二批滞留旅客400余名

恢复公交运营
有序推进465条涉险公交线路的恢复工作，满足市民出行需求

加快维修恢复
推进车辆机电安全排查、修复和场站信息化设备维修，对36处场站进行清淤，共计清理淤泥和垃圾600余吨

开展安全防护
加大场站消杀力度，强化食品安全管理，配齐配足防疫物资，组织志愿者前往受灾严重地区开展志愿活动

2023

累计慰问汛期受灾员工
4579人次

慰问抢险人员
6583人次

发动团员青年
1400余人次

开展志愿服务
80余次

转移受灾群众

灾后车辆清理

转移场站被困人员

清理场站淤泥

致敬 生命定格在防汛一线的公交人李万红

李万红生前工作照

2023年7月29日至8月2日,一场暴风雨席卷京城,山洪凶猛、交通受阻、人员被困……面对严峻考验,北京公交全系统迅速行动,穿越泥泞,无畏前行,基层车队员工昼夜驻守各个场站,李万红正是其中之一。

李万红是北京公交集团客八分公司第八车队行管员,近二十年的公交生涯中,她始终践行着共产党员的初心使命,扎根基层,恪尽职守,一心一意为乘客出行保驾护航。面对这场暴雨,李万红没有丝毫畏惧,主动请缨,与同事冒着风雨测量路面积水深度,观察周边环境变化,安抚乘客情绪,尽职尽责确保乘客出行安全。不幸的是,一场突发山洪让李万红的生命永远定格在了防汛一线,而此时距离她退休仅有两个多月时间。

在不幸遇难的那天早上,李万红一如既往地告别家人出门,绕道去接同事葛凤梅一起上班,聊天之际说到要站好最后一班岗,不给自己的职业生涯留下遗憾。面对李万红的主动请缨,她的同事也都习以为常,因为平常工作中的李万红也是这样一丝不苟、兢兢业业,但谁都没有想到这一去竟成永别。

进入公交行业近二十年,由于行业的特殊性,她很少能够与家人一起过团圆节,爱岗敬业的背后离不开家人对她的默默支持。在李万红儿子的眼中,母亲是一个对新鲜事物充满好奇的人,总是通过不断地学习提升工作能力,对周边所有人和物都抱有最大的热心与热情,在闲暇时间也会积极参与社区的公益活动,帮助社区老人和同事解决难题。

李万红将太多的时间交付给了工作和他人,自己的爱好和愿望只能为了这些她更在乎的事不断让步,她也曾想过自己的退休生活要怎么过,要多去看看祖国的大好河山,去体会不同的风土人情,可即便是这样简单的愿望,最终却也无法实现。

生命如阳,精神如光,即便短暂,亦能永恒。在这场暴雨中,李万红以生命赴使命,以己力护苍生,这座城市不会忘记她的付出,她的精神也会像她奉献一生的公交事业一样生生不息。

> 李大姐在平时总是冲在前、干在前,做的永远比说的多,当天能做完的事情从来不会拖到第二天,同事家中有事或者有什么难题的时候,我们都会去找她,她也很乐意帮我们解决问题,所以我们都叫她"热心李大姐"。这么好的人突然离去,我们至今还是接受不了。
>
> ——客八分公司第八车队葛凤梅

坚实保障，共襄盛举

我们以高度的政治使命感和责任感，勇挑重担，奋力前行，以全流程、全要素、高品质服务，确保重大活动保障安全有序高效，打造重大活动交通运输服务保障金字招牌，以首善标准高质量服务首都"四个中心"建设。2023年，我们以更高的站位、更严的标准、更大的力度，圆满完成第三届"一带一路"国际合作高峰论坛、夏季达沃斯论坛、全国两会等重大活动的交通运输服务保障工作。同时，多措并举做好重点地区运力保障，满足重要节假日人们的出行需求。

────── 重大活动保障措施 ──────

强化组织领导	精准细致筹备	平稳有序运营	安全服务到位
成立专项工作指挥部，召开动员部署会，全面梳理调度指挥、行车安全、应急值守、车辆维保等各环节流程	高标准选拔上会人员，全体签订保证书；全面摸排车辆设施，确保车质车安可靠；细化后勤保障，加强应急值守	加强指挥调度，启动重大活动保障行车时刻表；加强政治中心区运营线路管理	落实行车安全保障措施，强化驾乘人员安全纪律意识；加强巡查力量，重点地区现场值守；清理车辆站台，营造整洁环境

服贸会交通运输保障

国庆期间抢修救援车辆在核心区值守待命

北京公交人的服务心声

在服务乘客中展现"大国风采"

——北汽出租集团驾驶员 敬清波

"北京榜样·京城的哥"敬清波

城市交通是一座城市的"血脉",是城市的"流动名片",体现着城市的活力,承载着城市幸福感。公共交通服务人员作为交通服务最直接的窗口,他们的温情服务不仅直接提升乘客体验,更彰显着北京这座城市的温暖。

敬清波是一名来自北汽出租集团的出租车驾驶员,从业已经有16年了,说起与出租行业的缘分,敬清波感慨万千。最初是因为开出租时间相对自由,后来每日穿梭在城市的脉络之间,聆听着乘客的故事,每一次旅程都成为一段温馨而独特的相遇,这让他感受到了这份工作带给他的成就感和满足感。

用微笑和真诚传递城市的温暖和美好,每一个眼神交流、每一次点头示意,都为乘客带去信任和尊重,这种默契让敬清波的出租车里充满了和谐与温暖。敬清波是一个细节控,行驶过程中他会及时调整车内温度,让乘客感受春风拂面般的关怀;避开拥堵的路段,让旅程更加顺畅;时刻关注路况,确保每一次出行都安全无虞。"当我手中握紧方向盘的时候,我的心中就只有安全二字",这不仅是敬清波的内心独白,也是他外化于行的深刻实践。正是由于他的安全驾驶观和优质的服务理念,在北京奥运会、APEC峰会、"九三"大阅兵、中非合作论坛北京峰会、第三届"一带一路"国际合作高峰论坛等重大国际活动的保障一线都有敬清波的身影,他说:"这么多年能为国家举办的各种重大活动提供交通运输服务,我感到非常的幸运和自豪。"

用心服务每一位乘客是敬清波心中永恒不变的追求。"在我心中,每一位乘客都值得以最大的热情去服务,把每一位乘客安全、准时送到目的地是我们驾驶员最大的满足。未来,我将继续用真情服务乘客,续写更美好的'的士乐章',展示'北京榜样·京城的哥'的新时代风貌!"

"远山呼唤"为民线——富合线，保障"悬崖上的村庄"富合村群众出行，助力实现"村村通"。

相伴共享
幸福触手可及

响应联合国可持续发展目标

1 无贫穷	3 良好健康与福祉	5 性别平等	7 经济适用的清洁能源	8 体面工作和经济增长
10 减少不平等	11 可持续城市和社区	12 负责任消费和生产	13 气候行动	

一切为民者，则民向往之。身处社区之中、社会之内，北京公交始终秉承公交是人民的公交，车行万里，丈量民生。行之以躬，让人们净享低碳交通，助力城市发展宜行宜居；"村村通"公交畅通城乡路，用心守护民生温度，提升各方生活幸福指数；携手更多利益相关方群体共创可持续发展的美好图景，不断奏响公共出行的首善交响曲，让每一份善意能落地、有实效、可持续。

低碳环保,风景在路上

环境就是民生,青山就是美丽,蓝天也是幸福。北京公交牢固树立和践行"绿水青山就是金山银山"理念,以绿色发展为根本,坚持公交优先、绿色优先,编制并发布《公交集团公司碳达峰行动方案》,积极调整车辆结构,推进节能减排行动,不断构建绿色出行体系,助力打造低碳交通城市,描绘美丽中国的绿色底色。

2023

○ 公交充电站
251处

○ 已投运充电站
219处

○ 已建成充电桩
1727台

○ 已投运充电桩
1457台

○ 共有新能源车
16832辆

○ 清洁能源车
5242辆

○ 清洁能源和新能源公交车占比
94.7%

○ 启用加氢站
4座

氢燃料公交车

新能源充电站

"绿色公交"赋能美好出行

我们坚持绿色低碳发展理念,激活公共交通新能源引擎,推动车辆能源低碳化、车型小型化、车辆装备智能化,让公共交通发展更有韧性、更可持续。同时,加强充电桩、加氢站、智能电子站牌等配套设施建设,为乘客提供更加便捷、绿色、智能的出行服务。

2023

- 能源消耗总量
  453639吨标准煤
- 能耗强度
  3.94吨标准煤/万公里
- 开展碳交易
  2.01万吨
- 净收益
  234.35万元

- 入选生态环境部2022年全国绿色低碳典型企业案例
- 荣获中国设备管理协会"2023年度碳达峰碳中和标杆企业"
- 荣获中国城市公共交通协会"2022-2023年度城市交通低碳榜样单位"称号

类别	2021年	2022年	2023年
新能源车（辆）	13529	15137	16832
天然气车（辆）	7607	6799	5317
柴油车（辆）	2216	1557	1236
电力能源使用量（万度）	53208	37817	49345
天然气能源使用量（万公斤）	18414	15786	16329
柴油消耗量（万升）	7172	5113	6758
节电（万度）	7047	3862	4248
节气（万公斤）	940	338	334
节油（万升）	202	157	204

2021年 2022年 2023年

让蔚蓝天空成为永恒

我们积极贯彻落实碳达峰碳中和目标，牢固树立"以节能为己任，以节能促发展"的管理理念，科学制定能耗计划，挖掘数字价值提高能源利用效率，加强环境污染监控工作，强化日常节能减排管理和节能降耗培训教育，通过多维度多途径降低能源消耗、减少污染，为城市天空的一抹蔚蓝做出积极贡献。

2021—2023年污染物排放统计表

指标	2021年	2022年	2023年
碳排放量（吨）	288376	246261	280353
二氧化碳排放量（吨）	1057378	902957	1027962
氮氧化物减排量（吨）	123.41	57.05	236.86
颗粒物减排量（吨）	0.17	0.13	0.20
碳氢化合物减排量（吨）	80.78	30.72	60.21

低碳出行，共赴绿色之约

我们深耕绿色低碳出行服务场景，积极培育绿色出行新优势，满足乘客环保出行需求，聚力提升低碳出行服务。同时，以低碳环保理念为指引，广泛开展绿色环保行动，在全社会营造绿色低碳出行氛围，引导绿色出行成为风尚。

━━ 积极倡导绿色生活理念 ━━

推进绿色办公
全面落实"三体系"工作措施和"三不准"车辆制度，减少生产运营过程中的污染排放，不断提高绿色办公区域覆盖面

落实垃圾分类
提高生活垃圾分类收集、运输规范化水平，开展"混装混运"专项整治工作，开展多种形式的垃圾分类宣传培训

开展场站清洁
以"爱国卫生运动"等为契机，定期开展场站环境清洁活动，彻底清理场站及所属单位办公环境的卫生

推广绿色宣传
在重点路口、站台等开展世界无车日宣传、发放宣传册、秩序维护引导等活动，倡导文明乘车、绿色出行

2023

○ 环保培训
53589人次

○ 参与"桶前值守"活动比例达到
100%

○ 安装技防设施桶站
170个

开展"绿色出行宣传月活动"

每个人都有无限可能

员工与企业相向而行、共同成长、彼此成就，是企业行稳致远之基、永续发展之道。我们将员工视为企业最宝贵的财富和持续发展的不竭动力，致力于为员工创造一个充满信任、包容和激励的成长环境，让每位员工都能在工作中发光发热，真正实现员工个人理想与企业发展的"同频共振"。

员工权益落实落细

我们始终坚信员工是企业发展的内生动力，充分尊重并保障员工的各项权益，严格遵守《中华人民共和国劳动法》等法律法规，坚持为员工营造公平、包容的职场环境，不断畅通员工诉求表达渠道，通过有竞争力的薪酬体系及丰富的福利保障，留住并吸引更多人才。

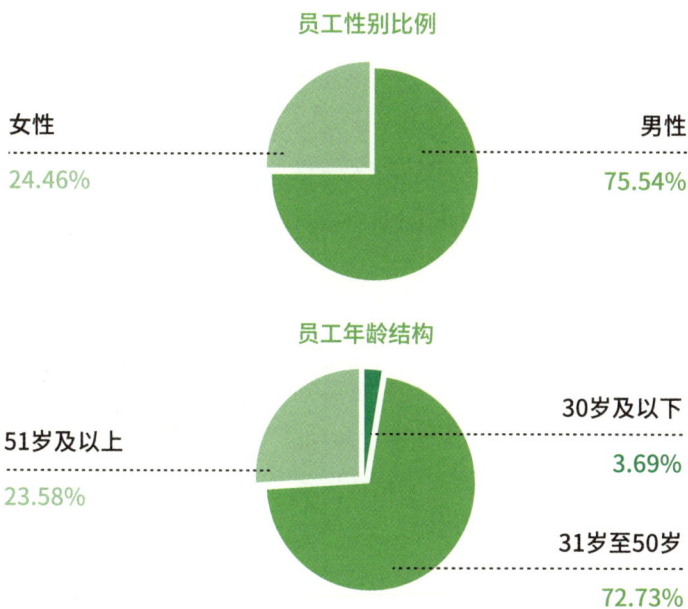

员工性别比例

女性 24.46%　男性 75.54%

员工年龄结构

51岁及以上 23.58%　30岁及以下 3.69%　31岁至50岁 72.73%

2023

吸纳就业人数 **1009**人

员工劳动合同签订率 **100**%

社会保险覆盖率 **100**%

人均带薪休假天数 **11**天

女性管理者比例 **41**%

开展员工座谈沟通会 **183**场

参与沟通 **5713**人次

■ 构建公平、尊重的工作环境

坚持公开招聘、公平发展的原则，严禁一切形式的强迫劳动和雇佣童工，严格落实《北京公交集团工作场所反暴力、歧视、性骚扰管理办法》等制度文件，为员工提供公平的发展机会，营造开放包容的工作氛围。

■ 完善薪酬福利体系

坚持足额、按时为员工缴纳五险一金，不断优化薪酬和激励政策，深化收入分配改革，与员工共享发展成果。

■ 持续推进民主管理

召开集团公司第三届职工代表大会第六次、第七次全体会议和第二次联席会议，定期开展员工代表座谈、专项检查、优秀提案征集等活动，不断激发广大员工参与企业管理的热情。

成就员工价值

企业的发展源于每个员工的劳动和创造。我们重视员工的长远发展,全力推进员工技能培训,持续深化劳动技能竞赛,以赛促学赋能员工成长。同时,积极搭建创新平台,激发员工创新活力,打造人人皆可成才、人人尽展其才的生动局面。

强化培训赋能

我们印发技能认定、在线学习平台管理、工作室建设等培训制度,持续开展岗前、适应性、职业化、专业技能等各类培训项目,不断加强员工素质能力建设,为处在不同职业和人生发展阶段的员工提供多样化的学习机会和资源,鼓励员工在职业道路上不断前行。

拓宽发展路径

我们不断深化劳动模范、职工创新工作室、技能大师工作室的创建,出台创新工作室联盟章程。同时,不断完善技能认定体系,形成司、售、调、保及保洁员五大工种体系,积极搭建涵盖"无等级—初级—中级—高级—助理技师—技师—高级技师—特级技师"的"新八级工"体系,为员工的成长和发展提供广阔的空间和平台。

培养技能人才

我们印发实施《公交集团公司深化职业教育体制机制改革总体方案》,制定实施《技能人才培育行动计划(2023—2025年)》,开发制作高技能人才培训课程,并推动各客运分公司形成"2023年高技能人才培训方案",让技能之美、工匠精神继续大放光芒。

2023

- 新增国务院特殊津贴、全国交通行业技术能手
  1人
- 培训
  15万人次
- 培训时长超
  1576688小时
- "公交云课堂"App累计激活用户
  77879人
- 累计组织考试
  899次
- 累计参考人数达
  5462641人次
- 完成驾驶员高级企业新型学徒培养工作
  1931名

2023年北京市职工职业技能大赛

职工创新工作室

案例:用创新成就职业梦想,让发明点亮公交人生

北京公交集团第二届职工创新成果大赛自2023年1月启动,共有922个创新项目参与报名。本次大赛通过展示各类创新成果实用价值及使用方法,切实增强了员工创新成果的应用转化力度,在赛场内外营造了浓厚的创新氛围,为广大员工成长成才、创新创造搭建了更加宽广的舞台。

公交集团第二届职工创新成果大赛决赛暨颁奖礼

案例:北京市公共交通技师学院正式获批成立

2023年9月5日,北京公交在北京市公共交通高级技工学校的基础上设立北京市公共交通技师学院,填补了首都城市公共交通领域技师学院的空白。自启动技师学院筹建以来,北京公交积极打造长阳校区、清河校区、王佐实训基地"两校区一基地"的办学格局。经过筹建,技师学院硬件设施水平显著提升,专业培养能力全面提高,专业结构更加合理。先后开设汽车驾驶、交通客运服务和汽车维修3个高技能人才培养层级专业,年均培训员工超2万人次,在校生人数超过3000人。

北京市公共交通技师学院

倾心关爱，情暖员工

我们重视每一位员工的工作与生活，落实员工健康关爱计划，持续开展各类员工关怀活动，通过全面的健康服务及丰富多彩的文体活动，用真情实意把温暖送到员工心底，让员工快乐工作、健康生活。

职工心理健康咨询热线

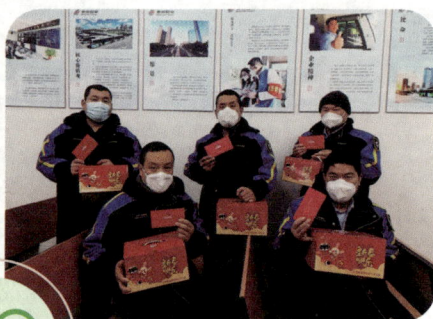

春节普惠慰问员工

好书阅享会

第八届职工运动会健步走活动

2023

员工体检覆盖率
100%

开展第二期"EAP专员"中级培训
75名

7x24小时员工心理健康咨询热线累计服务员工
829人次

完成驾驶员的年度心理测评工作
38494名

困难员工帮扶资金投入
485.12万元

困难员工帮扶人数
1702人

案例：筑起温情港湾，守护员工幸福

在第33个"全国母乳喂养宣传日"到来之际，北京公交电车分公司第九车队母婴室正式挂牌开放。母婴室的设计力求"屋尽其用"，将关心关爱融入细节，用温馨的布置、舒缓的音乐、便捷的设备和规范的制度为女员工们搭建了温暖的港湾。一间母婴室，是女性员工心灵的港湾，是车队的一抹暖色，更是企业文明的体现，彰显着北京公交对员工始终如一的守护和关怀。

车队母婴室

北京公交人的服务心声

用心守护乘客安全到站，也把人民的心声"送到站"

——电车分公司驾驶员 何少花

2023年，北京公交电车分公司BRT2线的驾驶员何少花当选全国人大代表，穿着公交制服、代表广大一线员工、带着民生所盼走进了人民大会堂。一路走来，何少花在北京公交担任过站务员、驾驶员，无论在哪个岗位上，她总是一心为首都的公交事业奉献着自己的全部力量，用初心与真情陪伴着乘客的每一趟出行。

在站务服务工作中，她便总结出一套"心勤"工作法：责任心、包容心、同情心、诚心、爱心，脑勤、眼勤、嘴勤、手勤、腿勤。2015年，她转岗成为驾驶员，将服务也带到了车厢里，刻苦钻研驾驶技术的她总结创新了"四字工作法"：克服"急"字、做到"稳"字、突出"让"字、牢记"法"字，确保乘客安全到达。在她驾驶的公交车上，乘客不仅出行更安心了，夏天还有了凉垫，冬天有了棉垫……很多常坐她车的乘客，都成了她的"粉丝"，主动热情地和她打招呼。

全国人大代表何少花

"每一位乘客的背后都是一份民意，作为人大代表，我不仅要把乘客送到站，也要把大家的心声'送到站'。"在当选上人大代表之后，何少花感受到了更大的责任。

一个早高峰，一位外地乘客上车后，一句句难懂的方言直接问懵了何少花，当时老乡无奈摇头下车的样子令她记忆犹新。如何更好地满足乘客需求？这个思考被她带到了全国两会：以前报站驾驶员一站一站按钮，现在进站就能自动报站，以后问路是不是也不用驾驶员回答，每台车都有"聪明的大脑"回答得又快又准？想到这儿，何少花豁然开朗，希望通过新质生产力赋能公交领域，让一线驾驶员能够开上更加"智慧的车"，同时提出了针对性建议："每到一站播报时能告诉乘客周边有哪些重要地点、最近的地铁是哪站。同时加大智能出行App的推广力度，让乘客们可以自主查询，满足个性化信息需求"，让市民能够享受到更加"数字的站"带来的出行便利。

作为一名驾驶员，握在手中的是守护乘客平安出行的方向盘，作为一名全国人大代表，握在手中的是为民发声、为民做事的那份沉甸甸的责任，"线路有终点，服务无止境""我来自老百姓，我就要回到老百姓当中去。"何少花始终这样要求自己。

心系家园,情牵社区

民生无小事,枝叶总关情。北京公交始终深刻洞察社会问题,关注社会责任重点领域,与乘客共同描绘文明出行的流动风景,助力城市更新,携手供应商打造可持续供应链,鼓励和支持员工参与到不同的志愿服务活动中,让人与人之间建立起传递善意的桥梁,推动社区更好发展,持续助力提升社会福祉。

文明出行,做路上"最美风景"

作为城市出行文明的守护者和引领者,我们坚持以倡导文明新风为重点,与政府部门联合举办"礼出文明,让出安全"实践活动,开展"我认领我服务"路口文明引导志愿服务活动,常态化推进礼让斑马线、公交站台秩序维护等工作,使每一个公共交通参与者都做到文明出行,让"关爱生命,文明出行"的意识深植于人们内心深处。

开展文明出行科普教育活动

开展文明出行宣传活动

📧 案例:文明交通 你我同行

为践行社会主义核心价值观,引导广大市民关注交通安全,共筑良好的交通环境,北京公交客八分公司于中小学开学首日开展"践行党的二十大 文明礼让斑马线 引领交通新风尚"交通安全宣传活动。公交员工手举"礼让斑马线"警示牌,提示驾驶员减速慢行;向过往行人发放交通安全宣传单,耐心讲解出行安全的重要性;在路口协助文明引导员指挥交通,劝阻不文明行车行为,以实际行动助力文明礼让,让文明出行理念深入人心。

开展交通安全宣传活动

更新城市，也更新生活

城市的生命在于其不断更新并持续进发的活力，更新是城市永恒的状态和不变的主题。我们聚焦北京城市更新存量项目，以民生保障、环境改善为导向的社会性更新为主线，深入研究老旧场站改造与城市更新条例政策的有机结合点位，高标准打造"1921城市智享空间"群落，与属地政府部门等共同探索小规模、渐进式、可持续的城市更新路径，持续增进民生福祉。

- 第一批试点花园胡同和南礼士路项目运行良好，入驻率平稳保持在85%以上

- 甘露园项目改造进入招标阶段，预招商加快推进，预计年底前出租率超10%

- 新风街项目被确定为"西城区重点数字经济产业园"并正式授牌，按既定计划将于2024年7月竣工交付

城市更新重点项目稳步推进

- 核桃园项目完成测绘勘察等前期工作，启动场地清理、设计方案报审等筹备工作，计划于2024年二季度启动改造

- 永定门东项目加快推进留驻企业续约，与东城区相关部门积极引纳优质入园单位

- 阜成门项目在保障集团使用需求基础上，提供部分空间支持西城区属地教育办学

"1921城市智享空间"群落

花园胡同项目

共建可持续价值链

我们以负责任、可持续的发展理念, 与供应商合作共同构建和维护阳光、廉洁、诚信、可持续的供应链, 不断加强供应商责任管理, 创建更加公开透明、公平公正的集中采购平台, 深入开展采购合规管理工作, 促使供应商提高责任意识, 携手共建可持续的供应链生态。

2023

○ 供应商审查覆盖率
100%

○ 开展供应商社会责任培训
4次

供应商准入与退出

▪ 公开招标录入供应商, 将服务团队业务水平、产品质量保证体系、物流配送等指标作为入库供应商的选择标准

▪ 供应商依据合同履约期限, 在完成委托采购项目后退出企业库, 发生违反法律法规和供应商考核管理制度的供应商将被清退

供应商动态管理

▪ 建立严肃的供应商考核评价体系, 对供应商考核实施分级认定、动态管理; 严格约束供应商采购行为, 定期组织对供应商进行评价, 按照发生问题性质对供应商采取约谈、考核扣罚、暂停资质、取消资格等分级管理措施, 确保库内采购活动依法合规开展

提升供应商履责能力

▪ 不定期开展库内供应商业务培训和专题培训, 组织需求单位对发生采购业务的供应商评价打分

志愿公益, 用心用情

小善渐而大德生。我们始终坚守公益性定位, 主动担当作为、服务社会, 广泛开展"爱满京城"学雷锋志愿服务活动、节日期间文明实践志愿服务活动, 并持续探索志愿服务新形式, 组织公交志愿者开展"23·7"特大暴雨洪涝灾害抢险救灾志愿服务、毛主席纪念堂志愿服务、第三届"一带一路"国际合作高峰论坛、春运等志愿服务活动, 让有爱者有力, 让奉献者发光。

开展毛主席纪念堂志愿服务

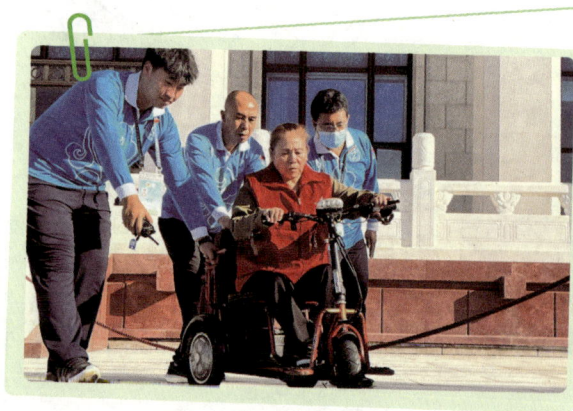

公交"路路通"志愿服务

站务设施清理

开展学雷锋志愿服务活动

2023

志愿者注册人数
16000余人

志愿服务
20余万人次

志愿服务活动
4.9万次

累计服务时长
68万小时

■ 被评为毛主席纪念堂志愿服务项目运行十周年"突出贡献单位"

案例：做雷锋式公交人

在学雷锋纪念日到来之际，北京公交组织员工与社区居民共同开展学雷锋共建活动。活动中，车队员工向居民们讲解了垃圾分类知识，并利用实物帮助居民们辨别处理各类垃圾，通过展示利用可回收垃圾进行二次创造的作品，号召广大居民投入到垃圾分类的行动中。同时，走进社区帮助居民清扫整理社区内的杂物和垃圾，擦拭消杀公共区域，将暖心服务从车厢延伸到了社区。

员工帮助居民清扫社区

助力乡村振兴正当时

公务用车及办公设备捐赠仪式

北京公交始终牢记国企责任担当,携手各方共筑乡村繁荣之路,绘就共同富裕新图景。我们聚焦京蒙协作和北京市"消薄"重点任务,多措并举助力乡村振兴,推进"村村通"线路开通,便利村民出行,携手北京邮政创新开展交邮合作,以实干"执笔"绘乡村振兴"满园春色",助力实现农村更富裕、生活更幸福、乡村更美丽。

2023

向西藏拉萨市交产集团捐赠乡村振兴资金
100万元

向内蒙古赤峰市巴林左旗捐赠乡村振兴资金
80万元

采购帮扶地区农副产品
832万元

新增脱贫地区就业人口
137人

新安置本市农村劳动力实现就业
223人

支援重点帮扶地区

我们立足资源禀赋,坚持优势特色,持续加强东西部劳务协作,提升对支援合作地区的帮扶力度,完成三个集体经济薄弱村年度"消薄"帮扶任务,全面支持乡村教育、交通、村居环境方面的改善,助力乡村构建令人向往的美好家园。

乡村振兴帮扶举措

对口支援	向国家乡村振兴重点帮扶县捐赠物资,并改善公交场站生产生活设备设施;向新疆和田地区捐赠价值约2.3万元的图书
产业帮扶	助力门头沟斋堂镇高铺村、黄岭西村和法城村实现村集体经济增收
消费帮扶	推进"以买代帮"消费帮扶工作走深走实,鼓励集团公司员工积极采购帮扶地区农副产品
就业帮扶	通过提供岗位、就业培训、帮助稳岗等方式,促进脱贫地区农村劳动力稳定就业,新招对口支援地区大学生就业5人
教育帮扶	公交技校新招录西部地区农村学生74人,增派公交技校汽车技术系教师孟庆科开展援疆支教活动

援疆教师孟庆科指导学生进行实习操作

交邮合作，畅通乡村物流

我们与北京邮政践行双方"一路同行、一心为您""情系万家、信达天下"的初心使命，共同探索交邮运输合作，利用既有郊区线路，让邮政物品"坐"公交按时抵达目标邮政所，提高乡村物流运输效率，畅通为民服务"最后一公里"，进一步满足郊区群众美好出行和用邮需求，合力打造公交、邮政运力资源融合的新发展模式。

谱好乡村邮政的"服务曲"

我们围绕"公交出行便捷化"和"物流快递最后一公里"，聚焦首都远山地区市民的出行和收发邮件的现实需求，规划双方交邮线路的设置与运行，尽可能加密发车班次，缩短邮件传递的时限，进一步提升山区百姓的用邮体验。

2023
开展交邮合作线路 **6**条
代运邮件 **100**余次
邮件数量近 **3000**件

开展交邮运力合作

奏响乡村振兴的"产业曲"

我们让农村地区的特色农产品也能顺利搭载上交邮合作班车，使山蘑、杂粮、蔬菜水果等农产品以最快时限配送至城区，充分激活乡村造血功能，不仅解决了山区农产品销售难、寄递难等问题，更为山区农民增收和服务当地经济做出了贡献。

> "交邮合作是北京公交与北京邮政携手践行乡村振兴工作、履行公共服务使命的一次探索与创新，不仅提升了公交线路的功能性，也进一步拓展了公交发展的可能性和服务市民的多样性。抓住交邮融合发展契机，紧密结合自身服务特点，有效提升公交服务效能，努力为沿途乘客提供更好的公共出行服务。"
>
> ——北京公交客六分公司运营管理部经理 李鹏

> "在解决当地村民'出行最后一公里'和'物流最后一公里'基础上，北京公交和北京邮政优势互补，把当地人文景观、地理风貌、地域特色、功能定位融入到运营线路里，突显了双方全方位服务首都乡村振兴工作的系统性和创新性，不断提升双方文化服务效能，为农民群众提供高质量的出行服务和邮政服务的同时注入精神营养。"
>
> ——北京邮政市场营销部总经理 丛树文

未来可期
共赴下一站

响应联合国可持续发展目标

9 产业、创新和基础设施　11 可持续城市和社区　17 促进目标实现的伙伴关系

为者常成，行者常至。站在历史与时代的交汇点，北京公交始终坚守初心不变，不断将"十四五"宏伟蓝图化为生动实践，用出色的时代答卷诠释着大国公交的担当。乘数字之帆向着自动驾驶公交持续进军，不断汇聚博士后人才智慧力量，用新的坚毅奋斗锻造出新的前行发展，用新的无限期待凝练出新的公交梦想，在"让更多的人享受更好的公共出行服务"的路上携手同行向未来。

战略导向,接续奋斗

未来已来,公共交通可持续发展的蓝图正跃然纸上、见诸成效。站在"十四五"发展承上启下的关键节点,北京公交坚持与时俱进,积极拥抱变革,在发展中审视过去、展望未来,努力携手更多利益相关方再绘美好出行新蓝图,引领城市交通可持续发展新征程。

蓝图在握,笃行实干结硕果

善谋者行远,实干者乃成。"十四五"已过半程,时间过半、任务过半,面对国家与公交行业发展的日新月异,我们始终立足更好满足广大乘客日益增长的美好出行生活需要,坚持"打造现代城市客运出行综合服务商"的定位,聚焦高质量发展、高品质服务和高效能治理,用亮眼的"十四五"中期成绩单给出对实干最好的诠释。

"十四五"规划主要目标任务进展与成效

- 公交运营服务取得新进展
- 重大交通服务保障和疫情防控取得新成效
- 基础设施和服务保障提供新支撑
- 资产管理和资本运营能力得到新提升

- 广告和汽车服贸业取得新进步
- 全面深化改革取得新突破
- 安全管理能力实现新提升

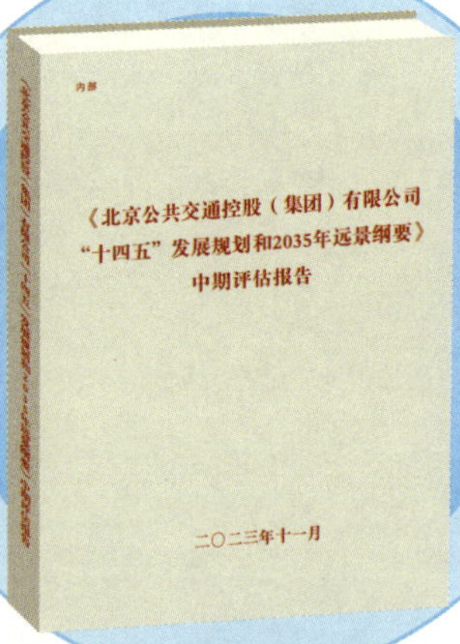

《北京公共交通控股(集团)有限公司"十四五"发展规划和2035年远景纲要》中期评估报告

二〇二三年十一月

- 数字化建设取得新成果
- 人才队伍建设得到新加强
- 人力资源管理实现新发展

- 企业文化展现新形象
- 企业管理实现新改善
- 党的建设迈上新台阶

"十四五"中期评估完成"十四五"目标值情况

- ▶ 资产总额完成**80.41%**
- ▶ 所有者权益完成**86.71%**
- ▶ 归属母公司所有者权益完成**86.16%**
- ▶ 国有资本保值增长率完成**99.54%**
- ▶ 线网优化完成**105.28%**

北京公交"十四五"规划中期评估工作通报会

锚定目标，奋楫扬帆展宏图

风至自灵动，策高当行远。迈向"十四五"发展的后半程，我们将继续坚持"十四五"战略目标任务，客观分析内外部环境，明确机遇与挑战，因势而谋、应势而动、顺势而为，奋力书写新时代大国首都公交改革发展新篇章、引领公交行业发展的新未来。

3 聚焦转型升级发展，促进质量效益有效提升

4 扎实推进改革深化提升，增强核心竞争力和核心功能

2 夯实服务保障根基，打造"硬核"服务保障

5 打造总体安全新体系，确保企业安全稳定

1 坚守服务初心，提高城市客运综合服务水平

6 坚持从严治党，全面加强党的建设

"十四五"规划后半程重点发展方向

自动驾驶，打造行业新质生产力典范

公交自动驾驶既是对新业态、新模式、新技术的成功探索和创新应用，也是主动融入全球新型智慧城市建设的生动实践。北京公交聚焦前沿科技领域提前布局，围绕自动驾驶项目加强产业上下游资源整合，加大创新链、产业链、人才链深度融合，高质量、高标准、高水平推进自动驾驶公交发展夯基筑底，以拓展公交自动驾驶的"加法"，带来北京公交高质量发展的"乘法"，不断实现传统服务转型升级、提质增效和智慧发展，让公交自动驾驶事业从听故事、讲故事变为真人真事，在京华大地落地生根。

自动驾驶公开道路测试顺时针环形路线

实地踏勘自动驾驶线路周边路况

北京公交自动驾驶1路测试车辆

自动驾驶安全员实时监测车辆运行

在自动驾驶示范项目推进过程中，我们充分发挥企业科技创新、产业控制、安全支撑作用，全局性谋划、统筹性设计、高质量推动公交"人、车、站、线、网、云、数"生产要素有效衔接、互联互通，让自动驾驶事业稳扎稳打、渐行渐近。北京公交高级别自动驾驶示范区建设专项工作组多次组织团队对国内外自动驾驶产业链进行系统学习、走访、调研，实地走访整车厂、自动驾驶技术提供商、通信商、高精度地图等企业，全面掌握自动驾驶产业发展的现状、经验和挑战。2023年9月，在多方共同努力下，通过感知系统标定、线控适配、控制调优、封闭场地考试、专家评审、应急演练、申领牌照等一系列准备，我们首次将8.5米公交车型投入城市公开道路进行常态化测试，更加契合了地面公交实际运营场景，实现自动驾驶公交智能化运行。

"新质生产力摆脱传统经济增长方式、生产力发展路径，由技术革命性突破、生产要素创新性配置、产业深度转型升级而催生，以劳动者、劳动资料、劳动对象及其优化组合的跃升为基本内涵，以全要素生产率大幅提升为核心标志，特点是创新，关键在质优，本质是先进生产力。在发展新质生产力的时代背景下，公交行业是发展新质生产力的重要场景，对北京公交这样一个传统的劳动密集型企业而言，对劳动者、劳动资料、劳动对象提出新的更高要求。我们积极发展公交自动驾驶，用新质生产力有效推动传统企业转型升级和高质量发展。"

——北京公交高级别自动驾驶示范区建设专项工作组
秘书处秘书长 徐正祥

2022年8月16日
《北京公交自动驾驶示范运营项目合作协议》正式签署

2023年3月至5月
开展自动驾驶车辆前期调试

2023年8月24日
完成专家评审

2023年9月13日
取得第一张大型普通客车自动驾驶路测牌照

2024年1月3日
两部自动驾驶公交车辆进入模拟载荷测试阶段

2022年11月22日至23日
选定4名公交自动驾驶测试安全员

2023年7月7日
两部自动驾驶公交车辆顺利通过封闭场地测试

2023年9月上旬
两部自动驾驶公交车辆开展应急演练

2023年9月22日
两部自动驾驶公交车辆开启空载测试

案例：北京公交取得第一张大型普通客车自动驾驶路测牌照

2023年9月，北京公交作为牵头单位，亦庄运营公司、福田欧辉公司、轻舟智航公司作为联合体，获得北京市公安局公安交通管理局颁发的路测牌照。这是北京公交取得的第一张大型普通客车自动驾驶路测牌照，意味着北京公交高级别自动驾驶车辆正式跨过封闭场地测试阶段，进入地面公共交通实际运营场景的开放道路测试阶段，将在北京市智能网联汽车政策先行区内开展上路测试。

功以才成，业由才广

博士后是重要的国家战略人才力量。北京公交高度重视博士后人才的引进与培养，以博士后科研工作站为创新平台，精准培育具有现代城市公共交通理念、专业实践能力的跨学科、复合型、战略型、高层次创新型人才，合力为公交行业培育创新驱动发展的生力军，让公交事业持续焕发新的生机与活力。

多渠道托举博士后成长发展

我们全力打造全国公交行业示范性产学研用协同创新基地，厚植高端人才沃土，持续建设具有全球视野、走在世界前列的行业高端智库，为建设现代化公交企业提供有力的智力支持和人才保障。

高标准遴选申请进站人员

多途径推送招聘信息，在坚持质量优先的前提下，兼顾适当扩大集团公司博士后工作站规模，严格考核、考察，综合考虑生源质量、专业背景、研究能力等多方面因素，成功招聘1名博士后研究人员

着力推进博士后工作站建设

主动与北京交通大学、对外经济贸易大学等单位交流，签署联合培养协议；组织在站博士后研究人员申报面上项目，积极参加全国博管办组织的创新大赛等活动

组织开展博士后中期考核

2023年11月，邀请政府主管部门、第三方专业研究咨询机构、产业链上下游企业和行业专家学者组成考核组，对2022年进站的首批两名博士后进行中期考核

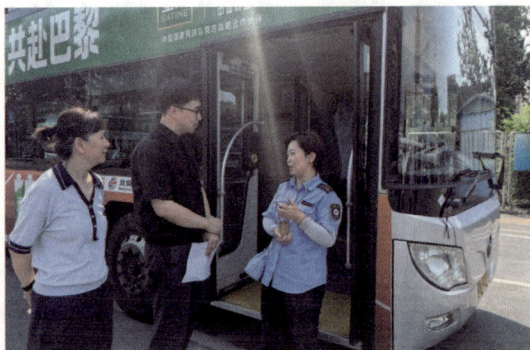

"驾驶员是公交企业与行业的核心人才资源。北京公交在驾驶员队伍管理与建设上积累了丰富的实践经验与海量的数据资源，未来，我将把职业研究热点——可持续职业生涯理论同驾驶员队伍发展相结合，更好地将'一心为乘客，服务最光荣'的精神融入到驾驶员队伍的建设中。"

——2023年入站博士后魏仕龙

让博士后人才发挥更多"光"和"热"

博士后科研工作站建立以来,我们从人工智能、自动驾驶等方面入手积极开展各类课题研究,有效促进了新理论、新技术和公交发展的深度融合,让博士后人才的创新成果在这里发挥出更多"光"和"热",为推动传统公交转型升级、激发公交行业创新创造活力持续赋能。

博士后中期考核评审会

深入研究

通过全面调研、国内外对标、前沿成果研究,刻画基于多源数据的北京公交线路运行特征画像、提出公交运营可靠性评价指标,探索更多运营调度新模式;总结自动驾驶公交的运行特性,在自动驾驶公交的伦理规则、自动驾驶法律责任、自动驾驶巴士使用者注意义务、激发司机驾驶意愿等方面提出对策建议;进行北京地面公交驾驶员可持续职业调查,展开公交驾驶员"体面工作"对标研究,为公交驾驶员队伍建设提出优化建议

形成报告

关注国内外公交行业和城市公交发展最新趋势,编制《国际城市交通发展战略与启示》《北京公交运营服务调研报告》《伦敦公交公司驾驶员管理政策及其思考》《香港巴士司机管理政策梳理报告》等研究报告,借鉴国内外先进经验,并提出相应对策建议

参与项目

查询、分析国内外大城市公交发展相关数据和指标,参与编制《北京公交集团构建和完善运营服务指标评估体系研究报告》

论文发表

公开发表《城市智慧公交云脑建设与应用》《北京地面公交运营服务提升对策建议》《自动驾驶时代:地面公交的挑战与应对》《基于TAM的自动驾驶公交司机接受度研究》等论文

扩大"朋友圈"，共绘"同心圆"

公共交通发展是一项全球性议题。北京公交深入领会"让可持续交通发展成果更好造福世界各国人民"的重要主张，积极参与国际公共交通领域的交流活动，不断扩大"朋友圈"，同时也努力在国际舞台传播中国声音、讲好中国故事，让世界看到中国公共交通领域的跨越式发展和成就，更好地"引进来"和"走出去"，为推动全球交通可持续发展贡献智慧和力量。

互联互通，携手探索未来出行蓝图

2023年，我们综合公交发展空间、规模、要素、业态和商业模式，着力发展国内国际产业生态圈，参与并出席UITP全球公共交通夏季峰会、COTA国际交通科技年会等活动，不断扩大国际公交朋友圈。同时，与UITP总部和西班牙当地企业开展商务洽谈，参观考察了巴塞罗那运输公司（TMB）、Mobileye盲区监测产品，并与新加坡公交公司SBST开展线上交流，携手各方合力构建客运出行全产业链相互促进、相互协同的开放式发展新格局，打造共创共享的公交新生态。

在国际公共交通联会（UITP）举办的2023年UITP全球公共交通夏季峰会上，北京公交区域智能调度改革项目荣获UITP大奖之特别荣誉奖（UITP Special Recognition Awards）

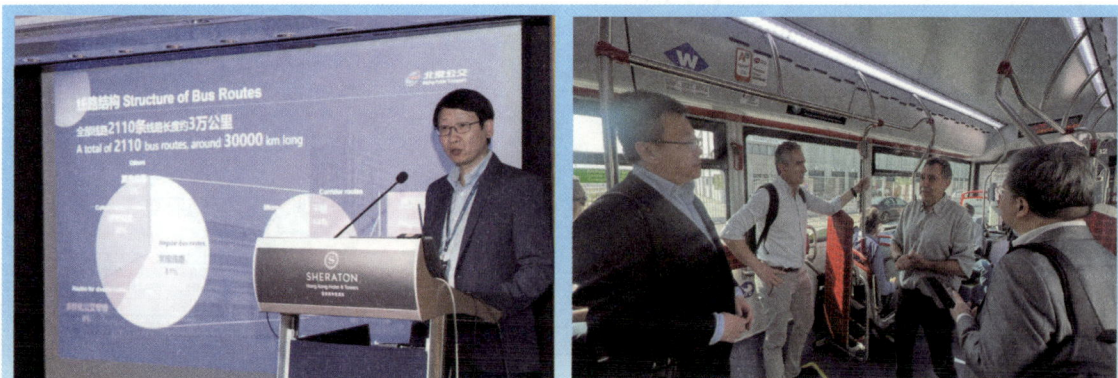

开展国际交流活动

对标一流,积极借鉴国际先进理念经验

我们始终保持对国际公共交通行业发展态势的密切关注,并深入推进国际研究,通过学习美国、英国、新加坡、日本等国公交行业最新研究成果和发展动态,及时掌握公交行业发展趋势。同时,积极开展国际对标分析研究,着重对比分析多个国际大都市出行结构、票价水平和公交运营商成本收入比,形成关于城市出行结构分析报告。通过深入研究和学习国际先进经验,为北京公交的发展注入新的活力和动力,全面推动公共交通朝着更加绿色、协调、可持续的方向发展。

案例:参加第23届COTA国际交通科技年会,为行业发展贡献北京公交方案

2023年7月16日,战略和改革发展部经理徐正祥代表北京公交参加第23届COTA国际交通科技年会(CICTP 2023)公共交通高质量发展特邀论坛,发表题为"以《北京宣言》为指引,推进超大城市公共交通治理"的演讲。在阐明《北京宣言》的诞生背景和核心要义的基础上,结合北京公交的实践,论述了对超大城市公共交通治理体系和治理能力现代化的认识,重点从"治理的根本立场:以乘客为中心""治理的体制机制:高层政治领导"和"治理的路径选择:科技赋能,打造智慧公交;低碳发展,打造绿色公交;利益相关方合作,共建公交发展共同体"等方面与国际公共交通行业学者展开互动交流。

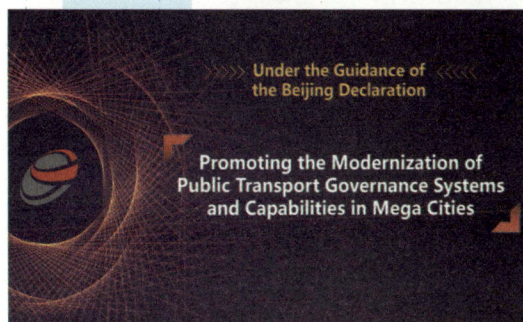

展望

岁序更替,华章日新。2024年,是新中国成立75周年,也是实现"十四五"规划目标任务的关键一年。新的历史坐标启动,北京公交将接续奋斗、赓续前行,主动担当时代使命,心系"国之大者",聚焦民生关切,践行"一心为乘客,服务最光荣"的价值理念,用一以贯之的初心和深情刻画为民服务的时代华彩,用开拓创新的精神和毅力塑造新时代的北京公交。

创造"出行即生活",践行"出行即服务"

我们将始终致力于为更多人提供更好的公共出行服务,聚焦人们日益增长的高品质、个性化、智能化出行需求,补短板、重衔接、优网络、提效能,加强地面公交、轨道交通"两网融合",深入优化线网布局,打造功能明确、结构清晰的地面公交线网。主动融入首都城市发展新格局,以首善标准打造符合首都城市发展需要,满足群众多样化出行期待的新时代公交出行服务新体系。积极服务首都功能建设,推进公交场站转型升级,补齐便民生活服务设施短板,探索提供城市公共服务的更多可能。持续推动京津冀一体化交通先行,献礼京津冀协同发展十周年。

更加深化绿色发展,守护"绿水青山"

我们将持之以恒深入贯彻习近平生态文明思想,坚定不移走生态优先、绿色低碳的发展道路,服务建设美丽中国、美丽北京。有力有序推进碳达峰碳中和行动,加大新能源车辆的投放力度,优化车辆能源结构。着力构建绿色交通体系,深入挖潜绿色交通,提高公交优先、绿色出行服务的覆盖度和可及性,让绿色出行蔚然成风。加大超级充电站、对外共享充电站等新能源应用力度,构建新能源电池维护、回收、拆解等产业链,推动多层次循环复合利用。主动履行碳排放控制责任,积极参与碳交易,为提升空气质量、保护生物多样性贡献公交力量,让蓝天白云绿水青山成为大国首都发展底色。

更加强化科技赋能,打造"智慧公交3.0"

我们将不断推进科技创新寻找发展最优解,落实"上云用数赋智"和"数字+"行动,释放数字化转型在生产、经营、管理、服务等领域的放大效应,努力构建智慧运营、智慧行车、智慧场站、智慧园区、智慧办公、智慧党建等智慧公交管理新体系。深入推进区域智能调度改革,着力培育"智慧的车""聪明的站""数字的线""动态的网"。紧抓北京市高级别自动驾驶示范区4.0阶段扩区建设契机,努力在公交自动驾驶示范应用、规模化、多场景上实现更大作为,打造北京公交自动驾驶运营的示范样板。锻造硬核强劲的人才力量,激发人才创新创造活力,为企业长远发展提供坚实的智力支撑。

更加开放和融共生,充实"公交生态圈"

我们将携手各方同心同行共赴美好未来,着力拓展与国内外组织开展更宽领域、更深层次的战略合作与交流互鉴,与合作伙伴共话共创新机遇,推动世界范围内的公交行业健康、可持续、高质量发展。发展成果与广大员工共享,让驾驶员职业更体面、更有尊严,让公交员工的获得感成色更足、幸福感更可持续、安全感更有保障。持续发力巩固脱贫攻坚成果,服务乡村振兴,加强对西部偏远地区、对口支援地区产业扶持,深化交邮合作,加深"大交通"框架下的跨界产业融合,提升城乡公共服务均等化水平。积极倡导文明出行,构建文明出行环境,助力全社会形成共建、共治、共享文明交通的良好格局。

一世纪风雨兼程,九万里风鹏正举。时代的浪潮奔涌向前,新时代的北京公交人始终胸怀梦想,无畏风雨,笃定前行,以真情服务为人民群众创造更加幸福美好的出行生活,以不懈努力建设人民满意、保障有力的首善公交,以无悔奋斗谱写新时代大国首都公共交通发展壮美华章!

关键绩效

	指标	2021年	2022年	2023年
经济绩效	年营业收入（亿元）	81.91	68.61	88.47
	企业总资产（亿元）	645.21	643.27	665.77
	企业净资产（亿元）	423.55	444.40	457.22
	资产负债率（%）	32.08	30.92	31.32
	纳税总额（亿元）	4.15	2.89	4.46
	运营车辆（辆）	32896	32783	33133
	运营线路条数（条）	1225	1299	1293
	公共电汽车年行驶里程（亿公里）	11.39	9.84	11.51
	公共电汽车年客运量（亿人次）	22.96	17.26	20.87
	投诉响应率（%）	100	100	100
	乘客满意率（%）	93.49	93.52	94.04
	报告期内供应商审查覆盖率（%）	100	100	100
	因社会责任不合规被否决的潜在供应商数量（个）	1	0	0
	因社会责任不合规被中止合作的供应商数量（个）	1	0	0
	供应商社会责任培训次数（次）	3	1	4

	指标	2021年	2022年	2023年
社会绩效	员工数量（人）	89014	84211	78936
	劳动合同签订率（%）	100	100	100
	社会保险覆盖率（%）	100	100	100
	女性员工比例（%）	26.49	25.43	24.46
	女性管理者比例（%）	39.30	40.54	41
	人均带薪年休假天数（天）	10	11	11
	员工体检覆盖率（%）	100	100	100
	员工流失率（%）	1.73	1.86	1.87

指标	2021年	2022年	2023年
安全生产投入（亿元）	24.08	21.64	22.98
安全培训覆盖率（%）	100	100	100
安全演练覆盖率（%）	100	100	100
交通违法率（%）	0.33	0.27	0.24
甲方责任事故死亡率（人/百万公里）	0.00307	0.0005	0.0026
累计志愿服务时间（万小时）	99	73	68
困难员工帮扶资金投入（万元）	209	303.15	485.12
困难员工帮扶人数（人）	1090	860	1702

社会绩效

指标	2021年	2022年	2023年
车辆报废淘汰数量（辆）	1071	1619	1642
碳排放量（吨）	288376	246261	280353
二氧化碳排放量（吨）	1057378	902957	1027962
非化石能源比重（%）	14.40	15.92	17.40
清洁能源和新能源公交车占比（%）	91.06	94.27	94.70
全年能源消耗总量（吨标准煤）	495424	418298	453639
单位产值综合能耗（吨标准煤/万元）	0.24	0.20	0.22
天然气能源使用量（万公斤）	18414	15786	16329
电力能源使用量（万度）	53208	37817	49345
柴油消耗量（万升）	7172	5113	6758
年度新鲜水用水量（万立方米）	263	208	223.7
氮氧化物减排量（吨）	123.41	57.05	236.86
颗粒物减排量（吨）	0.17	0.13	0.20
碳氢化合物减排量（吨）	80.78	30.72	60.21

环境绩效

指标索引

关于本报告

本报告是北京公共交通控股（集团）有限公司发布的第11份企业社会责任报告，旨在向各利益相关方披露公司在可持续发展方面的理念、行动和成效，深化与利益相关方的相互了解与协作，共同推进公司与社会的可持续发展。

报告变化

本报告新增了"初心传承，续写新的荣光"专题章节，集中展示北京公交践行初心、服务为民的创新与变革，重点展现2023年北京公交在深化服务理念，完善服务保障、延伸服务领域的生动实践。

时间范围

2023年1月1日至12月31日，为增强数据可比性、内容延续性、宣传时效性，部分内容超出上述范围。

报告范围

本报告主要披露了北京公共交通控股（集团）有限公司践行可持续发展、履行社会责任的意愿、行动和绩效。为便于表达和方便阅读，报告中，"北京公共交通控股（集团）有限公司"也以"北京公交集团""北京公交"和"我们"等称谓之。

数据说明

本报告中所使用数据均来自北京公交集团正式文件和统计报告，所引用的数据为最终统计数据。财务数据如与年度审计报告有出入，以年度审计报告为准。我们保证，本报告发布前所有数据和内容已通过北京公交集团管理层审核。我们承诺，本报告内容不存在任何虚假记载、误导性陈述和重大遗漏，对报告中数据的客观性和真实性负责。

参考依据

本报告编写参照国际标准化组织《ISO 26000：社会责任国际标准（2010）》、全球可持续发展标准委员会《可持续发展报告标准》（GRI Standards）、联合国《2030年可持续发展议程》、中国国家标准《社会责任报告编写指南》（GB/T 36001-2015）、中国社会科学院《中国企业社会责任报告编写指南之公共交通运输服务业》（CASS-CSR4.0之公共交通运输服务业）、香港联合交易所《环境、社会及管治报告指引》（HK-ESG），兼顾中国和国际准则。

编制过程

前期准备	报告撰写	内容审核	设计发布	反馈计划
• 组建工作小组	• 确认报告框架	• 审核报告内容	• 形成报告设计	• 收集各方反馈
• 同行报告对标	• 编制报告内容	• 确定报告内容	• 公开发布报告	• 部署下步计划
• 收集报告资料				

报告获取

本报告有中文和英文两种版本，均公开出版，您可通过线上购买，获取更多我们的社会责任信息。

联系地址：北京市丰台区莲花池西里 29 号

联 系 人： 兰亦帆

邮政编码： 100161

联系电话： 0086-10-63960088

扫一扫，期待您的反馈

SDG GOOD PRACTICES

SDG Solutions
源自SDG的中国行动

金钥匙·SDG领跑企业
GoldenKey·SDG Forerunner

北京公共交通控股（集团）有限公司

可持续发展是破解全球性问题的"金钥匙"。贵公司积极行动，精准识别问题症结，以创新的解决方案突破问题难点，为实现联合国2030年可持续发展目标贡献力量，入选"金钥匙·SDG领跑企业"。

Sustainable development is the "golden key" to solve global problems. The company has been selected as "Golden Key-SDG Forerunner" for its proactive actions to accurately identify the problems and provide with innovative solutions to contribute to the achievement of the UN 2030 Sustainable Development Goals.

可持续发展 经济导刊
CHINA SUSTAINABILITY TRIBUNE

图书在版编目（CIP）数据

北京公交社会责任报告. 2023 ／ 北京公共交通控股
（集团）有限公司编著. -- 北京 : 经济管理出版社，
2024. -- ISBN 978-7-5243-0130-1

Ⅰ. F512.71

中国国家版本馆CIP数据核字第2025HN2648号

责任编辑：张莉琼

责任印制：许　艳

出版发行：经济管理出版社
　　　　　（北京市海淀区北蜂窝 8 号中雅大厦 A 座 11 层　100038）
网　　址：www. E-mp. com. cn
电　　话：(010) 51915602
印　　刷：唐山玺诚印务有限公司
经　　销：新华书店
开　　本：889mm×1194mm/16
印　　张：13.25
字　　数：382 千字
版　　次：2024 年 12 月第 1 版　2024 年 12 月第 1 次印刷
书　　号：ISBN 978-7-5243-0130-1
定　　价：138.00 元（全二册）

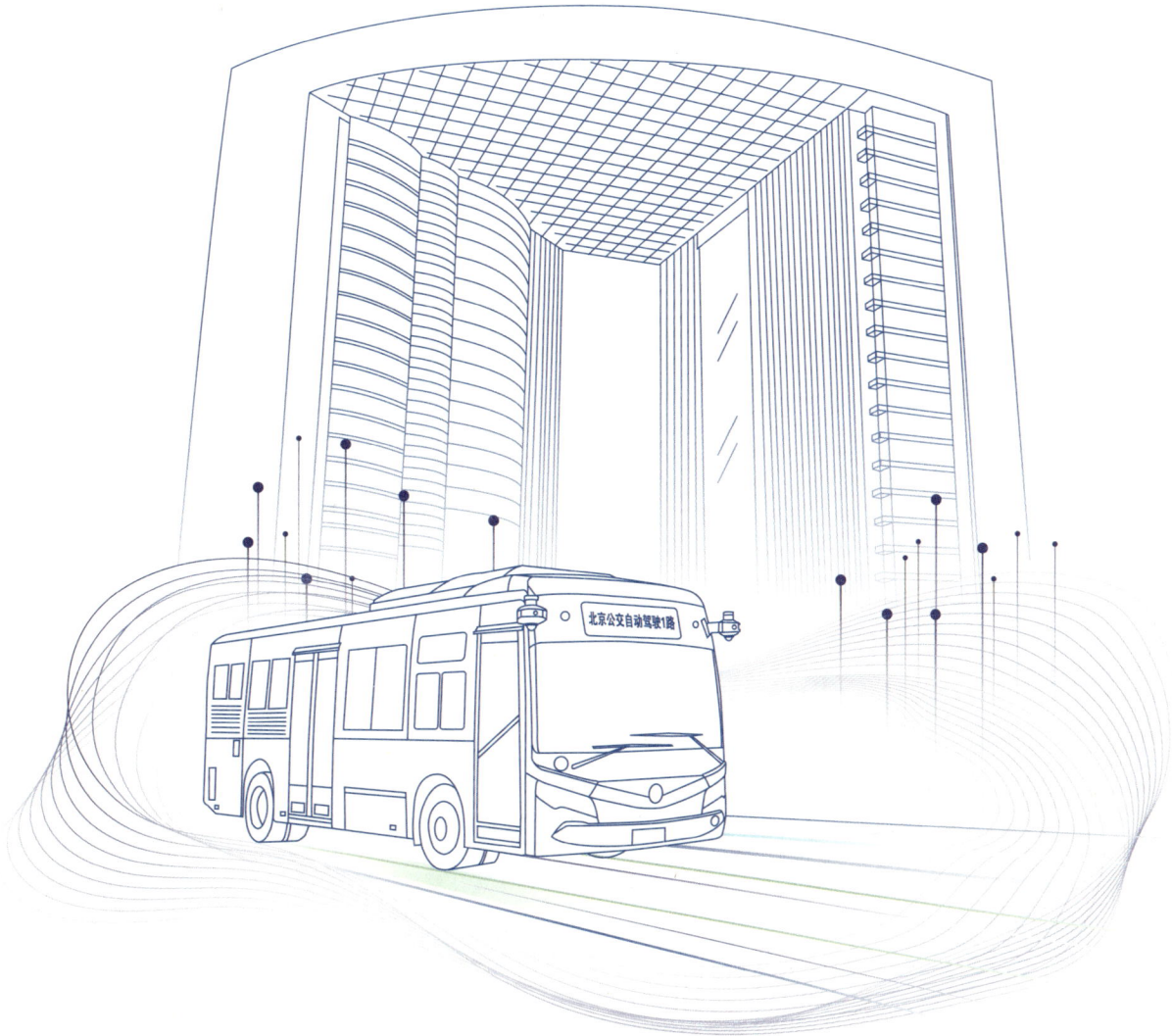

Serving passengers, the commitment of all BPTC's employees, is an everlasting theme in the Corporation's development. Our sense of dedication derives from our history. The slogan "Putting Passengers First" was coined in the passion-filled early years of the PRC when the bandwagon of services for passengers started to roll at BPTC. Since then, providing people with higher-quality public transport services has become a shared pursuit. We have thus been improving our service quality and have produced role models one after another, adding great glory on the Corporation. Keeping abreast of the times and Beijing's development, BPTC's employees remain committed to and inspired by this spirit. In the new era, we shoulder responsibility at different positions and provide better public transport services to more passengers sincerely, meticulously, and courageously. Our efforts will ensure that the corporate spirit of "Putting Passengers First, Serving With Honor, Contributing Sincerely to Society, and Taking Responsibility With Courage" remains evergreen and shining.

This report includes five chapters: Unchanged Aspiration, Enjoyable Travel, Mission Delivery, Shared Development, and Promising Future. The chapter "Unchanged Aspiration" is a new CSR section designed to illustrate highlights in 2023; the chapter "Enjoyable Travel" focuses on our primary businesses and the main responsibilities of our operations and services; the chapter "Mission Delivery" emphasizes our transport services for major events and important moments; the chapter "Shared Development" concentrates on public welfare activities; and the chapter "Promising Future" highlights the innovative development of BPTC.

CSR Management Committee of BPTC

Directors

Jin Qiuhong   Wu Shijiang

Deputy Directors

Sha Yong   Jiang Xiao   Gao Ming   Wang Xiuying   Chen Wancheng
Geng Zhencheng Cui Di   Ji Langchao

Committee Members

Xu Zhengxiang   Zhang Bin   Liu Huizhong   Gao Yuan   Kong Weifeng
Zhao Chao   Li Jinpeng   Xu Liquan   Tian Qi   Shao Qiang
Han Congbi   Zhou Jianyong   Shao Dan   Tian Guihong   Li Lifeng
Wang Yongjie   Zhang Zheng   Zhao Mingjun   Wang Feng

CSR Reporting Preparation Committee of BPTC

Chief editor

Xu Zhengxiang

Deputy editors in chief

Hu Liwen   Han Yunzhe

Members

Lan Yifan   Pu Xiaomin   Feng Shuai   Li Jingya   Ji Peilong
Che Xun   Zhao Ying   Zhao Liuyin   Zhao Yipu   Zheng Ying
Li Beini   Geng Zihou   Liu Tongzheng   Wei Shilong   Zhang Fushun
Zhang Jie   Tang Wenlan   Li Zujie   Wang Chao (Operational Dispatch Control Center)
Liu Xiang   Zhao Yu   Wu Shuang   Fan Siqi   Jing Ran
Tian Jiamiao   Yang Shunyu   Tian Qingxia   Liu Yingkai   Xu Yichen
Sun Dandan

Photography

Wang Chao (Publicity Department)   Li Tianci

Proofreading

Li Jingya   Lan Yifan   Liu Tongzheng

CONTENTS

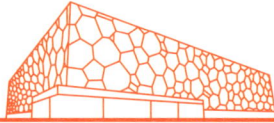

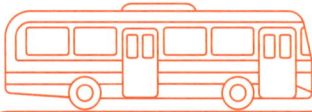

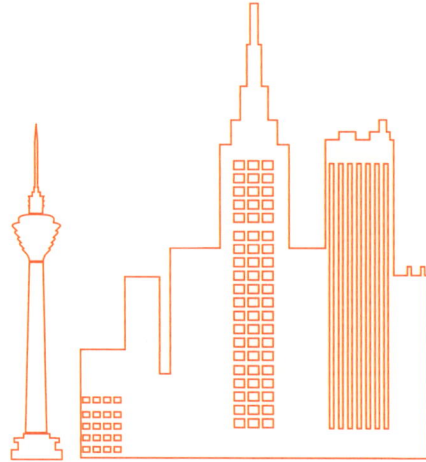

Enjoying the safe and joyful space

In the starry night of winter

Our night buses traveled through streets and alleys

Around the corner, bus convenience stores left lights on for exhausted passengers ...

The service of BPTC employees

Is responsive to people's needs

The honor of BPTC employees

Comes from our dedication to enabling more people to enjoy better transport services

In the future

For greater honors to come

BPTC will remain true to our original aspiration and take courageous actions

We will pursue upgraded public transport services featuring high quality and diversity

With first-class facilities, technology, management, and service

We will support every passenger's travel and daily life

And dedicate ourselves to the ever-evolving development of the capital

People and the capital will witness that

Our spirit in the new era is alive and everlasting

Preface

Public transport is a public utility for the people

BPTC's gene of serving the people has been

Ingrained in the corporate spirit of "Putting Passengers First, Serving With Honor,

Contributing Sincerely to Society, and Taking Responsibility With Courage"

Since the corporate spirit was proposed in the 1950s

It has been adhered to till today in 2023

Six decades on

BPTC employees' sincerity has remained undiminished

Three-hundred and sixty-five ordinary days of "Putting Passengers First, Serving

With Honor"

Made up the extraordinary year of 2023

In the comfortable breeze of spring

We conducted a survey with over ten thousand employees

Going to the communities to investigate and inquire about passengers' needs

Despite the heavy rain in summer

We delivered every order and mission

Acting in harm's way, we supported Beijing and Hebei where we reached out to

people affected by the natural disaster

As the sun rose in autumn

Students took our green school buses

Message From the Senior Management

Putting Passengers First, Serving With Honor

In 1959, BPTC first proposed the corporate spirit of "Putting Passengers First, Serving With Honor". Inspired by the spirit, BPTC employees were actively engaged in professional training to dramatically improve service quality. As a result, we produced a large cohort of national and municipal advanced crews and individuals, making BPTC the cradle of role models. The spirit of service added infinite glory to BPTC. In 1988, "Putting Passengers First, Serving With Honor" was established as the public transport industry spirit in the capital, which has encouraged generations of public transport staff to fulfill their missions and provide quality public transport services for the people.

Rapid changes over the past decades do not alter the spirit of BPTC to serve passengers. In response to the urban development in Beijing, BPTC seeks continuous innovation, transformation, and upgrade, enriching the connotation of "Putting Passengers First, Serving With Honor". We have transitioned from route-oriented operations to passenger-oriented operations, from conventional stop signs to intelligent electronic stop signs, and from carriage services offering "fans, water, and comic books" to social services encompassing "public transport convenient stations, supercharging stations, and shared parking lots". In the new era, modern public transport development is up to high standards, with diversified quality public transport service products. We have repeatedly proven to passengers that we adhere to the principle that "public transport is a public utility" and that "public transport is for the people". The simple yet profound value concept of "Putting Passengers First, Serving With Honor" holds the most vigorous and lasting strength forward.

Strong tailwinds speed up our actions and surging tides motivate us to get ahead

The year 2023 marked the beginning of fully delivering the guiding principles of the 20th CPC National Congress and the first year of building a modern socialist country in all aspects. In 2023, guided by the passenger-centered service concept, we offered high-quality and diversified public transport service products and set the model of public travel to improve urban life quality. Following the new development philosophy and putting the development of the capital in the new era as our overarching goal, we adhered to innovation-driven reform and high-quality development, creating a new development dynamic. In 2023, we shouldered the responsibility of a state-owned enterprise, responded to people's needs, and worked with stakeholders for a happier life and a new chapter of public transport that supports the development of the capital in the new era.

Putting passengers at the center, we optimized our services sincerely. We launched the theoretical study programs on studying and implementing Xi Jinping Thought on Socialism with Chinese Characteristics for a New Era and conducted a survey with over ten thousand employees going to communities, villages, and stations to investigate and inquire about passengers' needs. The results of the survey have been applied to our operations. We continued to optimize the bus route network. In 2023, we extended our network coverage by 134.2 kilometers to facilitate the travel of 313 residential communities. Given passengers' diverse needs, we launched 107 premium bus routes to enrich bus travel experiences. We also expanded the scale of customized bus routes. In 2023, we added 428 customized bus routes, and in total, we operated 660 such routes. We also introduced 19 flexible bus routes, raising the total number of such routes to 139. We accurately responded to the passengers' common and urgent needs, and opened new special lines for medical treatment and sightseeing. We operated 48 school bus routes, serving 21 schools with a daily average of 100 buses for more than 4,600 students. To deliver the coordinated development strategy of the Beijing-Tianjin-Hebei region, in 2023, we operated 38 cross-Beijing-Hebei bus routes, 20 regular bus routes in Xiong'an New Area, and 7 customized bus routes to build an integrated Beijing-Tianjin-Hebei transport pattern.

> **We put into practice that 'public transport is a public utility' and that 'public transport is for the people'. BPTC will strive diligently to play a crucial role in the capital city's comprehensive transport system, which aims to be well-structured, seamlessly connected, convenient, and orderly, with rail transit serving as the backbone, the ground public transport providing solid support and a variety of travel modes acting as supplements.Through all these endeavors, we will persist in polishing the golden service brand of BPTC.**

While upholding our core principles, we strive for innovation and advance through continuous reform. To contribute to the development of the capital city, we expanded our services that benefit the general public and took the lead in the industry to share bus depot resources to the public. We have opened up 30 bus convenience stores and shared 21 bus depots that offered 366 parking spaces at staggered times, and built 18 supercharging stations. To explore the development of new quality productive forces in the public transport industry, we piloted autonomous driving bus. We obtained the first autonomous driving road test license for large-scale ordinary passenger buses and our two autonomous driving buses accumulated over 4,000 kilometers of test driving. Committed to the strategy of strengthening the Corporation with talent, we have taken various approaches to vocational education and talent training. Beijing Public Transport Technician College was approved to be established, striving to train great professionals for the transport industry. We also advanced the development of a post-doctoral research center, attracting PhD graduates from Tsinghua University and Renmin University of China, etc. The Corporation has reached joint postdoctoral training agreements with the University of International Business and Economics and the Beijing Jiaotong University to build up a world-class new-type public transport think tank. As we deepened international exchanges, we participated in international exchanges and cooperation in the public transport industry through multiple channels and in different scenarios, communicating the message of BPTC globally.

Bearing the big picture in mind, we demonstrated loyalty in accomplishing our missions. Shocked by the unprecedented downpour and the subsequent floods in July 2023, we acted on government orders and fulfilled our responsibilities by mobilizing the whole Corporation to support flood control and disaster relief, going all out to safeguard the lives and properties of the affected. With a strong sense of political mission, we delivered transport services for the Third Belt and Road Forum for International Cooperation, the Summer Davos, and the Two Sessions, etc. Our paired assistance programs were rolled out in Inner Mongolia, Xizang, and Xinjiang, helping three villages with a weak collective economy to address their weakness and consolidate the results of poverty alleviation. We have built a model route that integrated bus and postal services to improve the efficiency of rural logistics and the satisfaction of rural residents in using postal services, which contributed to the capital's rural vitalization initiatives. Guided by the concept of green development, we have accelerated the elimination of outdated buses, with the proportion of clean energy and new energy buses reaching 94.7%. We also upgraded green and low-carbon equipment and installed more supporting facilities such as charging piles and hydrogen refueling stations. Our engagement in carbon emissions trading has generated a transaction of 20,100 tons with a net profit of RMB 2,343,500. Our pursuit of low-carbon public transport serves green development and contributes to a better environment.

Ongoing efforts shape the new-era public transport in the capital

The year 2024 is significant to implementing the guiding principles of the 20th CPC National Congress. It marks the 75th anniversary of the founding of the PRC, and is critical to realizing the goals and tasks of China's 14th Five-Year Plan. The best way to bear our legacy forward is to take action. BPTC will remain committed to the spirit of "Putting Passengers First, Serving With Honor" and make concerted efforts to work even harder. We will follow the principle that "public transport is a public utility" and that "public transport is for the people". Guided by major decisions and deployments of the CPC Beijing Municipal Committee and Beijing Municipal People's Government, we will contribute to building a public transport system with rail transport serving as the backbone, the ground public transport providing solid support, and a variety of travel modes acting as supplements. When serving the development of the capital, we will shoulder our responsibility and pool strengths for high-quality development to make ourselves a domestically leading and world-class modern comprehensive service provider of urban public transport, winning greater honors in the new era.

Party Secretary, Chairwoman, BPTC

About BPTC

Corporate Profile

Beijing Public Transport Corporation (BPTC) is a large-scale wholly state-owned public transport enterprise group. The Corporation integrates services of passenger transport, vehicle repair, tourism, vehicle rental, advertising, etc. In April 2020, the CPC Beijing Municipal Committee clarified the strategic positioning of the Corporation as a "comprehensive service provider of urban public transport." Focusing on this development orientation, the Corporation has identified two primary business sectors, namely comprehensive urban passenger transport service, and automotive service and trade, for the "14th Five-Year Plan" period.

By the end of 2023, we had total assets of RMB 66.577 billion, net assets of RMB 45.722 billion, and 78,936 employees. With a fleet of 23,385 buses and trolleybuses, we operated 1,285 scheduled bus routes, two modern tram lines-Xijiao Line and ETOWN Line, and 799 customized bus routes and routes for flexible services (660 customized bus routes and 139 routes for flexible services). Additionally, we opened 48 school bus routes. We had 25 secondary companies and public service organizations, including 14 public welfare-oriented companies, 9 market-oriented companies, and 2 public service organizations directly administrated by BPTC. In 2023, we covered a distance of 1.151 billion kilometers, with 2.087 billion annual passenger trips, playing a principal role in Beijing's ground public transport.

During the reporting period, BPTC achieved excellent performance in Social, Environmental, and Governance (ESG) dimensions. In the Governance dimension, we had 7 Board members, with women making up 28.57% of the Board. We conducted 595 anti-corruption training sessions, covering 21,837 participants. In the Environmental dimension, we engaged in carbon trading amounting to 20,100 tons, resulting in a net profit of RMB 2,343,500. In the Social dimension, we invested RMB 2.298 billion in work safety, with women making up 41% of management positions. Our employee training totaled over 1,576,688 hours and the volunteer service we offered amounted to 49,000 times.

Corporate Culture

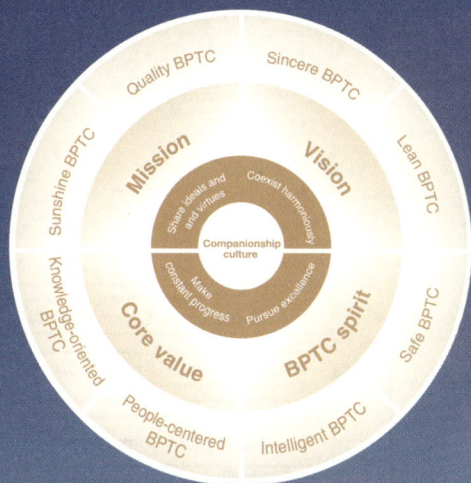

Mission
Deliver better public transport services to more people

Vision
Lead the way for the public to travel, raise the quality of city life, and build a world-renowned modern comprehensive service group for urban public transport

Core value
Put people first   Give utmost care to passengers
Promote innovation   Pursue excellence

BPTC spirit
Putting Passengers First, Serving With Honor, Contributing Sincerely to Society, and Taking Responsibility With Courage

Organization Structure

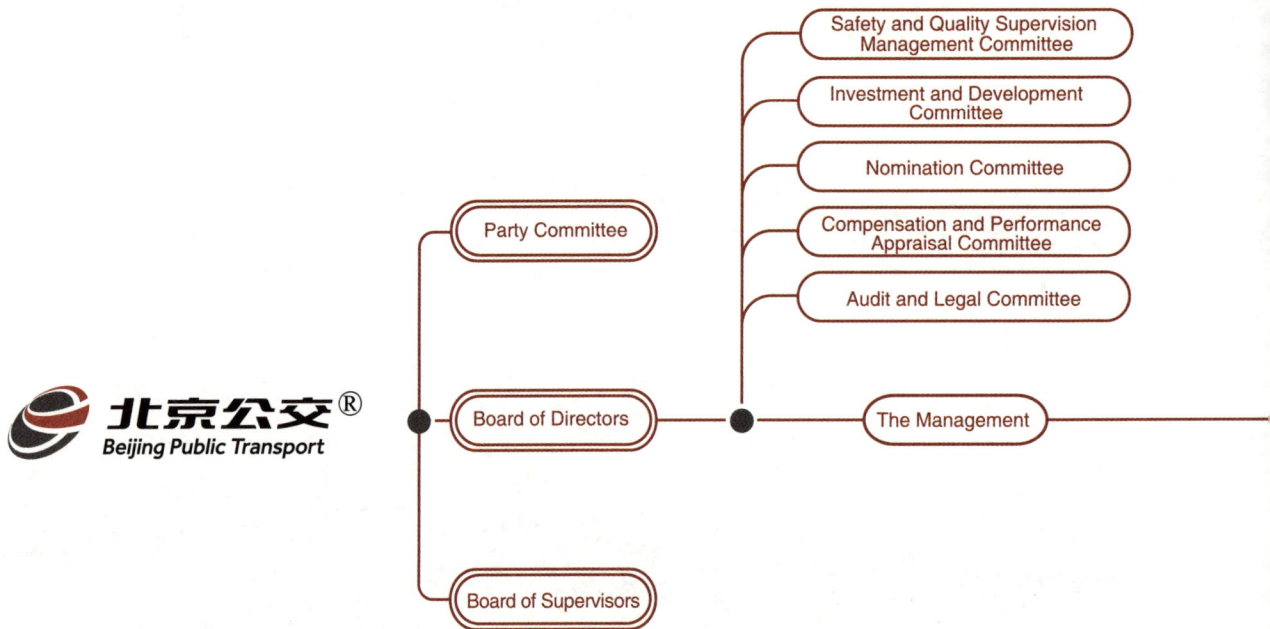

北京公交®
Beijing Public Transport

- Party Committee
- Board of Directors
  - Safety and Quality Supervision Management Committee
  - Investment and Development Committee
  - Nomination Committee
  - Compensation and Performance Appraisal Committee
  - Audit and Legal Committee
  - The Management
- Board of Supervisors

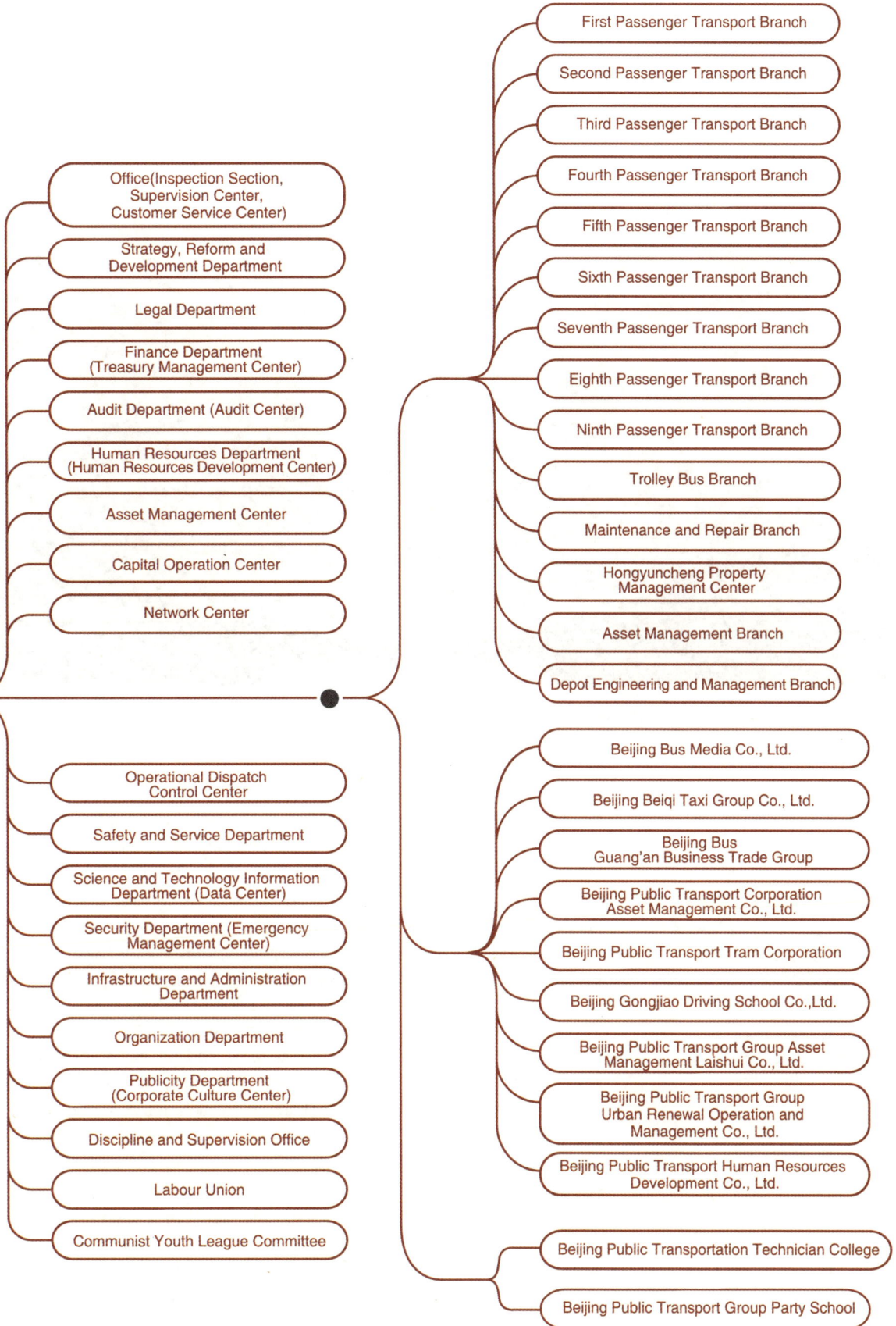

First Passenger Transport Branch

Second Passenger Transport Branch

Third Passenger Transport Branch

Fourth Passenger Transport Branch

Fifth Passenger Transport Branch

Sixth Passenger Transport Branch

Seventh Passenger Transport Branch

Eighth Passenger Transport Branch

Ninth Passenger Transport Branch

Trolley Bus Branch

Maintenance and Repair Branch

Hongyuncheng Property Management Center

Asset Management Branch

Depot Engineering and Management Branch

Office(Inspection Section, Supervision Center, Customer Service Center)

Strategy, Reform and Development Department

Legal Department

Finance Department (Treasury Management Center)

Audit Department (Audit Center)

Human Resources Department (Human Resources Development Center)

Asset Management Center

Capital Operation Center

Network Center

Beijing Bus Media Co., Ltd.

Beijing Beiqi Taxi Group Co., Ltd.

Beijing Bus Guang'an Business Trade Group

Beijing Public Transport Corporation Asset Management Co., Ltd.

Beijing Public Transport Tram Corporation

Beijing Gongjiao Driving School Co.,Ltd.

Beijing Public Transport Group Asset Management Laishui Co., Ltd.

Beijing Public Transport Group Urban Renewal Operation and Management Co., Ltd.

Beijing Public Transport Human Resources Development Co., Ltd.

Operational Dispatch Control Center

Safety and Service Department

Science and Technology Information Department (Data Center)

Security Department (Emergency Management Center)

Infrastructure and Administration Department

Organization Department

Publicity Department (Corporate Culture Center)

Discipline and Supervision Office

Labour Union

Communist Youth League Committee

Beijing Public Transportation Technician College

Beijing Public Transport Group Party School

Corporate Governance

BPTC strengthened Party leadership while improving corporate governance. We continue to improve the modern corporate system with distinctive Chinese features, build an advanced corporate governance structure, and continuously enhance the modernization of our corporate governance system and governance capacity. With strategic thinking, we strive for high-quality and sustainable corporate development.

Party leadership

Conducting the collective learning session by the Party Committee's Theory Learning Center Group

2023

30
Meetings of the Standing Committee of the Party Committee

236
Issues studied

12,903
Party members

369
Party branches

4,428
Party-building activities

1223
Hours of training on Party building

Adhering to the Party leadership and strengthening Party building are glorious traditions, the "root" and "soul", and unique advantages of state-owned enterprises (SOEs). BPTC deeply understands and grasps the general requirements for Party building in the new era. With firm political beliefs as a foundation, we continue to study, publicize, and implement the guiding principles of the 20th CPC National Congress, strengthening the deep integration of Party building with daily work. This ongoing effort transforms the political advantages of SOEs into development advantages, forming a vivid example of implementing the guiding principles of the 20th CPC National Congress within BPTC.

We thoroughly study and implement General Secretary Xi Jinping's important thoughts on Party self-reform, applying strict steps, measures, and atmospheres throughout the entire process of our reform and development. We continuously deepen efforts to improve Party conduct, enforce Party discipline, and fight corruption, resolutely addressing corruption and misconduct that occur on the people's doorsteps. By strengthening oversight on "leading bodies" and the key few, we enhanced supervision around key tasks such as bus network optimization and safe bus operation of the Beijing Municipal Administrative Center, and improved our supervision system. We implement the CPC Central Committee's eight-point decision on improving work conduct, making consistent and sustained efforts to improve work conduct. We promote a culture of integrity in the new era, guiding Party officials and employees to fight corruption in both thinking and action.

Profound and real measures for theoretical study programs

BPTC adheres to Xi Jinping Thought on Socialism with Chinese Characteristics for a New Era as its guiding principle, and conducts theoretical study programs with great political awareness and a sense of responsibility. We firmly grasp the general requirements of theoretical study programs: "Learning Party's New Theories, Strengthening Party Consciousness, Putting Practice First, and Making New Achievements." By deeply understanding the significance of theoretical study programs and highlighting our unique characteristics, we have formulated work plans to establish the "56741" work tasks: our theoretical study should embody the "Five Orientations", our Party building research should focus on the "Six Concentrations", our high-quality development should emphasize the "Seven Strengthenings", our inspection and rectification work should concentrate on the "Four Aspects" and by doing so we should form "a series of" long-term mechanisms. Additionally, we have developed 23 specific measures tailored to our actual conditions, formulated a weekly plan for the leadership team's theoretical study programs, detailed a task list for theoretical study programs, and identified 52 key tasks.

Symposium on Theoretical Study Programs

2023

167
Learning sessions conducted by the Party Committee's Theory Learning Center Group during theoretical study programs

5,211
Learning sessions for Party members organized by grass-roots Party branches during theoretical study programs

2,756
Suggestions and opinions solved when we conducted the survey to investigate and inquire about people's mobility needs.

460+
Measures beneficial to the public launched

Corporate governance

BPTC continues to promote a corporate governance mechanism that is defined by legal responsibilities, transparency of responsibilities, coordinated operations, as well as effective checks and balances, with an aim to consolidate and enhance the governance of legal entity. We have formulated the *Key Decision List for the Board of Directors* and the *Authority Process Table for Key Decision Matters for the Board of Directors*. We strictly implemented the decision-making system and advanced the establishment of the control platform of "decisions on major events, appointments and removal of important officials, important project arrangements, and use of large amounts of funds" by the State-owned Assets Supervision and Administration Commission of People's Government of Beijing Municipality. With the release of the *Implementation Plan for Benchmarking with First-Class Companies,* we steadily advance governance of legal entity of the entire system, and the Boards of Directors of subsidiaries at all levels are being matured. A strong synergy to promote high-quality, healthy, and sustainable development is taking shape.

2023

11
Board meetings

69
Issues discussed by the Board

63
Issues discussed by specialized committees

26
Meetings of Management Office

202
Issues discussed by the Management Office

Deepening reform in all respects

BPTC adheres to innovation in reform and development. We thoroughly reviewed the work of the three-year action of state-owned enterprise reform conducted from 2020 to 2022, and planned the new round of corporate reform. This approach is aimed at adapting to new development, policy requirements, and market changes, thereby creating a synergy for the deepening of reform across the board. The goal is to make new contributions to building a domestically leading and world-class modern integrated service provider of urban passenger transport.

Law-based corporate governance

BPTC adheres to Xi Jinping's Thought on the Rule of Law as its guide, continuously deepening the construction of law-based public transport and compliance management system. This effort aims to enhance our capabilities in lawful and compliant business management and risk prevention. We have issued the *Assessment and Evaluation Index on Rule of Law (2023 Edition),* effectively prompting the key few, the primary responsible persons in all subsidiaries, to coordinate and supervise law-based governance practice in person. In terms of key dates such as "National Constitution Day", we widely and thoroughly conduct legal publicity and education, fulfill the responsibility of promoting legal knowledge, and communicate the rule of law. Besides, we actively build a culture of legal compliance in public transport, and create a favorable legal environment.

We have further clarified our policy of compliance management and the concept of "everyone complies, everything complies, compliance at all times, compliance everywhere." We have issued the *Compliance Code of Conduct and established a team of compliance administrators (compliance liaisons) for the BPTC*. We have advanced the preparation and improvement of the "Three Lists of Compliance Management" and have held the "First Compliance Joint (Expanded) Conference and Mobilization Meeting on Compliance Management System Construction Evaluation". Successfully passing the on-site evaluation of the compliance management system by the State-owned Assets Supervision and Administration Commission of People's Government of Beijing Municipality, we promoted the establishment of the Corporation's compliance management system across the board. Additionally, we have been actively advancing standardization. For example, we have formulated the *Three-Year Improvement Plan for Standardization (2023-2025)*, and launched a series of promotional activities for World Standards Day to enhance the standardization of the Corporation.

The Meeting of Compliance Managers and Compliance Liaisons

Commitment Letter of Compliance Code of Conduct

Bus to publicize the rule of law

2023

12

Corporate standards released

4

Revisions of industry and group standards participated

58

Issues of updates on rule of law published

4

Invention patents authorized

75

Patents authorized in total

60

Utility patents obtained in total

Audit supervision

BPTC fully leverages audit-based supervision to provide strong support for deepening corporate reform and quality development. We have comprehensively implemented the "three-year full coverage" for supervision and evaluation of internal control, and significantly increased the scope of inspections. Focusing on central and key reform initiatives, goals of management, cost reduction and efficiency improvement tasks, key infrastructure projects, and major funds, we precisely and efficiently implemented the audit plans. Additionally, we have intensified the education of audit regulations and carried out skills and knowledge training. A total of 12 professional online business knowledge training sessions were held, effectively enhancing the dissemination of audit policies, regulations, and higher-level directives. In 2023, we completed 68 annual audit plans, conducted 166 audit activities, audited 96 units, issued 167 audit reports, and proposed 412 suggestions. This has provided strong support for standardizing enterprise operations, and promoted the establishment and standardized operation of our internal control system.

CSR Management

Urban public transport is a major livelihood project, ensuring the normal operation of cities. With a history of over a hundred years of serving the people, BPTC is always dedicated to public welfare initiatives. We integrate CSR philosophy into corporate development strategies, operation and management. We work to establish a sound CSR management system, continuously promoting the CSR philosophy both inside and outside the Corporation. We have provided ideas and made contributions to economic, social, and environmental development, serving as a textbook example of sustainable development.

CSR Philosophy

Sustainable development has become the prevailing consensus in the new era. The UN Sustainable Development Goals (SDGs) are the blueprint for achieving a better and more sustainable future for all. Always bearing in mind the country's most fundamental interests, BPTC continuously makes innovative practices and positive contributions in the field of sustainable transport. We have been committed to the CSR philosophy of "safe, convenient, efficient and comfortable" to serve passengers wholeheartedly, enabling more people to enjoy better public transportation services.

Deliver better public transport services to more people

Safe　Convenient　Efficient　Comfortable

1 NO POVERTY　3 GOOD HEALTH AND WELL-BEING　4 QUALITY EDUCATION　5 GENDER EQUALITY　7 AFFORDABLE AND CLEAN ENERGY　8 DECENT WORK AND ECONOMIC GROWTH　9 INDUSTRY, INNOVATION AND INFRASTRUCTURE　10 REDUCED INEQUALITIES　11 SUSTAINABLE CITIES AND COMMUNITIES　12 RESPONSIBLE CONSUMPTION AND PRODUCTION　13 CLIMATE ACTION

CSR philosophy and contributions to SDGs

Management Approach

As a proactive practitioner of sustainability philosophy, BPTC integrates environmental, social, and governance (ESG) standards into corporate management, production and operations, forming a scientific and professional CSR management system as well as a clear and transparent governance structure, making CSR-related work more systematically. Meanwhile, we continue to enrich the disclosure forms of CSR information and strive for excellence to improve the quality of CSR information disclosure, conveying our CSR value.

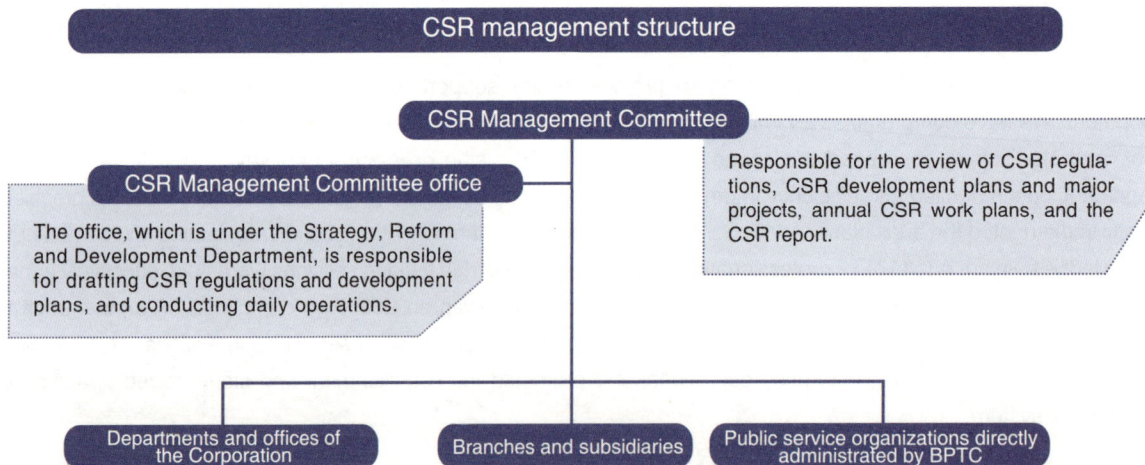

CSR management structure

CSR Management Committee

Responsible for the review of CSR regulations, CSR development plans and major projects, annual CSR work plans, and the CSR report.

CSR Management Committee office

The office, which is under the Strategy, Reform and Development Department, is responsible for drafting CSR regulations and development plans, and conducting daily operations.

Departments and offices of the Corporation

Branches and subsidiaries

Public service organizations directly administrated by BPTC

CSR Communication

CSR communication creates value. BPTC is well aware that CSR communication is expected by various stakeholders for the Corporation. It acts as an important bridge for all parties to work together to build consensus and create diverse value. At BPTC, we achieve collaboration with stakeholders through survey on material topics, "Beijing Transport Open Day" activities, new media channels, etc. We also comprehensively present our responsibilities and corporate value through CSR reports.

Material topics

Material topics reflect the significant impacts of organizations on the economy, society, and environment. Based on the industry development environment and important strategic directions in 2023, we benchmarked against domestic and international social responsibility guidelines and standards. Accordingly, we have identified material topics that are significant to both the Corporation and stakeholders from two dimensions, "Significance to economic, environmental and social impacts" and "Impact on stakeholder assessment & decisions", and have drawn a materiality matrix. The matrix provides important references for improving the report's transparency and our sustainability management.

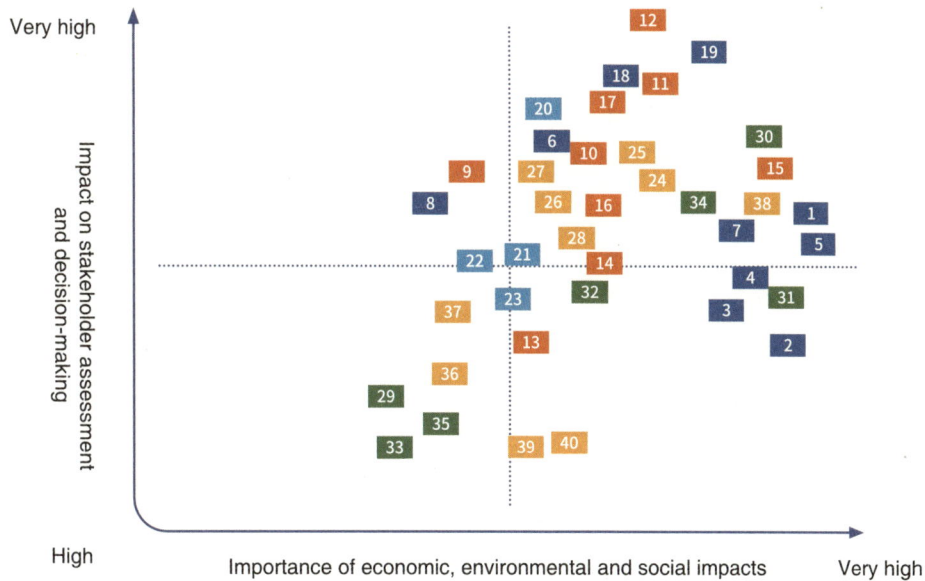

Material topic matrix

1	Improving corporate governance	11	Convenient bus service	21	Enhancing ability to handle emergencies	31	Carbon neutrality
2	Strengthening Party building	12	Passenger satisfaction	22	Strengthening safety and security management	32	Energy conservation and emission reduction
3	Law-based corporate governance	13	Serving Beijing-Tianjin-Hebei regional development	23	Securing safety through technologies	33	Green office
4	Implementing macro policies	14	Technological innovation	24	Protecting employee rights and interests	34	Addressing climate change
5	Deepening the SOE reform	15	Digital transformation	25	Equal employment	35	Charity on environmental protection
6	CSR management	16	Delivering transport services for major events and in important period	26	Occupational health management	36	Promoting employment
7	Party leadership	17	Contributing to the development of the capital	27	Staff training and development	37	Rural vitalization
8	Leading industry development	18	Ensuring passenger safety	28	Employee care	38	Emergency rescue
9	Diversified services	19	Strengthening public security	29	Advocating green travel	39	Advocating responsible travel
10	Accessibility services	20	Creating safety culture	30	Optimizing energy structure	40	Volunteer service

Note: In the review of CSR topics in 2023, based on industry development trends and the Corporation's strategic planning, we elevated the importance of Topic 8 "Leading industry development", Topic 9 "Individualized services", and Topic 12 "Passenger satisfaction".

Stakeholder communication

Placing a high value on communication and collaboration with stakeholders, we keep paying attention to their expectations and core demands. We use various communication channels to respond to their keen concerns, continuously bringing wisdom and strength into sustainability management. Together, we strive for a better future.

Stakeholders	Expectations and appeals	Responses
The government	Complying with laws and regulations Implementing transportation plans of the government Contributing to regional economic develop ment Increasing employment	Compliance management and risk control Paying tax Accepting the supervision of the government proactively Contributing to Beijing-Tianjin-Hebei integrated development
Passengers	Quality and considerate services Ensuring safe travel	Providing diversified travel services Promoting accessibility Passenger satisfaction survey Handling of customer complaints Driving safety training Safety and emergency management
Employees	Basic rights and interests Employee development Employee care	Improving compensation and benefit system Labor unions and worker representative congress Occupational health and safety management Launching staff trainings Assisting needy employees
The industry / partners	Abiding by business ethics Promoting shared development among the industry	Responsible purchasing Combating unfair competition Promoting technological innovation Conducting strategic collaboration with partners Actively supporting the work of industrial associations
Communities	Enhancing community co-construction Contributing to public welfare	Providing volunteer service Facilitating rural revitalization Promoting social employment Advocating responsible travel
The environment	Abiding by environmental laws and regulations Environmental protection	Conserving energy and reducing emissions Promoting new energy vehicles Waste sorting and Clean Your Plate Campaign Advocating green travel Public welfare activities on green development

BPTC signed a strategic collaboration agreement with Capital Airports Holdings Co., Ltd.

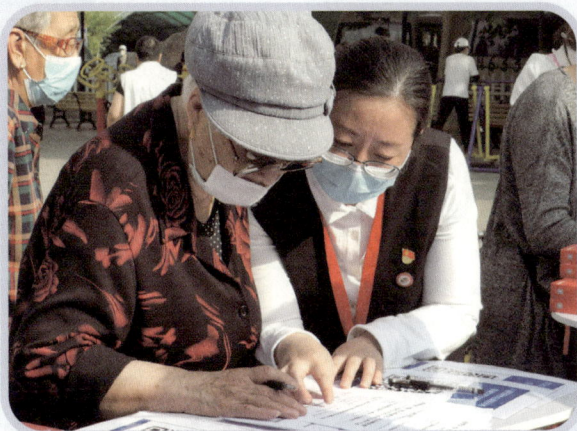

BPTC carried out the survey involving over ten thousand employees going to communities to investigate and inquire about people's mobility needs

BPTC implemented the "Little Bus Drivers" professional experience activity

BPTC collaborated with the Beijing Postal Branch of China Post Group Corporation Limited on transporting parcels by scheduled buses in rural areas

Highlights in 2023

January

We ensured smooth public transport operation during the New Year and Spring Festival period.

Wangzuo Bus Maintenance Yard was adjusted for the production layout and put into use.

February

BPTC convened the 2023 Party and Government Work Conference to make a comprehensive summary and arrangements for key tasks.

BPTC convened the sixth session of the Third Worker Representative Congress.

In the spring semester, BPTC carried out the "Responsible Driving and Pedestrians Going First" activities.

March

BPTC held the launch ceremony for the bus route T115, themed as the route only with female bus drivers.

We accomplished the task of providing transport services for the "two sessions", namely the annual sessions of the National People's Congress and the National Committee of the Chinese People's Political Consultative Conference.

We undertook the finals of the Second National Urban Vocational Skills Competition for Bus Drivers in the Public Transport Industry.

We inaugurated a mental health consulting hotline for employees to continuously ensure they have sound psychology.

BPTC signed a *Supplementary Agreement to the Strategic Cooperation Framework Agreement* with Beijing Automotive Group Co., Ltd., to fully leverage advantages for both parties, further expand cooperation, and achieve coordinated development.

Bus convenience stores at Liufang was put into operation.

September

School bus routes were piloted to open.

Beijing Public Transport Technician College was approved for establishment.

We delivered the transport services for the 2023 China International Fair for Trade in Services.

BPTC collaborated with the Beijing Postal Branch of China Post Group Corporation Limited for Route H16 and Route H31 carrying parcels in Huairou District.

We obtained the first autonomous driving road test license for large-scale ordinary passenger buses in Beijing. Our two Level 4 autonomous driving buses, with L4 autonomy, with a length of 8.5 meters, a width of 2.4 meters, 19 equipped seats, have been conducted public road testing.

August

We supported the recovery and reconstruction of targeted assisted villages after extremely heavy rainstorms. Our technical school provided logistics support for armed police officers and soldiers stationed on the levee for flood control and disaster relief.

The first batch of 100 school buses were delivered for use.

We organized a parent-child experience activity for employees in the summer themed with "Hand in Hand for Growth Accompanied by BPTC".

BPTC signed a strategic cooperation framework agreement with Beijing Financial Holding Group Co., Ltd. to deepen the common development strategy of the ecosystem, so as to give play to complementary advantages and achieve win-win cooperation.

April

Route F82 in Fangshan District and Route 929 in Mentougou District were selected as the first batch of pilot routes to carry parcels in rural areas.

We carried out promotional and educational activities for World Intellectual Property Day on April 26.

Seven subsidiaries, including the Ninth Passenger Transport Branch, BPTC Driving School and Beijing Beiqi Taxi Group Co., Ltd., participated in the "Beijing Enterprise Direct Sales - SOE Consumption Season" activity.

We held the opening ceremony of the Eighth Workers' Games and the Fifth Staff Culture Festival, as well as the Spring Sightseeing and Walking Event for Thousands of People.

May

We had an investigation carried out by more than ten thousand employees to inquire about people's needs.

We held the Second Employee Innovative Achievement Competition to fully promote the transformation and application of innovative achievements.

BPTC participated in the 2023 ZGC Forum as a typical representative of digital transformation in the field of public transport services in China.

The documentary *Reform of BPTC During the Past Century* was released nationwide.

Bus convenience stores at Maguanying was put into operation.

July

The "1921 Smart Space" Xinfeng Street Project was awarded the title of Digital Economy Industrial Park in Xicheng District.

We held the 2023 Driver "Gold and Silver Steering Wheel Award" ceremony.

The "Standardization Pilot Project for Beijing Ground Public Transport Operation Services" received funding from the Subsidy Fund for Capital Standardization Strategy.

We effectively organized the operation of public transport during the "23·7" heavy rainfall period, sparing no effort in carrying out flood prevention and disaster relief.

We released the *Implementation Plan for Improving Public Transport Services in Zhangjiawan Design Town (2022-2035)*.

June

We launched an experience and promotion month activity for customized bus routes.

We launched a free medical diagnosis activity themed with "Heart Warming and Health Caring to Promote Rural Vitalization".

The first batch of 11 bus depots shared space to the public.

We signed an agreement with Baarin Left Banner, Inner Mongolia, to establish a poverty recurrence prevention fund, and donated to assistance projects such as job creation and the setup of public welfare jobs.

The *Digital Transformation Practices of Ground Public Transport Operation Control and Vehicle Technology Support* was selected as one of the "China's Top 10 Cases of Enterprise Digital Transformation in 2023".

The first supercharging station, Muxiyuan Supercharging Station, was put into use.

BPTC convened the seventh session of the Third Worker Representative Congress.

October

BPTC signed a strategic cooperation framework agreement with Beijing Yiqing Holding Co., Ltd. to jointly strengthen business integration and resource sharing, further expand the influence of brand linkage, and improve the capability and level of serving people's livelihood in the capital.

Beijing Beiqi Taxi Group Co., Ltd. delivered the transportation services for the Third Belt and Road Forum for International Cooperation.

We undertook the finals of the "Beijing-Tianjin-Hebei Railway" Vocational Skills Competition for Coach Bus Drivers.

We successfully completed the compliance for annual carbon emissions by submitting 900,741 tons of emissions through the Beijing carbon emission management platform.

November

The buses of the Route Y16 in Yanqing District started to carry parcels as part of the collaboration between BPTC and the Beijing Postal Branch of China Post Group Corporation Limited.

We replaced bus stop poles and signs across the Tongzhou District.

The mid-term evaluation report of *Outline of the Development Plan During the 14th Five-Year Plan Period and Vision 2035 of Beijing Public Transport Corporation* was approved by the eighth review of BPTC's Board of Directors, and submitted to the State-owned Assets Supervision and Administration Commission of People's Government of Beijing Municipality for the record.

December

Beijing Public Transport Hall was opened to the public for trial operation.

BPTC signed a strategic cooperation agreement with Capital Airports Holdings Co., Ltd. to jointly explore to establish a new comprehensive framework for the "land and air" transport system.

CSR Honors

Our collective honors and accolades (partial)

BPTC's Regional Intelligent Operation Control Reform Project won the Special Recognition Award of the UITP Awards.

BPTC won the first prize in the "SOE Digital Scene Innovation Professional Competition" hosted by the State-owned Assets Supervision and Administration Commission of the State Council (SASAC).

BPTC's green and low-carbon development practice was selected as a "2022 National Green and Low Carbon Typical Case" (Enterprises) by the Ministry of Ecology and Environment.

BPTC was selected in the "China's Top 10 Cases of Enterprise Digital Transformation in 2023" at the Second National Enterprise Digital Transformation Forum of the Global Digital Economy Conference.

BPTC was chosen as a "Typical Scene of National Enterprise Digital Application" at the First National Enterprise Digital Application Ecology Conference of the 2023 China International Digital Economy Expo.

BPTC was honored with the "Second Prize of Annual Excellent Achievements of National Corporate Culture in 2022-2023".

BPTC was awarded the "National Safety Culture Building Demonstration Enterprise".

BPTC won the title of "2023 Benchmark Enterprise for Achieving Carbon Peaking and Carbon Neutrality by the China Association of Plant Engineering".

BPTC got the honorary title of "Annual Low-Carbon Model Unit for Urban Transportation in 2022-2023" by the China Urban Public Transport Association.

BPTC won the title of "Unit to Promote Green Activities" jointly awarded by Beijing Social Enterprise Quality Association, Beijing Society of Energy, and Beijing Society for Environmental Science.

BPTC's two achievements, including the *Innovative Management Practice of the Construction and Operation of the "Dual System" of Beijing Ground Public Transport Operation Service Standardization*, were awarded the First Prize of the 37th Beijing Innovation Achievement in Corporate Management Modernization.

BPTC's *Firm Political Direction, Services for the Workers, and Hard Efforts for a New Chapter for the Work of BPTC's Labor Union – "Five-type" Achievements of BPTC's Labor Union Construction* won the "First Prize of Excellent Achievements in Staff Culture Building" issued by the China Enterprise Culture Improvement Association.

The First Passenger Transport Branch's *Integrated Brand, Management and Services to Create a Corporate Culture of Thoughtful Care* got the Second Prize of Annual Excellent Achievements of National Corporate Culture in 2022-2023.

The Second Passenger Transport Branch was honored with the title of "National May 1st Labor Award" by the All-China Federation of Trade Unions.

The "Male Spirit" culture brand of the Third Passenger Transport Branch won the "Top Ten Cultural Brands" in national transportation industry.

The Party branch of the 18th Fleet of the Third Passenger Transport Branch got the award of "the Second Top 10 Innovative Cases of Enterprises in Grassroots Party Building in the Transportation Industry".

Route 877 of the Eighth Passenger Transport Branch was given the honorary title of "Model Collective for Youth Work Safety Demonstration Post in Beijing".

The youth task group of the Eighth Passenger Transport Branch for flood prevention and disaster relief was awarded "Beijing Youth Task Group".

The Xijiao Line of the Beijing Public Transport Tram Corporation won the "21st National Youth Civilization Award".

Beijing Bus Media Co., Ltd. participated in the Urban Transport Media (Advertisements) Forum and was awarded the title of "The Most Influential Enterprise".

Our employees' honors and accolades (partial)

Wang Kun from the First Passenger Transport Branch was awarded the title of "Most Charming Volunteer in the Capital".

Cui Zhiyong, driver from the Third Passenger Transport Branch, was awarded the "National May 1st Labor Medal".

Chen Meng and Liu Ran from the Third Passenger Transport Branch, Guo Sen from the Fourth Passenger Transport Branch, and Fan Lubin from the Fifth Passenger Transport Branch were honored with the title of "Most Charming Voluntary Service Family in the Capital".

Cui Man, operation controller from the Fifth Passenger Transport Branch, got the title of "National Women's Model for Contributions".

Zheng Da from the Security Department of the Fifth Passenger Transport Branch received the Excellent Individual Award for the "Third Safe Transport Striver · Beijing Model in 2023".

Nian Zhikuan, driver from the Sixth Passenger Transport Branch, won the 35th "Beijing Youth May 4th Medal".

He Shaohua from the Trolley Bus Branch was recognized as the 2023 "National Women May 1st Model", the "SOE Model · Beijing Model" dedicated to work, and the first place in the Capital SOE Staff Publicity Competition of "Individual Contribution to Country Strengthening and Rejuvenation".

Li Yuehua, employee from the No. 1 Workshop of the Maintenance and Repair Branch, was awarded the honorary title of "National Transportation Technology Expert" by the General Office of the Ministry of Transport.

Xiang Shuo from the First Passenger Transport Branch, Zhang Zheng from the Second Passenger Transport Branch, Li Xuejie from the Third Passenger Transport Branch, Liu Shuo from the Fourth Passenger Transport Branch, Shen Xuesong from the Fifth Passenger Transport Branch, Zhao Ang from the Sixth Passenger Transport Branch, Dong Zhuo from the Maintenance and Repair Branch, Guo Zhiqiang from the Property Management Center, Zhang Chen from the Beijing Public Transport Tram Corporation, and Gu Xi from the Beijing Public Transport Group Party School were honored with the Fifth "Beijing Public Transport Youth Model in the New Era".

Jing Qingbo, Zhao Zhiguo, Li Guoqing, Xie Hongge, and Li Liang, five drivers from the Beijing Beiqi Taxi Group Co., Ltd., were awarded the title of "Beijing Model · Beijing Taxi Driver" in 2022.

The news column *Accompany You All the Way* submitted by Wang Chao, Zhang Xuan and Li Tianci from the Publicity Department of BPTC got the first prize of the 2022 Beijing professional newspaper.

Zhang Shuai from BPTC won the title of "Outstanding Information Officer in the Beijing Organizational System".

Unchanged Aspiration
and New Glories

Contribution to UN SDGs

4 QUALITY EDUCATION

9 INDUSTRY, INNOVATION AND INFRASTRUCTURE

11 SUSTAINABLE CITIES AND COMMUNITIES

12 RESPONSIBLE CONSUMPTION AND PRODUCTION

"Putting Passengers First, Serving With Honor" is our duty, mission, and commitment. Deriving from our history, the spirit is alive with generations of BPTC employees, showing its lasting vitality. The spirit is reflected in our bus routes and the glory of BPTC employees. In Beijing, a city with 16 districts covering an area of 16,419 square kilometers, every departure of BPTC buses is to serve the city and its millions of residents. Our action revolves around what people need. With considerate services, our buses travel day and night on routes knitted intricately to serve passengers. Embarking on the long journey ahead, we will maintain a glorious sense of dedication and hard work and support the public's daily travel with sincere commitment and service to depict a picture of happiness in people services.

北京公交馆

BEIJING PUBLIC TRANSPORT HALL

Services Throughout the Day

Changing times do not alter our commitment and an impressive mileage record witnesses our unchanged aspiration for better services. Day in and day out, BPTC buses never stop. Our vertical and horizontal bus routes contribute to the capital's rapid development. We sincerely listen to people's voices, reflect them in our services and always be there for our passengers.

At 05:00

When the dawn is about to break, drivers of the first buses begin to prepare for the departure, which wakes up the whole city for a new day.

At 09:00

When the sky is clear, customized buses are ready to go in the direction tailored to passengers' needs.

At 12:00

At noon, the supercharging station at the corner enables a worry-free and relaxing journey.

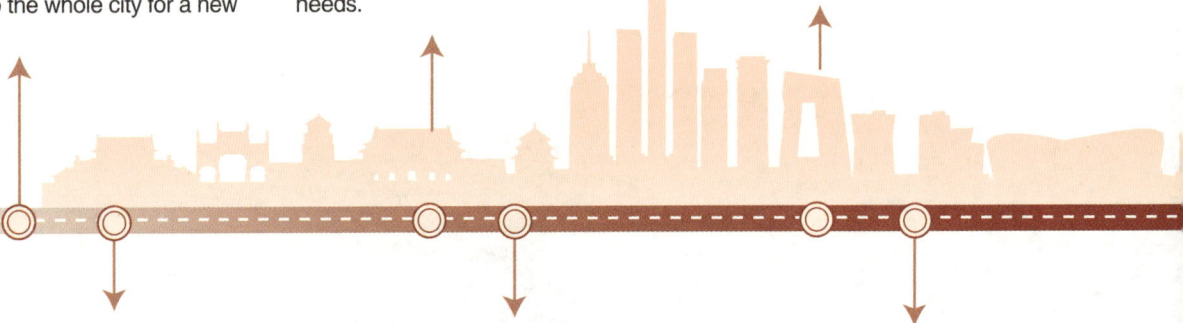

At 07:00

When the sun rises, the school bus waits as scheduled, sending students to school safely, adding a special green color in the traffic.

At 10:00

When the sun shines brightly, the Beijing Public Transport Hall welcomes visitors to have a glimpse of the past and the present of BPTC.

At 15:00

During the season of mild wind and sunshine with blossoming flowers, passengers can take the tram along the most beautiful Xijiao Line to enjoy the beautiful scenery.

At 17:00 ------------------

When dusk is approaching, bus convenience store at people's doorstep makes it easy to get daily necessities.

At 21:00 ------------------

In the middle of the night, we stagger the use of shared parking spaces to save people time finding places to park their cars.

At 03:00 ------------------

In the long night, our service staff still greet passengers who carry their luggage and are about to depart to other places.

At 19:00 ------------------

When it is gradually dark outside, the intelligent bus operation control center manages traffic during the evening rush hour behind the scenes. They sincerely contribute to every passenger's journey.

At 01:00 ------------------

When lights are still bright, our night buses send passengers home safely.

07:00 **Expectations for Sunrise**

School Buses Warmly Send Students to Their Schools

As the sun rises, students looking joyful for a new day at school gather from different directions in the waiting area for their bus to school. School bus services concern all walks of life and reflect the level and warmth of urban public services. Building a public transport operation and management system for primary and secondary schoolers in the capital is an innovative approach to addressing a special issue as the capital enters a new stage of development. It is a practical project that cares about and benefits students. In response to people's needs, we harness our resources and advantages to operate school buses as a pilot project, promoting the high-quality development and operation of a public transport operation system for schoolers in the capital and making cities more children-friendly.

On September 1, 2023, in Chaoyang, Haidian, Fengtai, and Xicheng districts, we rolled out high-quality bus routes for 13 pilot schools. Each student was assigned to a seat and was required to buckle up. These bus routes are express direct routes with each link closely managed...The opening and operation of school bus routes enable an increasing number of students and their parents to have a greener, safer, and more convenient option and effectively alleviate traffic congestion around schools.

Pilot program scale:

13
Pilot schools

25
School bus routes

47
School buses

1,599
Daily passengers on average

Gradual expansion:

21
Pilot schools

48
School bus routes

100
School buses

4,600
Daily passengers on average

Customized bus routes precisely meet the needs of each student

Adhering to the principle of "customized policy for each district, school, and bus route", we thoroughly investigate the needs for school buses and plan routes and stations accordingly. Given the arrival and departure times provided by schools, traffic conditions, safe driving requirements, and the number of expected passengers at each station, etc., we determine the travel time between stations and settle the location of pick-up. The departure time of each station is sent to passengers through the "Jingtong" mini program on WeChat and buses stick to the schedule strictly. Meanwhile, for different roads and student demand, we introduce 8-meter and 12-meter vehicle models, which are put into use according to local conditions to improve resource utilization and efficiency.

Students take school buses

Safety is paramount in each journey

Safety is our priority for the school bus operation. At the beginning of designing the school bus, we put safety at the core, ensuring that every detail reflects the importance of safety. The vehicle models selected feature excellent stability, precise control, and thoughtful consideration of safety protection devices. School buses are equipped with comprehensive and advanced safety emergency warning systems, and softened interior decorations to provide a safe and comfortable traveling space for young passengers.

Exterior color:

"Spring green" is the standard color, which is taken from "The Dragon Star Ushers in the Spring" in *Sunny Spring Poem,* symbolizing youth and hope

Interior design:

Rounded corners, no screws exposed
Flame retardant materials prevent fire and explosion

Windows:

Sliding windows are set in the upper part to prevent students from sticking out their heads and hands

Doors:

Low floor and reduced steps for a safer and more convenient experience

Driving safety:

360-degree panoramic cameras and equipped with onside BSD blind spot warning: Eliminate blind spots
Driver assistance warning system: Lane departure prevention, distance monitoring and warning, speed limit recognition

Emergency devices:

Fireproof compartment design: Build up the firewall of the whole vehicle structure
Safety emergency switch: One-key emergency response
Automatic door opening and power cut-off: Emergency lighting is activated inside the car

Seats:

Softened seats with two-point lap seatbelts effectively prevent collision

Real-time monitoring:

Camera guarding against students left behind: Camera detecting students left inside the vehicles will automatically give warnings
Inspection button: Drivers inspect vehicles to ensure that no student is left behind
Abnormal behavior monitoring system: Warnings of driver fatigue

Improving the emergency plan

We have formulated the *Handling Plan for School Bus Emergencies.* Given that all the passengers are students, we have designed the handling process for "8+1" possible school bus emergencies.

Bettering the management system

We have established 26 polices covering route setting, transport management, driving safety, emergency transport, personnel management, vehicle maintenance, IT-based operation and maintenance, etc.

Monitoring the whole process in real time

Intelligent technology realizes real-time positioning, and the ID card swipe system compares the data of students boarding and disembarking the bus, ensuring information transparency for schools and parents. We also leverage the function of the operation monitoring platform to guarantee that the service personnel of each link cooperate smoothly.

Selecting drivers and bus attendants

Our internal selection chooses the best personnel with a great sense of responsibility, professionalism, emergency handling ability, and mental toughness.

Multiple measures guarantee students' travel

At the same time, before a pilot bus route is opened, we conduct several transport and emergency drills on routes and stations to fully simulate transport scenarios such as students going to and leaving school and emergency transfer. Our drills involve drivers, crew members, bus dispatchers, students, parents accompanying students on the same bus, volunteers, teachers, etc., covering all the elements of operating vehicles, bus operation control platforms, repair, and rescue, etc. We focus on practical drills in scenarios, such as, traffic safety, service flow, organization, boarding and alighting at bus stops, smooth transfer, and emergency handling. For emergencies such as vehicle breakdowns, emergency evacuation, ride transfer, and vehicle rescue, we carry out drills according to the operating procedures of each key position and make sure that not a single detail is missed.

Inspecting the safety of school buses during the school season

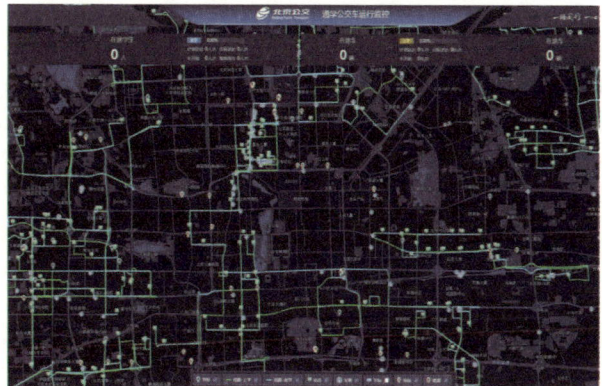

Monitoring school bus movement

Meticulous service makes the journey to school more comfortable

To provide meticulous and considerate service to students, we have selected friendly female bus attendants, who are offered specialized training in theory and practical skills, including primary and secondary schoolers' psychological education and communication skills, wound treatment, Heimlich Maneuver, and other common first aid knowledge. Meanwhile, given the knowledge and cultural needs of primary and secondary schoolers, we enhance their cultural experience during the journey by decorating our bus interiors on five themes of safety common sense, traditional Chinese culture, moral education stories, traditional festivals, poems and songs according to the requirements of pilot schools. We make our school buses mobile classrooms integrating knowledge into daily travel.

Comfortable and cozy school buses

Since our pilot school bus project, an important initiative to improve people's life, was rolled out, our school buses have been well applauded for their safety, comfort, convenience, punctuality, and the functionality of addressing school bus challenges and easing congestion around schools. The Central Government Rotating Inspection Team, the CPC Beijing Municipal Committee and Beijing Municipal People's Government, and relevant commissions and bureaus have recognized our school buses. Schools and parents have praised the service we provide.

12%
Decrease in cars picking up students since the trial operation of school buses was rolled out.

4.91
Traffic index average value, suggesting a level of "mild congestion", and congestion around campuses has eased during peak hours.

Source: Beijing Municipal Commission of Transport

"BPTC has advanced bus route surveys, stop settings, supporting facilities optimization, and online operation platforms to ensure the smooth operation of school buses on September 1. Since the operation of school buses, both parents and schools have given their thumbs up to BPTC's operation management and service. School buses operated by the municipal SOE, BPTC, symbolize a higher standard of safe operations. At the same time, BPTC's bus attendants and drivers have received strict and meticulous training, and their attitude and professionalism have left a deep impression on parents. Children are very happy on their way to and from school, and everyone is reassured."

—The person in charge of the Chaoyang District Education Commission's special program for school buses

"After I experienced multiple school bus routes, I discovered firsthand the magic of school buses. Children like taking these buses and are no longer late for school. In addition, they are taught to follow rules and have self-management in these small buses, marking their first step to independent traveling."

—A Beijing Daily's reporter note

"At first we didn't choose to take the school bus because there were some safety concerns. My kid wanted to have a try, and soon we found out that the bus was convenient, safe, and affordable. All our previous concerns were gone, and we are satisfied."

—A parent of a student at Chaoyang Elementary School Affiliated with Capital Normal University

"My classmates and I like to take the school bus. There will be a bus attendant to check students' presence and help us buckle up. Usually, on the way, we will chat and read books on the bus, which is very fun."

—A student at the Chaoyang Elementary School Affiliated with Capital Normal University

10:00 In Touch With History

A Small Hall Carries Our Past

In the daytime, a visit to the Beijing Public Transport Hall leads you into a journey spanning over 100 years. The Beijing Public Transport Hall is a condensed exhibition hall of approximately 5,000 square meters, *A Hundred Years of Grand Line 1* features the integration of public transport into urban development and *the Reform of BPTC During the Past Century* is a 95-minute documentary. They record the collective memories of the city created by BPTC's travel services in the past 100 years and reflect the unchanging aspiration of BPTC employees to serve the people.

Time leaves its mark while old items keep our aspirations alive

Beijing Public Transport Hall

Entering the Beijing Public Transport Hall, visitors can understand our progress step by step in the past century and witness the power of time. Stories of how our past links with our present are a new way of connecting passengers and BPTC employees in the new era. Here, visitors can get on the tram on display, listening to the bells that echoed in Beijing a century ago. They can also see the old bus stop sign with a pull-out hook used in the last century, a design to inform passengers about the end of daily services. In technology-enabled scenarios, visitors can realize how our bus routes are interwoven into a network that shines throughout the whole city of Beijing...

Following the logic of social development, we present six carriers: people, vehicles, routes, tickets, stations, and stories in eight thematic sections: a century of leadership, a century of development, a century of change, a century of glory, a century of memories, a century of evolution, a century of engraved moments, and a century of key moments, panoramically displaying the glorious history of Beijing's public transport in the context of times and the development of Beijing. The hall is also the first comprehensive medium-sized industry museum in Beijing that focuses on ground public transport and integrates display, collection, research, education, and interaction, which will provide strong support to Beijing in building a "City of Museums".

The hall houses more than 6,000 collections and 16 main vehicle models and includes over 10 interaction areas strengthened by sound, films, objects, and stories. Full-scene immersive interaction, tactile experience, and cloud travel VR technology vividly present memories of the past. As of December 31, 2023, the hall had received 453 visits, totaling 19,651 visitors.

"Top Ten Museum" and "Popular Museum" in China's transport industry

Honors

Six carriers of the Beijing Public Transport Hall

Case: Bus stop signs that can "talk"

In the 1950s, information technology was undeveloped and most passengers did not wear a watch. To allow passengers to accurately know the times of the first and last buses and avoid passive waiting, BPTC set up a bus stop sign with a pull-out hook. Specifically, stops poles were equipped with double-layered round iron plates, which sandwiched a curved iron arrow containing the white words "the last bus has departed" on a red background. As the last bus traveled, the bus attendant would get off at each stop and pull out the iron hook, which was withdrawn the next day when the first bus passed by to start a new day of operations. Therefore, passengers often said that "hook up, no bus; hook down, bus running." A small hook embodied the value of BPTC employees who put passengers first and offered services as promised. Today, an increasing number of smart bus stop signs with electronic displays are appearing around us, telling passengers more information and bringing great convenience.

Bus stop sign with a pull-out hook

The first group of visitors in the Beijing Public Transport Hall took a group photo

"When I was a child, buses were my first option. I was curious about what the first generation of buses looked like. I also wanted to see the development of BPTC over the years, so I made an appointment to visit. In addition, I grew up influenced by the story of Li Suli (a former conductor in BPTC known for her sincere service). Although I never took her bus, I can see and get on the bus on display where she used to work, picturing how she worked over those years. Her work was special and not easy."

—The first visitor to the Beijing Public Transport Hall

A century of development depicts the memories of a city

Public transport in the last 100 years witnessed a happy life and carried the collective memory of a city. On February 20, 2023, the documentary *A Hundred Years of Grand Route 1* was broadcast on China's CCTV-9 documentary channel as the first of 110 key literary and artistic programs under the "Superior Audio-visual Beijing" mechanism to be released on CCTV. The documentary shows the historical charm of BPTC and the development of Beijing, and for the first time features the "Grand Route 1", the shared memory of generations of Beijing residents. Through the window of the Grand Route 1, the documentary follows a timeline of more than a century, from *Waking up to the Old Capital, Old City Takes a New Look, Spring Sunshine Sprinkles All the Way, Living Together in the Global Village,* and *Together to the Future,* telling the history of BPTC in the last century and changes of the times in collective memories. In this documentary, the wheel of history connects the past and present, presenting a picture of people's life in Beijing, an ancient but vibrant metropolis.

We are always moving forward and continuing the story of Beijing and public transport in the new era toward a bright future.

A Hundred Years of Grand Route 1

A century of changes collects moments of happiness

In a hundred years of changing landscape, BPTC grows and matures together with passengers, all reflected in the documentary *Reform of BPTC During the Past Century.* It illustrates the aspirations of BPTC employees who selflessly dedicate themselves to making progress and serving the people.

On May 29, 2023, the documentary J*ourney of Joy: Reform of BPTC During the Past Century* was screened in cinemas nationwide. The unique and moving documentary tells touching stories of BPTC employees in generations striving for people's happiness. It depicts that BPTC employees persevere in taking their responsibilities to support the public transport development throughout all seasons and at all hours over the century. The documentary indicates the challenges in delivering convenient bus services and the significance of passing on BPTC's spirit. Since it was released, the movie had been widely watched and highly recognized by our industry counterparts and citizens from all walks of life across China with a box office of more than RMB 5.8 million. It has been collected by the National Film Collection Project, a major cultural project of the *Cultural Development Plan Set for the 14th Five-Year Plan Period,* demonstrating the modern corporate image of BPTC.

The poster of *Journey of Joy: Reform of BPTC During the Past Century*

Honors

- Outstanding Documentary at the 9th China Jiayuguan International Short Film Festival
- Best Documentary Film of the Year and Golden Angel Award, 19th Chinese American Film Festival, 2023
- Outstanding Documentary Re-evaluation (Documentary Feature Section) of the 20th Guangzhou International Documentary Film Festival Golden Kapok Award
- Recommended Work and Special Recommended Editing Award of the Cultural and Historical Category of the Second Chinese Documentary Film Festival

♡ The voice of BPTC employees

"Driving a bus is what I am proud of in my life"

——Song Shuhui, the female driver of the first-generation trolleybus

The road to happiness requires wholehearted dedication. Looking at the past enables one to savor moments of happiness. The development of BPTC starts with trams, whose rails only existing in a few locations today. They are an irreplaceable symbol of Beijing's culture, bearing special commemorative significance and value for the city and its residents. So how did trams work and who was the first female trolleybus driver? What were the buses like in those days and what was the point in passenger service? For these questions, Song Shuhui, a 90-year-old retired bus driver who served for 30 years, can give her answers.

Song Shuhui, a trolleybus driver in the "Hulan Group"

In 1951, Song Shuhui started to work at the tram company and soon she became a bus conductor popular among passengers. She still vividly remembers scenes of the past. "We treat passengers as friends and make them feel at home. We always smile, say 'please', and introduce bus routes quickly. There was a bowl of water inside the bus. The water could not be spilled out as we pulled in and pulled away. This means keeping a steady speed."

Trolleybus "Hulan Group" drivers
(The first driver from the left in the second row is Song Shuhui)

Thanks to several years of excellent performance as a conductor, in 1954, Song was recommended to the driving class to learn how to drive a tram. After systematic training, she became a tram driver. "The tram ran on a track. We could only slow down to stop when a situation arose. It had no steering wheel and no glass windows. The doors were slid open. The tram bell was on the tram floor, and when I pressed the bell with my feet, it rang 'Diang Diang'. That was why trams were called 'Diang Diang Vechiels'. Although it was slow, driving a tram was not easy, because I was not tall enough to reach the joystick when seated. I stood all the way when I was working. My legs were almost numb after a day of work. It was challenging, but I loved the job and I was satisfied. On May Day or the National Day, I drove through Dongdan and Xidan, Tiananmen Square. Seeing all those special light and flower decorations, I was more than proud and happy," she said excitedly.

In 1958, the Beijing Municipal People's Government issued a call to replace trams with trolleybuses, ushering in the vigorous development of trolleybuses. In the same year, inspired by the spirit of self-dependence, Chinese workers created China's first trolleybus within one year. The twelve female drivers who drove the first domestic "Jingyi" trolleybuses were widely reported by media. They were divided into two groups of six. Song Shuhui's group was named the "Hulan Group" by themselves as they hoped to inspire everyone to overcome difficulties and learn from the female role model Liu Hulan's tenacity.

"Since everything is hard-won, today's young employees should cherish what they have, polish their skills, and serve passengers wholeheartedly. Buses are an image of a city and bus drivers should be proud of their work," Song said firmly. From her career, we feel the passion and hard work of generations of BPTC employees who forge ahead along the way.

17:00 The Harbor at Dusk

Convenient Services Support a Better Life

As the sun sets, a day's work is coming to an end. Beijing at dusk, however, is bustling again. To meet people's aspirations for a better life, Beijing improves the quality of life in its development and builds an effective mega-city governance system so that the benefits of development are shared among all more equitably. This raises higher requirements in social governance for Beijing due to its special status as the capital. Amid the trend of new-era development in Beijing, BPTC pinpoints our position and serves the general picture, providing high-quality services to build Beijing into "four centers" (the national political center, cultural center, center for international exchanges, and center for technological innovation). We also strive to explore a transformation from "a provider of urban public transport" to "a provider of urban public services". By creating a high-quality transit experience that blends travel with lifestyle, BPTC is expanding its role to better meet the people's desire for a fulfilling life.

We are committed to bringing more benefits to people and resolving their concerns. Thus, we tap into the value of bus depots and practice the concept that public resources are reserved for the public. We promote the sharing of bus depot resources in an orderly manner. For example, bus convenience stores are installed at well-equipped bus depots. We also provide supercharging services for new energy vehicles (NEVs) and share parking spaces with private cars by staggered use, meeting people's urgent needs. These efforts enable us to meet people's service demands, and supplement urban functions, so as to support a better life.

30 bus convenience stores opened, serving more than **644,100** customers.

The first group of supercharging stations built and operated in **18** bus depots in Muxiyuan and Liucun,
with a total of **2,598,200** kWh of electricity charged for **105,200** orders.

21 shared bus depots providing **366** parking spaces for staggered sharing.

Bus convenience stores are a scenery bustling with life

In response to the 15-minute radius livelihood service circle in the capital, we expand our service coverage to shore up community convenient services by utilizing our bus depots. On March 31, 2023, the Liufang Public Transport Convenience Store was launched on a trial basis, which marked the official beginning of the bus convenience stores project.

We have set up a special team to make coordinated planning. Bearing in mind the needs of community residents, the team comes up with thoughtful and detailed planning under the principle that "once a pop-up stall is put in place, it should develop steadily and become successful." It visits different locations with government departments and communities to choose the right place. Under the premise that bus depot operations are not compromised, the team opts for places where residents concentrate, the transport is convenient, and convenient services are not sufficient. It utilizes the spare space of bus depots and plans all kinds of business formats based on the principle of "making up for what is missing" to maximize the value of convenient services. To meet the needs of people to purchase what they want, we operate bus convenience stores from 7:00 a.m. to 10:00 p.m. so that more residents feel the warmth and care we provide.

We sell fruits and vegetables at affordable prices to meet people's daily needs, reflecting our responsibility and commitment. In the future, we will explore the sustainable development path of convenience services, tap the potential of existing spaces, and enrich the formats of convenient services to meet residents' needs, translating the list of needs into the list of satisfactions. We will strive to satisfy residents by getting close to people and enlarging the circle of happiness so that more residents can enjoy a more convenient and comfortable urban life.

Maguanying bus convenience store

Supercharging stations become a harbor for car owners

As NEVs are increasingly adopted, charging piles, an important supporting facility, are frequently seen. However, the use of NEVs is inevitably accompanied by "charging anxiety" problems such as a small number of charging piles and lengthy waiting times.

To alleviate people's "charging anxiety", at the end of June 2023, the first supercharging station we operated at the Muxiyuan bus depot was opened to the public. Making full use of the depot's power resources, we provide 24-hour vehicle charging services to the surrounding residents, effectively addressing the problem of charging piles being few and far between in communities. This makes charging as fast and convenient as refueling and truly realizes "charging for a quarter of an hour and traveling 800 miles." In addition, we equip each charging pile with a QR code, through which the current power price and service fees can be seen. The charging pile screen also displays real-time charging volume, fees, current, and the time still needed, helping car owners easily complete the charging process themselves.

In addition to providing car owners with all-weather charging services, we also set up car owners' service centers in supercharging stations, which are equipped with air-conditioners, seats, microwave ovens, mobile batteries, and other facilities. Every detail shows our warmth and consideration for car owners, making supercharging stations a happy harbor for car owners in their green travel.

Muxiyuan Longrui Sanyou Supercharging Station

"It is convenient. No parking fees are charged. I only need to wait for half an hour to get my car fully charged, during which I can have my lunch. I can also go to the Car Owner Service Center to rest for a while. There are seats, air conditioners, and hot water available."

—Taxi driver Mr. Zhao

Scan the QR code to watch the news about the opening of BPTC's supercharging stations to the public

Staggered sharing of parking areas saves time in finding available places

Late at night, the Tiancun Banbi Bus Depot in Haidian becomes quiet. It houses operating buses and keeps 20 parking spaces for surrounding residents. They can park their cars there at night only. We share public resources with the community to give real benefits to the people.

Under the premise of guaranteeing the safe operation of buses, we allow residents to park their cars at night at the corners of bus depots where it is impossible to park large buses. This enables staggered parking, and resource sharing, alleviating the imbalance of supply and demand for parking, promotes the circulation of parking resources. Meanwhile, to ensure the orderly management of shared parking, we adopt advanced digital technology to empower intelligent parking facilities, put in place a variety of data-sharing mechanisms covering vehicle information, parking space information, payment information, etc., and accurately supply parking spaces to the demand side. This mode facilitates the transition from "management by human" to "management by human and machine". We also require the parking demand side, parking management side, local communities, and other stakeholders to jointly sign the Agreement on Staggered Sharing of Parking Space to ensure parking safety and coordination.

Parking spaces for staggered sharing in Tiancun Banbi Bus Depot

"In the past, when I came home, I had to drive around the neighborhood looking for a parking space. I was anxious when I couldn't park my car. Now, I have rented a parking space for staggered sharing at the bus depot near my neighborhood and no longer have to worry about parking issues."

—Mr. Lin, a resident

23:00 The Companion at Starry Night

Night Buses are a Warm Guardian of Passengers

As people hurry around the capital, which is still bustling and dynamic at night, BPTC offers all-journey considerate services to meet passengers' expectations. Running buses make up the flowing light in Beijing.

We initiate night bus services, weaving dreams with our passengers

In 1958, to meet the needs of night-shift workers, we opened two bus routes at night, making Beijing the first city in China where public transport was operated day and night. In the 1990s, the number was increased to 15. Since 2014, we have re-planned and established a night bus network of 37 routes in a mesh-shaped checkerboard pattern. Since then, the network has expanded, allowing passengers to travel freely and conveniently even late at night. Today, we have enriched the services of night buses. We have put in place the warm-hearted "late-night bus route" so that our spirit of "putting passengers first, serving with honor" continues to shine at night.

Our timely services meet people's needs, bringing them the expected comfort

To shorten the waiting at night, we coordinate the planning of the night bus route network, accurately and carefully summarize the travel and transfer needs of passengers at night, and always refine the night bus timetable. With better support of information technology, we enable passengers to have real-time information about bus movements. We strictly select skilled and experienced drivers who are required to perform their job responsibly and committedly, and monitor real-time situations through the driver behavior monitoring system to ensure travel safety at night. At the same time, we pay close attention to small details in creating a cozy environment. With bus interior decorations themed "Warmth of Bus" and "Warmth in the Way Home", we make passengers feel the passion and care of BPTC.

Warm-hearted "late-night bus route" (Night Line 7)

"Warmth of Bus" bus culture

♡ **The voice of BPTC employees**

The guardian of shimmering light
——Lv Zhen'an, driver of Night Line 7

Night bus drivers, like a lamp lighting up passengers' way home, always fulfill their responsibilities and accompany passengers amid the dim light of night buses. As an experienced night bus driver, Lv Zhen'an has witnessed the development and changes in Beijing and the life of people busy with their work late at night.

Twenty-two years of career achieves a mileage of 350,000 meters. In 2001, Lv Zhen'an started to work as a bus driver. Before the night bus schedule adjustment in September 2014, to take care of his bedridden father in the daytime, Lv applied to drive the night bus. He has been working as a night bus driver for over nine years, during which he did not ask for a day off or miss a shift. He always turns up at 21:00 to take over his shift and gets everything ready before the departure time at 23:20.

Driving on Liangguang Street all year round, Lv Zhen'an shapes his overall impression of passengers. "Those who take the night buses include designated drivers, major railway transfer hub passengers, outpatients, drinkers, sanitation workers, morning exercise people, and tourists to Beijing. We will provide targeted services, such as waking up sleeping drinkers, and offering what passengers need." To provide passengers with more comfortable and warm services, the Night Line 7 team to which Lv belongs summarizes the work method of "three hearts, three diligence" and the work concept and principle of "following standards, ready to help, observing passengers, treating them well, and carrying out operations." We serve late bus passengers with meticulous service.

"Satisfying passengers is the goal of our night bus drivers, and we all work for that goal." At BPTC, there are more night bus drivers like Lv who provide warm services to passengers. Their considerate services are as bright as stars in the sky, illuminating the way of passengers to their homes and warming every corner of the city.

Lv Zhen'an patiently answers passengers' questions

Enjoyable Travel
Offering More Options

Contribution to UN SDGs

BPTC intends to help every passenger reach their destination, and embrace innovation for providing people more travel options. We are committed to securing excellent services heart and soul and safeguard every trip day in and day out. We are looking forward to a future where people's life is made better because of our travel services.

全面深化改革
全面建设社会主义现代化国家

全面从严治党
全面依法治国

北京城市副中心

XJ 011

Easy Travel in a Prosperous City

Bearing in mind the mission of "delivering better public transport services to more people", we provide more and better travel options that link up each stop in Beijing. Constantly upgraded travel services make public transport warmer and higher quality. As we go forward, our century-old brand takes a new look. Our high-quality brand bus routes in the new era bear some hallmarks of urban culture in an extended network that carries exclusive moments and warmth.

Interweaving a "network of happiness" for urban travel

Prioritizing the improvement of passenger experience, we are committed to building a high-quality bus network and improving the bus service in key areas. We also promote bus-metro connection and complementarity for better public transport accessibility.

2023

144
Conventional bus routes opened, adjusted, or extended

134.2 km
Additional bus route length

99.07 %
Bus schedule adherence in rush hour

—— **Route and network optimization priorities** ——

Strengthening connection with metro
- We have adjusted Route 390 to connect with Dajing Station of Metro Line 14, helping passengers transfer to the nearest subway station on Chengzhuang Street.
- We have added the Lianhuaqiao bus station to Route 62 to enable efficient connection between rail transit and buses.
- By opening or adjusting routes and adding bus stops, etc., we guarantee that bus stations with a transfer distance of less than 50 meters from metro station exits account for 86%.

Optimizing micro-circulation routes
- We have opened Special Route 125 to meet the travel needs of the newly built neighborhood in the Guogongzhuang area.
- We have opened Route S102 to facilitate the daily travel of residents in the Mapo New Town.
- We have adjusted the direction of Special Route 155 and Special Route 189 to attract more passengers.

Steadily advancing the punctuality project
- We improved the monitoring technology of punctual departure and install new fences at 680 bus depots and 1,105 route stops to improve the accuracy of monitoring the punctuality of buses.
- We set up midway control points of all eligible bus routes and utilize the statistics of the operation report to strengthen the monitoring of midway punctuality.
- We strengthen the punctuality management of fixed route timetables and evaluate fixed route performance based on the operation punctuality report.

2021-2023 Operational Indicator Table

	Index(unit)	2021	2022	2023
Routes in operation	Total number of routes in operation	1,225	1,299	1,293
	Number of scheduled bus routes	1,217	1,291	1,285
	Length of scheduled bus routes (km)	28,579.7	30,173.9	29,738.5
	Length of route network (km)	7,771.3	8,180.6	8,314.8
	Number of bus stops	19,262	20,469	20,792
Optimized route network	Total number of optimized routes	151	100	144
	Length of overlapping routes reduced (km)	384.6	276.0	1,069
	Number of overlapping stops cut	941	700	2,099
	Length of bus routes on the road not covered before (km)	142.7	82.5	134.2
	Number of communities benefited	186	118	313

Offering customized travel

To satisfy passengers' desire for better travel services, we track current trends, innovate in customized buses, and provide differentiated and diverse travel services for passengers. Meanwhile, we updated digital management means and adopted a variety of new media channels for customized bus experience promotion month activities to improve customized bus brand awareness and user engagement. Our customized bus services cover different scenarios, such as commute, tourism, daily leisure, short-distance connection, etc., allowing passengers to book buses and travel anytime and anywhere.

Carrying out the customized bus experience promotion month activity

2023

428
New customized bus routes

660
Total customized bus routes

19
New flexible bus routes

139
Total flexible bus routes

The moving customized bus

Case: Hailing a bus to travel around Beijing

It is difficult to hail a taxi in Beijing's core area during the tourism peak season, so tourists have no option but to wait in a long queue. In June 2023, the No. 9 Passenger Transport Branch introduced the on-demand shuttle bus service in the core area for tourists headed to the Forbidden City. For group tourists, they can also reserve the guide service. So far, our on-demand shuttle buses have covered 28 areas. Many tourists have opted to "hail a bus", which brings them greater satisfaction.

Enjoying quality travel

Despite changing times, we remain committed to our mission of improving services. Focusing on passengers' expectations for diverse, high-quality, and interactive travel experiences, we introduced the Branded Route Project that consists of 10 benchmark routes, 100 quality routes, and N special routes. With the interior decorated with different themes, the branded buses become mobile publicity platforms, museums and lecture halls.

━━━ BPTC's branded bus route system ━━━

Benchmark routes

These routes are the flagship of BPTC's bus services, including the routes passing the Chang'an Avenue and those in the core area.

Quality routes

These are the embodiment of BPTC's quality bus routes in terms of service, safety, or operation, with strong social influence. These routes feature themes such as quality service, safety, respecting the elderly and disabled, convenient commuting.

Special routes

These routes have 15 special themes, such as the central axis, the ancient capital, the mountain area service, the nighttime service, legal publicity, as well as women's contribution.

2023

107
Branded bus routes rolled out in total

Among them, Route 1, Route 563, Route 141,Night Route 7, Route 5, and Senshui Route are honored with title of National Excellent Premium Routes.

Case: Newly painted Route 23 buses catch people's eyes

BPTC's Route 23 opened in 1949, as old as the PRC, carries a profound Beijing culture. In 2023, BPTC painted the exterior of the Route 23 buses with Beijing Opera characters, such as Mu Guiying and Zhao Yun, and photos of Beijing's past in bright colors and exquisite styles that amaze people along the way. Today, Route 23 has become a "mobile exhibition hall" of traditional culture both inside and outside.

Newly painted Route 23 bus

The route themed Chang'an Avenue

The route themed mountain area service

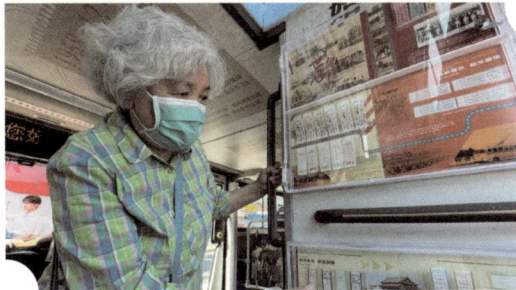

The route themed the history of the ancient capital

The route themed education on the history of revolution

The route themed women's contribution

The route themed the central axis culture

Case: Taking the Route 107 to experience the ancient capital

The Route 107 is of profound historical and cultural significance. Traveling from west to east, the route passes through the most representative landmarks of Beijing, hutongs, and prosperous and bustling urban streets, linking up classic cultural symbols of the ancient city. The beauty of ancient Beijing unfolds in front of passengers when they take Route 107. Today, Route 107 has become one of the iconic routes in Beijing.

The Route 107 trolleybus themed the history of the ancient capital

Responsiveness to Passengers' Needs

We cater to the needs of people and live up to their expectations. We conducted a survey with over ten thousand employees going to the communities to investigate and inquire about passengers' needs. We also deepen the "efficient handling of complaints" mechanism, respond to every demand, and deliver high-quality and warm services to small details, illuminating people's journeys with our passenger-oriented services.

Ten thousand employees involved in passenger surveys

Practical actions deepen our understanding, which in turn guide our efforts. In May 2023, under the theme of "visiting the front line with sincerity, listening to people's opinions whole-heartedly, and meeting people's needs with concrete actions", we mobilized nearly 13,000 Party members to inquire about passengers' needs at bus stops, communities, and distant villages across the city and get to understand their troubles and urgent expectations. Informed by the survey results, we took targeted measures and introduced initiatives to benefit the people, which optimized the "last kilometer" service, improving passengers' sense of gain, happiness and safety.

Our efforts in passenger surveys

A map of the survey scope
We divided the survey scope into different regions and designated a person in charge. We maintained district, region or nature-based hierarchical planning and management.

A plan of balanced coverage
Nearly 370 Party branches covered about 1,000 survey locations in prosperous neighborhoods, remote villages, bus depots with difficult conditions and distant bus stops to cater to a wider group of passengers.

A list of questions to understand people's thoughts
We compiled internal and external questionnaires respectively. For passengers, we care about opening, adjusting, or extending bus routes, improving services, and the construction of bus convenience stores, while the internal version highlights the contents of employee care and problem solving.

A list of people's voices
Through methods such as on-site visits, on-site questionnaire distribution, online surveys, random interviews, and seminars for exchanges, we fully understand social expectations, people's opinions, and community experience, which are collected in the list.

A plan of realistic and effective actions
Based on the list above, we formulated action plans and called for coordinated efforts to address common problems to ensure effective results.

2023

Nearly
13,000
Party members visited

50
Villages

220
Enterprises

212
Communities

107
Schools

33
Hospitals

43
Government agencies at all levels

333
Community-level organizations and stops

620
Seminars held

32,000
Questionnaires distributed

2,756
Issues addressed

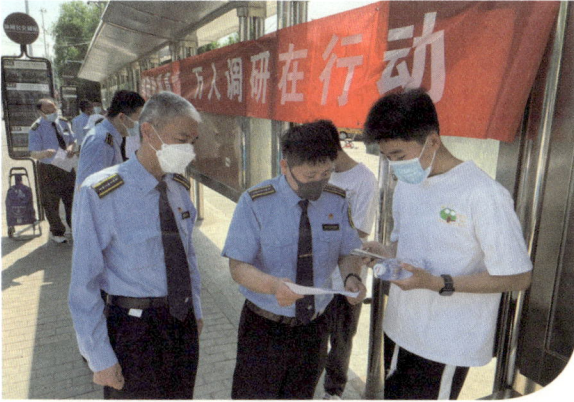

Investigating passenger demand at a bus stop

Visiting communities to conduct passenger surveys

Adding a new bus stop at a school entrance after a school survey

Adjusting the first and last bus stops based on passengers' feedback

Case: Building a "service rainbow bridge" based on survey results

On May 17, 2023, the fourth Party branch of the Trolley Bus Branch surveyed the Dongjiaominxiang Primary School in Dongcheng District. Teachers and students there hoped to have a new bus stop, Taijichang stop, set on Route 103 to reduce students' walking distance and time. After an on-site visit, the Trolley Bus Branch introduced a popular and distinctive rainbow decorated Taijichang stop, on June 9, bringing convenience to teachers and students. A simple bus stop acts as a bridge for BPTC to serve the public and facilitates the "last kilometer" in passenger services.

The newly added "rainbow stop" on Route 103

Efficient handling of complaints

Committed to providing warm services to people, we strive to meet the public's pursuit of high-quality travel services and deepen the mechanism of "efficient handling of complaints". By formulating special work programs, implementing the system of contacting and serving the public, and improving the assessment and incentive mechanism, we help our service personnel improve their knowledge and practical skills. At the same time, an in-depth analysis of passengers' complaints enables us to understand their needs and work with other stakeholders to solve problems. We respond quickly to passengers' complaints, take targeted initiatives, and achieve the results we want. We are shifting from "efficient handling of complaints" to "addressing complaints before they emerge".

BPTC customer service center

2023

94.04%
Passenger satisfaction rate

100%
Complaint resolution rate

99.83
The overall evaluation of "efficient handling of complaints" averaged

263,706
Customer communications (hotlines, mailboxes, etc.)

Unhindered channels collect people's opinions

At the forefront of travel services, we act as the considerate guide for passengers, providing them with accurate and timely information to facilitate every trip. Under the "one issue per month" campaign, we go to bus stops and into the compartment to listen and respond to passengers' demands. We also improve the 24/7 hotline mechanism to answer passengers' questions instantly and ensure that every call gets timely and satisfactory responses. Employing a wider group of new media platforms, we interact with passengers in real-time through various channels such as Weibo, WeChat, Douyin, and Weishi. Online influencers are also invited to visit our workplaces to witness BPTC's efforts and achievements in facility renovation and service upgrading that bring convenience to the public.

2023

848,265
Calls on the 96166 hotline answered

1,220
Visits through the "into the community and bus stops" surveys

Heartfelt services create warm and pleasing journeys

To allow wider access to better public transport, we continue to improve overall service quality, deliver seven service norms, and maintain order at stops. We also clean bus compartments every day and optimize services and facilities for aged passengers. Our care resolves travel obstacles to make every trip full of care and warmth. This improves travel satisfaction and life quality.

Crews clean up bus compartment

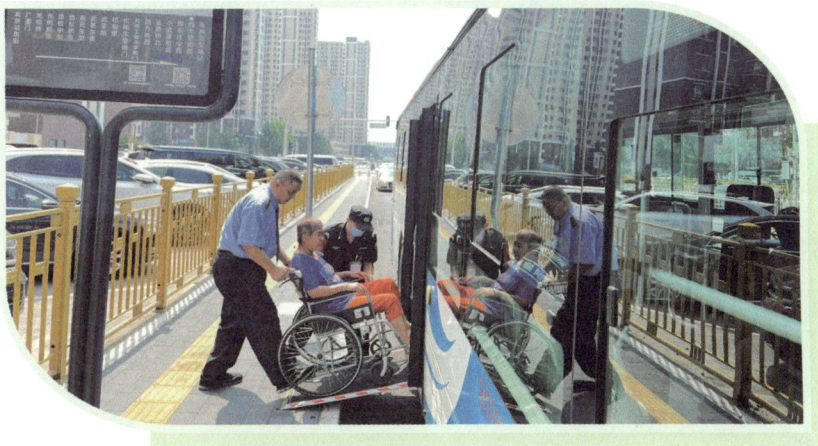

Helping an elderly passenger get on

2023

21,000+
Personnel organized for

96,000+
Times Vehicle cleaning

120
Bus routes designed with cultural interiors

3,500
Vehicles designed with cultural interiors

11,158
Commendations for returning lost money

4,000+
Praises for respecting the elderly and helping the disabled

53,000+
Elderly or disabled passengers assisted in their journeys

Sincerity shown at details

Our spirit nurtures our corporate culture.

BPTC's spirit of "Putting Passengers First, Serving With Honor, Contributing Sincerely to Society, and Taking Responsibility With Courage" has been upheld by generations of BPTC employees. It shapes a unique corporate culture system and motivates BPTC employees to forge ahead proudly. Inspired by the century-old spirit and the "shared journey" culture of BPTC, the First Passenger Transport Branch has summarized a unique brand culture that advocates everyone should offer sincere services in detail.

细微真情
XIWEIZHENQING

"Sincerity Shown in Details" logo of the First Passenger Transport Branch

A grand career begins with small endeavors.

Committed to sincere services, the First Passenger Transport Branch optimized bus route design and bus stop allocation to addresses passenger concerns. The branch is a good guide and a map of passengers, striving to improve all the details and to ensure zero driving accidents. The culture of "subtle sincerity" is translated into employees' self-recognition and action to realize sincere, detailed, and quality passenger services of the branch.

Digital Empowerment for Intelligent Travel

Embracing the wave of digitization, we accelerate digital development, and innovate in regional smart operation control and monitoring. Supported by a digital system, we advance overall digitalization to bring smarter services for passengers.

"Smart brain" realizes accurate operation control

Deeply integrating information technology into our operation management, we upgrade regional smart operation control in all aspects to realize greater resource efficiency, compatibility between bus capacity and mobility demand, and a better balance between occupancy rate of the bus and the comfort of passengers. We aim to offer smoother, smarter, and more comfortable travel experiences.

Improving regional smart operation control

We have established a timetable evaluation system to improve the function of the vehicle scheduling assistance system.

We have formulated 32 comprehensive reports, including daily operation reports and real-time monitoring reports, to efficiently analyze and monitor daily operation data and other information.

We have formulated rules and procedures on bus interlining and promoted the interlining of buses for 167 routes.

We have downsized or integrated 12 regional operation control centers to improve the level of integration.

We strengthen operation evaluation and guidance to primary management. In 2023, we organized more than 20 operation control meetings and issued 41 operation evaluation reports and 18 operation control reminders.

We keep optimizing the smart operation control system to adapt to the scenarios of multi-route departure and command, as well as long-distance monitoring.

BPTC operation control and emergency command center

Digital transformation gathers momentum

Intensifying our efforts in the field of intelligent public transport, we adopt a variety of information technologies for network security monitoring and warning, and unleash the powerful potential of digitalization to provide passengers with high-efficient and safe experiences, raising passengers' sense of gain, well-being, and safety.

Honors

★ The *Application and Practice of Digital Transformation of Ground Public Transport Operation Control and Vehicle Technology Support* was selected as one of the "China's Top 10 Cases of Enterprise Digital Transformation in 2023".

★ The *Simulation Platform for Public Transport Vehicle Resource Utilization Based on Data Middle Platform* was selected as "Typical Scenario of National Enterprise Digitalization Application" in the First National Enterprise Digitalization Application Ecology Conference of China International Digital Economy Expo 2023.

★ The innovative project titled "Digital Empowerment for Urban Bus Operation Control and Vehicle Technical Support" won the first prize in the "SOE Digital Scene Innovation Professional Competition".

— Upgrading digital transformation —

We have established a digital business middle platform and launched comprehensive business digitalization.

We have launched the operation and monitoring platform for school buses, providing efficient and convenient transport services for primary and secondary schoolers in Beijing.

We have built a smart fueling management platform to promote digital energy management and settlement.

We have advanced the development of an online management and control platform, human resources system, bus stop poles and signs management platform, and major event command platform, deepening the efforts in digitalization.

We have improved and released data security management methods, monitored network security situation, warned and reported network security vulnerabilities. We blocked malicious IPs more than 50 times, and hired network security experts to promote network security and IT training.

Safety Regarded as Our Priority

As the life line of public transport, safety is the basic requirement of every passenger, the cornerstone of public transport system stability, and the bottom line of public transport employees. BPTC embeds the concept of safety into every link of operation and every detail of service and joins hands with all stakeholders for safe and harmonious public transport.

Worry-free and safe services for passengers

We are convinced that every trip bears the trust and expectations of passengers. Therefore, adhering to the concept "life foremost, safety first", we comply with strict standards and a high level of responsibility in every journey, inspection, and maintenance to ensure that our vehicles are in the best condition so that passengers can feel safe and well-protected.

Driving behavior monitoring system

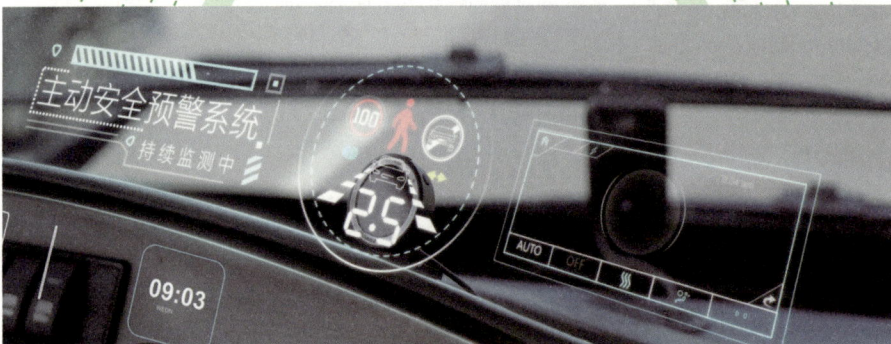

Advanced driving assistance system

Smart voice safety reminder system

2023

11,000
Vehicles installed with the advanced driving assistance system

13,000
Vehicles installed with driving behavior monitoring system

563 sets of
A-pillar blind spot warning systems installed at key vehicles, such as double-deckers and long vehicles

3,762
Emergency cases on the bus handled, with

4,147
People involved

Strengthening preventive driving safety management in all respects ////////////////////

- According to the adjustment of bus lanes, we summarize the traffic patterns along our bus routes, take effective measures to address discovered risks, and promptly revise the manual for driving safety.
- We strengthen the preventive management of driving safety, quickly activate emergency plans, and proactively address the impact of cold waves and snow on driving safety.
- According to traffic features in different festivals, we carry out education on seasonal changes and strict implementation of festive safety driving measures to improve drivers' safety awareness and adaptability during special periods.

Maintaining vehicles and guaranteeing transport for smooth travel ////////////////////

- We have carried out the "zero midway breakdown" campaign (meaning to prevent breakdowns during bus operation) and improved vehicle management by troubleshooting and eliminating safety hazards and setting up "zero midway breakdown" bus routes, teams, and crews.
- We optimize the maintenance system, supplement inspection tools, and introduce training materials for hidden danger detection and troubleshooting to ensure standardized policies and no mechanical and electrical accidents.
- Given seasonal changes, we carry out vehicle maintenance at different periods to improve vehicle quality and provide passengers with a more comfortable and safer environment.

Empowering driving safety with technologies ////////////////////

- We have updated existing vehicles with technological preventive system or introduce new vehicles, with vehicles installed with the advanced driving assistance systems and driving behavior monitoring systems.
- We have established a regular reporting mechanism based on the data from drivers' smart wearable devices and installed safety smart voice reminder systems on 176 major routes.
- We pioneer the driver's driving safety digital portrait, covering nearly 100 indicators in five aspects such as safety awareness, physical and mental health, and driving skills to accurately identify the level of driving risks.

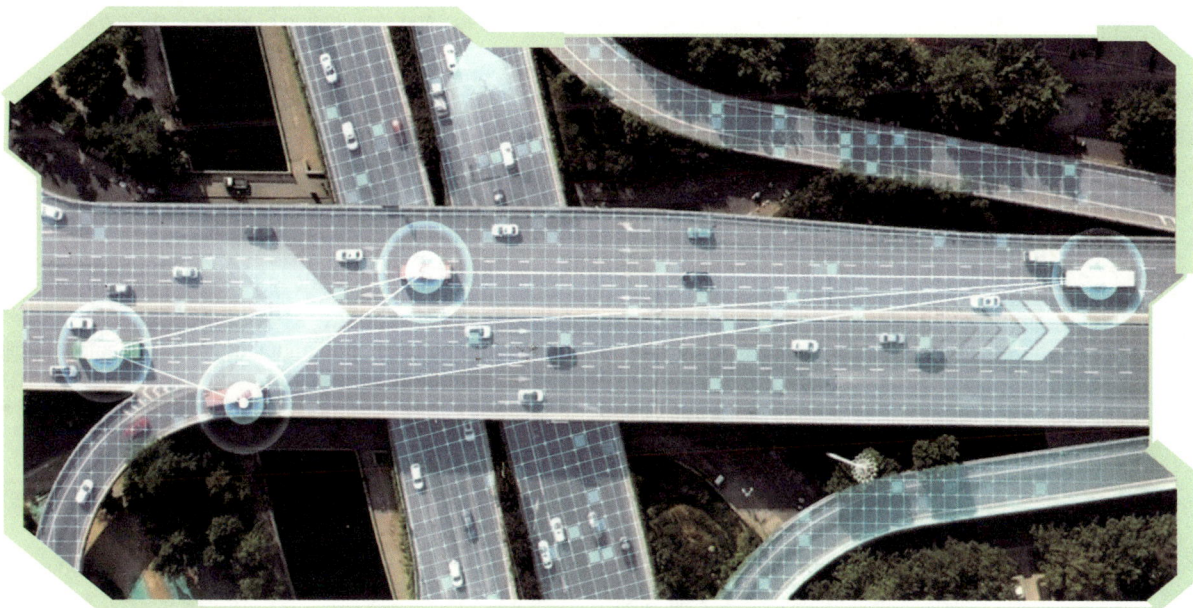

Technology-empowered digital safety guarantee

Safe public transport in our mind

As a public transport enterprise, we see safety as our responsibility and our solemn commitment to passengers. We unswervingly implement the strictest safety standards, enhance hidden danger investigation & treatment and emergency drills, and systematically carry out safety training and education. These efforts help employees develop a high degree of safety awareness and professional skills to safeguard public transport safety together.

2021-2023 Safety Efforts in Personnel, Facilities and Technology

	Project	2021	2022	2023
Personnel	Number of on-bus safety personnel	36,679	31,630	35,803
Facilities	Number of closed electronic fence	500	500	500
Technology	Vehicles with one-button alert system	17,271	21,500	21,354
	Vehicles with automatic identification system	17,249	24,043	14,500

2023

100%
Rectification rate of hidden hazards

438
Emergency plans for secondary subsidiaries revised

6,212
Emergency drills carried out, with

86,232
Participants involved

265,000
Participants in safety education and training

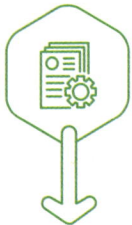

Reinforcing the safety foundation

- We have revised the *Provisions on Work Safety Accountability*, implemented the new work safety law, and finalized all-employee work safety requirements.
- We carry out internal safety audits, strengthen work safety supervision during and after production, and improve safety management in all respects.
- We improve safety management at bus depots and stops, and organize the line marking of bus depots.

Investigating and addressing hidden dangers

- We have revised systems such as the *Management Measures for Identification of Work Safety Hidden Risks* to strengthen hidden risk investigation and management.
- Based on the special action of large-scale investigation and rectification of work safety and fire hazards, we work to eliminate all kinds of fire dangers.
- We have strengthened the hidden risk identification system and adopted the "Corporate Safety" system to report and solve all kinds of hidden risks.

Strengthening emergency management

- We standardized the process and content of reporting emergency information.
- We guaranteed transport services for key periods and flood seasons and shoulder emergency duties during the "Two Sessions" and BRI summit periods.
- We carried out fire emergency evacuation and handling drills and conducted "119" fire safety publicity and training activities.

Enriching safety training

- We organized the police-enterprise joint training workshop and invite external experts to give lectures to security management personnel to improve our emergency response.
- We organized annual training workshop for security professional managers, and the orientation and skill improvement training for on-bus safety personnel.

A solid foundation for work safety culture

Safety culture is nurtured from daily routines, perseverance, and an unshakeable sense of responsibility. We persist in strengthening work safety culture, enhance safety education in multiple aspects, and regularly conduct campaigns such as "Golden and Silver Steering Wheel Award" commendation, "National Traffic Safety Day" publicity and education, and "Work Safety Month" campaign to create a sound atmosphere of safety. At the same time, the Corporation strives to create a national work safety culture demonstration enterprise, effectively improves corporate safety culture, and embeds safety culture into production and operation.

Fire Prevention Month activity

Case: United as one for forging safe buses and paying tribute to a golden decade

On July 28, 2023, BPTC held the 10th anniversary ceremony of "Golden and Silver Steering Wheel Award" for drivers. The theme of the ceremony was "Paying Tribute to a Golden Decade". Over the past ten years, a total of 1,293 drivers have been awarded the "Golden Steering Wheel Award", which demonstrates a decade of dedicated safety management reform and the influence of a safety culture.

2023 "Golden and Silver Steering Wheel Award" ceremony under the theme "Paying Tribute to a Golden Decade"

2023

10
Subsidiaries of BPTC honored with the title of Beijing Safety Culture Demonstration Enterprises

168
Drivers won the "Golden Steering Wheel Award", the highest honor for safe driving in BPTC

1,055
Drivers won the "Silver Steering Wheel Award"

51,096
Employees participating in the Work Safety Knowledge Competition

2023

24
Publicity stations set up for the Work Safety Month campaign

375
Information booths installed

65,443
Knowledge manuals distributed on work safety publicity

21,156
Inquiries received from passengers

Coordinated Beijing-Tianjin-Hebei Development in the Last Decade

BPTC has actively responded to the coordinated development strategy of the Beijing-Tianjin-Hebei region since it was proposed. We have implemented the Beijing-Tianjin-Hebei transport coordination policy, served the development of the Beijing-Tianjin-Hebei city cluster, and acted as a pioneer to lead the development of the public transport industry in the three areas. We endeavor to build a new pattern of ground public transport development compatible with the capital's strategic position and the coordinated development of the Beijing-Tianjin-Hebei region. Since the 14th Five-Year Plan, we are determined to build a domestically leading and world-class modern comprehensive service provider of public transport based in Beijing and serving the Beijing-Tianjin-Hebei region. After ten years of transformation, more than 2,500 kilometers of cross-city bus routes have brought Beijing, Tianjin, and Hebei closer, making Beijing-Tianjin-Hebei transport integration from a blueprint to a reality.

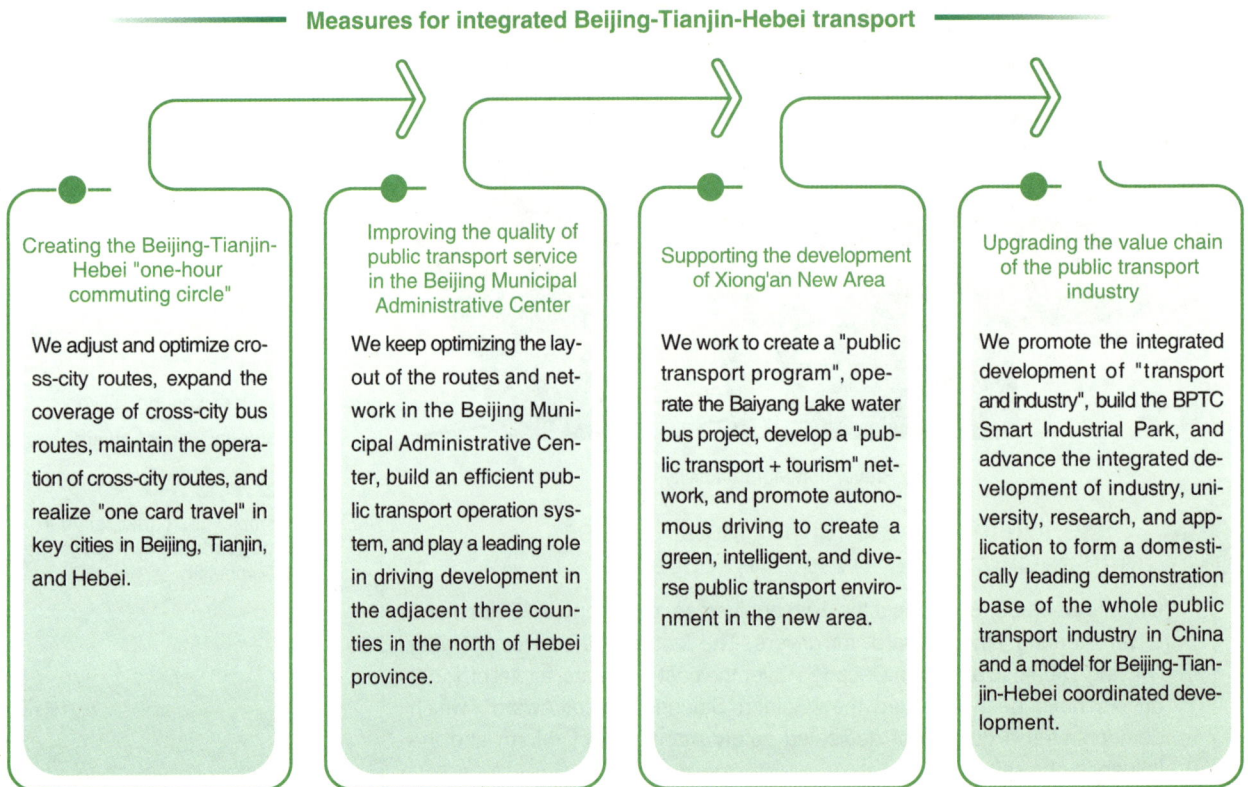

Measures for integrated Beijing-Tianjin-Hebei transport

Creating the Beijing-Tianjin-Hebei "one-hour commuting circle"

We adjust and optimize cross-city routes, expand the coverage of cross-city bus routes, maintain the operation of cross-city routes, and realize "one card travel" in key cities in Beijing, Tianjin, and Hebei.

Improving the quality of public transport service in the Beijing Municipal Administrative Center

We keep optimizing the layout of the routes and network in the Beijing Municipal Administrative Center, build an efficient public transport operation system, and play a leading role in driving development in the adjacent three counties in the north of Hebei province.

Supporting the development of Xiong'an New Area

We work to create a "public transport program", operate the Baiyang Lake water bus project, develop a "public transport + tourism" network, and promote autonomous driving to create a green, intelligent, and diverse public transport environment in the new area.

Upgrading the value chain of the public transport industry

We promote the integrated development of "transport and industry", build the BPTC Smart Industrial Park, and advance the integrated development of industry, university, research, and application to form a domestically leading demonstration base of the whole public transport industry in China and a model for Beijing-Tianjin-Hebei coordinated development.

Case: "Water buses" take visitors to Baiyang Lake

To support the coordinated development strategy of the Beijing-Tianjin-Hebei region, BPTC contributes to the development of Xiong'an New Area by carrying out the Baiyan Lake water transport project with 100 customized LPG boats and 200 ecological wooden boats. In addition, we set up the Baiyang Lake water bus operation control and command center and a centralized monitoring and management platform for boat safety, with emergency boats and safety officers hired to improve Baiyang Lake water transport services. Today, it has become a new way of touring around Baiyang Lake by cleaner "water buses" to enjoy the harmony between human beings and nature.

Operate Xiong'an ground bus lines

2023

38
Cross-city bus routes

2,500+ km
Route length

178
Bus routes operated in the whole Beijing Municipal Administrative Center

20
Regular bus routes operated in the Xiong'an New Area

7
Customized bus routes operated in Xiong'an New Area

Baiyang Lake "water buses"

Mission Delivery
Going Through Thick and Thin Together

Contribution to UN SDGs

As an important public transport system of Beijing, BPTC mirrors the city's heartbeat, growing and supporting alongside it. At every important moment, we leverage professional competence and deliver high-quality services to conscientiously fulfill our responsibilities, embodying the responsibility and commitment as a national public transport enterprise.

No Fear of Challenges and Devotion to Guard

Unity is our shield against challenges. Facing the rare heavy rainfall, BPTC has made careful arrangements according to orders and responded calmly to spare no efforts to cope with the rainfall and ensure safe travel for passengers. Amid this great challenge, BPTC's staff emerged as the city's guardians, with their perseverance and selfless actions creating a heart-warming beacon in the rainstorm. After the storm will finally come the rainbow.

Calling for unity for flood control and disaster relief

For the sudden and extremely heavy rainfall weather, we have made early judgments and deployments and initiated the Level I (red alert) flood-control emergency response. With a high sense of responsibility more scientific, accurate, and powerful measures, we have coordinated the entire company to respond efficiently with scientific, accurate, and powerful measures. All employees grouped as a whole unity to charge forward to resolutely make emergency rescue and tackle the challenges in flood control and disaster relief.

■ Systematic layout for flood response ■

Strong organization and sound mechanism

We established the Flood Control Headquarters to coordinate a three-tier command system, strictly implementing a leadership-driven shift schedule. We also developed the *2023 BPTC Flood Control Work Plan* to guide the entire company for efficient flood response.

Decision-making consultations and multi-party actions

We convened multi-departmental and trans-disciplinary decision-making consultations to align expertise, including with the city's flood control office and fire and rescue corps to carry out professional emergency rescue.

Better scheduling and rapid response

We intensified route monitoring and dispatch control, made decisions timely, and handled emergencies decisively. We also took measures such as stopping running, short-turning operations, service suspension, etc. to strengthen the identification and rectification of hidden dangers and ensure safe bus operation.

United efforts and focus on key points

We arranged our flood-control support forces in advance, reserving over 200 vehicles and organizing 130 technical service teams (354 people in total). We conducted strong inspections and repairs on vehicles at 116 key stations and areas. We also adjusted the rescue layout of the emergency repair and rescue centers, concentrating resources in the western region. Comprehensive assessments were performed and ample flood control materials were stockpiled.

2023

200+
Flood-control emergency transport buses deployed

50+
Rescue buses dispatched

1,000+
Emergency repair personnel mobilized

2,000+
Management personnel on standby

425
"Party member vanguard teams, task teams, and volunteer service teams" established

466
bus routes

744
Temporary dispatch measures taken for

20,000+
Trapped individuals transferred

Working in harm's way in the flood peak

Adversity reveals resilience. We have spared no effort in flood control and disaster relief, with Party members bravely leading the charge as the "main force". Employees braved to excel in emergency transport, vehicle repair, depot rescue, emergency transfer, etc. BPTC's staff has built a solid defense line of life through their practical actions, including measuring water depths with their feet, repairing rescue vehicles in the rain, and racing against wind and rain to transfer trapped people.

Rescue for trapped people in the rainfall

A bus runs in the rainfall

Case: "No one should be missing or injured"

On July 29, 2023, with the onset rainfall, BPTC activated emergency protocols and deployed staff for emergency rescue. On July 31, the peaked flood stranded four member of Li Jie's team, Captain of the Eleventh Fleet of the Fourth Passenger Transport Branch, in rising waters. As they anxiously awaited the return of outstanding 20 buses, Li Jie's concern deepened. She didn't take an umbrella and someone wanted to drag her into the house, but she shook her hand and said, "I can only relax when all the buses come back. No employee should be missing, and no passenger should be injured." At 4 am on August 1st, when the last bus returned, tears streamed down Li Jie's face.

Li Jie, Captain of the Eleventh Fleet of the Fourth Passenger Transport Branch,
commands a bus to run into the depot

Pulling together to make concerted efforts

While the storm was indifferent, our compassion was not. We swiftly resumed operations to ensure the safe travel of citizens, optimizing routes for efficient emergency transport. Actively participated in rescue and disaster relief, we supported disaster-stricken units in rebuilding and united our efforts to overcome difficulties, calling for resumption of work and production.

Recovery and reconstruction after the disaster

Evacuation of affected people
Over 6,000 residents were urgently transported from Matou Village and Beilu Community in Matou Town, Zhuozhou, Hebei, and over 400 stranded passengers from the second batch of K396 train were relocated.

Resumption of bus operations
We orderly promoted the restoration of 465 risky bus routes to meet the travel needs of citizens.

Acceleration of maintenance and recovery
We promoted bus mechanical and electrical safety inspection and repair, as well as the maintenance of information equipment at bus depots. We also cleaned up silt and garbage for 36 depots, with a total of over 600 tons.

Safety protection
We strengthened depots disinfection and food safety management, provided sufficient epidemic prevention materials, and organized volunteers to carry out volunteer activities in severely affected areas.

2023

4,579
Flood-stricken employees visited

6,583
Rescue personnel visited

1,400+
Members of the Communist Youth League mobilized

80+
Volunteer services conducted

Transfer of disaster-stricken people

Bus cleaning after the disaster

Transfer of trapped people in the bus depot

Clearing away the silt at the bus depot

Salute: Li Wanhong, a bus practitioner whose life ended on the front line of flood control

A portrait of Li Wanhong at work

From July 29 to August 2, 2023, a storm swept through Beijing, causing flash floods, traffic gridlock, and trapped people... Faced with these formidable challenges, BPTC acted quickly, crossed the mud, and moved forward fearlessly. Our primary-level fleet employees maintained an unwavering presence at their depots day and night. Li Wanhong was one of them.

Li Wanhong was the fleet manager of the Eighth Fleet at BPTC's Eighth Passenger Transport Branch. In nearly 20 years of public transportation, she practiced the original mission as a Party member, rooted in the grassroots, and fulfilled her duties, wholeheartedly protecting passengers' travel. In the face of this rainstorm, Li Wanhong fearlessly volunteered to measure the depths of waterlogs with her colleagues in the wind and rain. They observed the changes in the surrounding environment, reassured passengers and dutifully safeguarded their well-being. Tragically, on the front line of flood, Li Wanhong lost her life in a sudden flash flood, just over two months before her retirement.

On the morning of that fateful day, Li Wanhong said goodbye to her family as usual before setting off to collect her colleague, Ge Fengmei. During their conversation, Ms. Li expressed her determination to complete her final shift, leaving no regrets for her career. Her colleagues were familiar with her cautious and conscientious approach to work, so her volunteering spirit came as no surprise. However, no one expected that this departure would become a permanent farewell.

Having worked in the public transport industry for nearly 20 years, the particularity of the industry often prevented her from reuniting with her family at festivals. Her dedication to her job was fueled by her family's silent support. In the view of Li Wanhong's son, his mother was a curious person for new things, always improved her work competence through continuous learning, and had the greatest enthusiasm for everyone and things around her. She actively participated in the community's public welfare activities in her spare time and helped the elderly in the community and colleagues to solve their problems.

She poured her time into her work and helping others, often sacrificing her hobbies and desires. She had also thought about how to live after her retirement. She would explore China's beautiful rivers and mountains and experience different customs and traditions. Sadly, even such a simple wish cannot be realized in the end.

Even if life is short, the spirit can be eternal. In this rainstorm, Li Wanhong fulfilled her mission with her life and protected the citizens with her strength. Her dedication will be remembered, her spirit as enduring as the bus routes she served.

Ms. Li always worked at the front line in her daily life, always doing more than she promised. No task was ever postponed if it could be done on that day. Our go-to person in times of trouble, both at work and home, she was always ready to lend a helping hand. Therefore, we called her "heart-warming Ms. Li". We still can't accept the sudden death of such a nice person.

—— Ge Fengmei from the Eighth Fleet of the Eighth Passenger Transport Branch

Exceptional Services for Grand Events

We shoulder heavy tasks with a high sense of political mission and responsibility to strive to move forward. We provide full-process, all-element, and high-quality services to ensure the safety, orderliness, and efficiency of major events. Aiming to create a golden signboard for transport services for major events, we adopted the highest standards to serve the construction of the "Four Centers" of Beijing with the highest quality. In 2023, taking a higher position and stricter standards and making greater efforts, we provided transport services for major events such as the Third Belt and Road Forum for International Cooperation, Summer Davos, and the "Two Sessions". Meanwhile, we took multiple measures to ensure transport capacity in key areas and meet the travel needs of people during important holidays.

Measures to ensure the security of major events

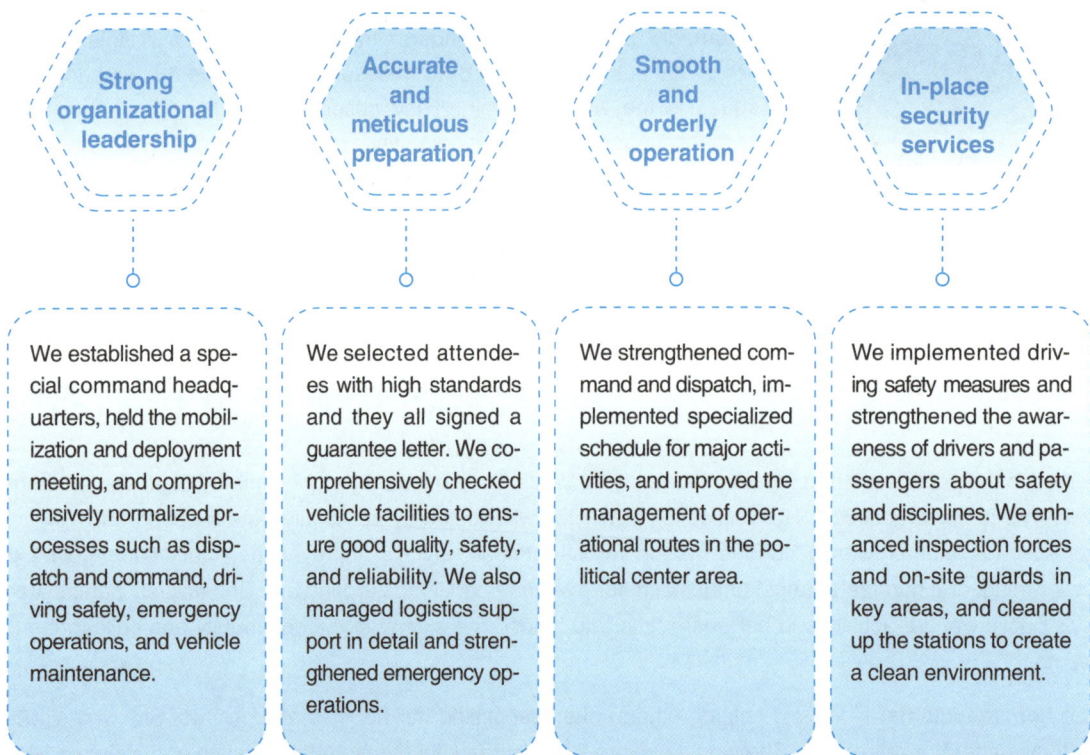

Strong organizational leadership	Accurate and meticulous preparation	Smooth and orderly operation	In-place security services
We established a special command headquarters, held the mobilization and deployment meeting, and comprehensively normalized processes such as dispatch and command, driving safety, emergency operations, and vehicle maintenance.	We selected attendees with high standards and they all signed a guarantee letter. We comprehensively checked vehicle facilities to ensure good quality, safety, and reliability. We also managed logistics support in detail and strengthened emergency operations.	We strengthened command and dispatch, implemented specialized schedule for major activities, and improved the management of operational routes in the political center area.	We implemented driving safety measures and strengthened the awareness of drivers and passengers about safety and disciplines. We enhanced inspection forces and on-site guards in key areas, and cleaned up the stations to create a clean environment.

Transport services for the China International Fair for Trade in Services

An emergency repair and rescue vehicle is on standby in the core area during the National Day holiday

♡ The voice of BPTC employees

Demonstrating the "appearance of a great power" in serving passenger
——Jing Qingbo, Driver from Beijing Beiqi Taxi Group Co., Ltd.

Jing Qingbo, "Beijing Role Model · Beijing Taxi Driver"

Urban transport is the lifeblood of a city, and also its "mobile name card", reflecting the city's vitality, bringing happiness to the city. As the most direct window of transport services, the kind services of public transport service personnel not only enhance passengers' experiences directly but also highlight the warmth of Beijing.

Jing Qingbo, a sixteen-year veteran driver of Beijing Beiqi Taxi Group Co., Ltd., speaks with deep connection about his career. At first, he involved into the industry due to its flexibility of driving a taxi. Later, driving in the city every day and listening to the stories of passengers, he realizes that each journey is a warm and unique encounter. Over time, these interactions became a source of immense fulfillment and satisfaction.

Using smiles and sincerity to pass the warmth of and share the beauty of the city, every eye contact and nod brings trust and respect to passengers. This tacit understanding makes Jing Qingbo's taxi full of harmony and warmth. With meticulous attention to detail, he timely adjusts the temperature inside the taxi, avoids congested routes, and always pays attention to road conditions to ensure safe travel without worries. "When I hold the steering wheel, safety is my sole focus." This is not only Jing Qingbo's inner monologue, but also his profound practice in his travel. His dedication to safe driving and high-quality service has positioned him at the front line of transportation for major international events such as the Beijing Olympic Games, APEC Summit, the Military Parade on September 3, the Beijing Summit of the Forum on China-Africa Cooperation, and the Third Belt and Road Forum for International Cooperation. He said "I feel very lucky and proud to be able to provide transport services for various major events held by the nation for so many years."

Providing wholehearted service to every passenger is an eternal pursuit in Jingqingbo's mind. "In my mind, every rider deserves the utmost care and attention. Dropping every passenger safely and on time to their destinations is the greatest satisfaction for us as drivers. In the future, I will continue to serve passengers with sincerity, crafting memorable passenger experiences, and embodying the spirit of 'Beijing Role Model · Beijing Taxi Driver' in the modern era."

We run the Fuhe route to serve the residents of Fuhe village, the cliff-side village in southwestern Beijing. This initiative was implemented to improve transportation for the local community and connect rural and urban areas.

Shared Journey
Creating a Brighter Future

Contribution to UN SDGs

Whoever is for the good of the people, they will, in turn, earn the people's trust and support. Firmly rooted in the community and society, BPTC always adheres to the principle that public transport serves the people. Traveling thousands of miles, we work to benefit the people's livelihood. We provide low-carbon transportation and contribute to the city's sustainable development, making it more travel-friendly and livable. Additionally, our "Village Transport" project connects urban and rural areas, improving people's livelihoods and enhancing the overall well-being. Committed to creating a better vision of sustainable development in partnership with various stakeholders, we continue to lead the way in public transport with the highest standards, ensuring that every act of goodwill and every best wish makes a lasting impact.

Enjoying the Beautiful Scenery on the Eco-friendly Trip

The environment, such as green mountains and blue skies, is essential for people's well-being. Adhering to the philosophy of "lucid waters and lush mountains are invaluable assets", we prioritize green development and public transport. We have formulated the Carbon Peaking Action Plan to adjust our fleet structure and promote energy-saving and emission reduction efforts. By building a green transportation system, we contribute to a low-carbon city and underpin the environmental protection initiatives for a beautiful China.

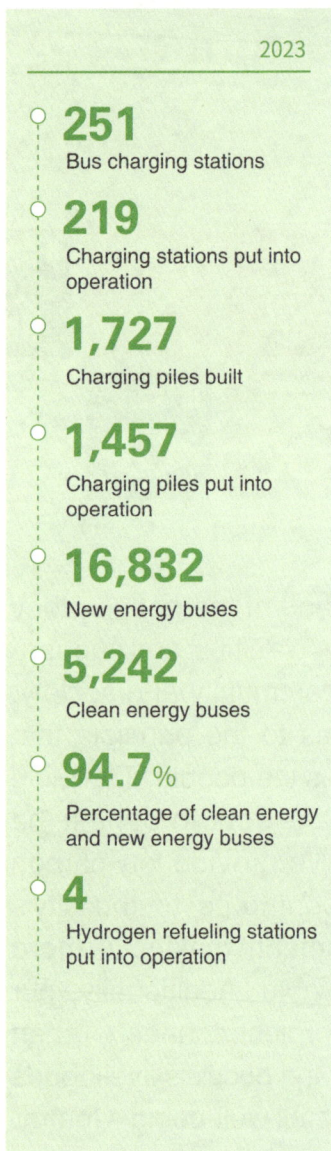

2023

251
Bus charging stations

219
Charging stations put into operation

1,727
Charging piles built

1,457
Charging piles put into operation

16,832
New energy buses

5,242
Clean energy buses

94.7%
Percentage of clean energy and new energy buses

4
Hydrogen refueling stations put into operation

Hydrogen fuel cell bus

New energy charging station

Green public transport for better travel

Committed to green development, we are now driving the shift towards new energy sources in our vehicles by promoting low-carbon energy options, designing smaller vehicle models, and incorporating intelligent technology. This approach enables more resilient and sustainable development of the public transport. Additionally, we enhance our supporting infrastructure by installing more charging stations, hydrogen refueling stations, and intelligent electronic stop signs. These facilities provide a more convenient, green, and intelligent travel experience for our passengers.

2023

453,639
Tonnes of standard coal equivalent in total energy consumption

3.94
Tonnes of standard coal equivalent/10,000 km Energy use intensity

20,100 tons
Carbon trading

RMB 2.3435 million
Net carbon trading income

- BPTC was awarded the *2022 National Green and Low Carbon Typical Case* by the Ministry of Ecology and Environment.
- BPTC was awarded *2023 Benchmark Enterprise for Achieving Carbon Peaking and Carbon Neutrality* by the China Association of Plant Engineering.
- BPTC was awarded *Annual Low-Carbon Model Unit for Urban Transportation in 2022-2023* by the China Urban Public Transport Association.

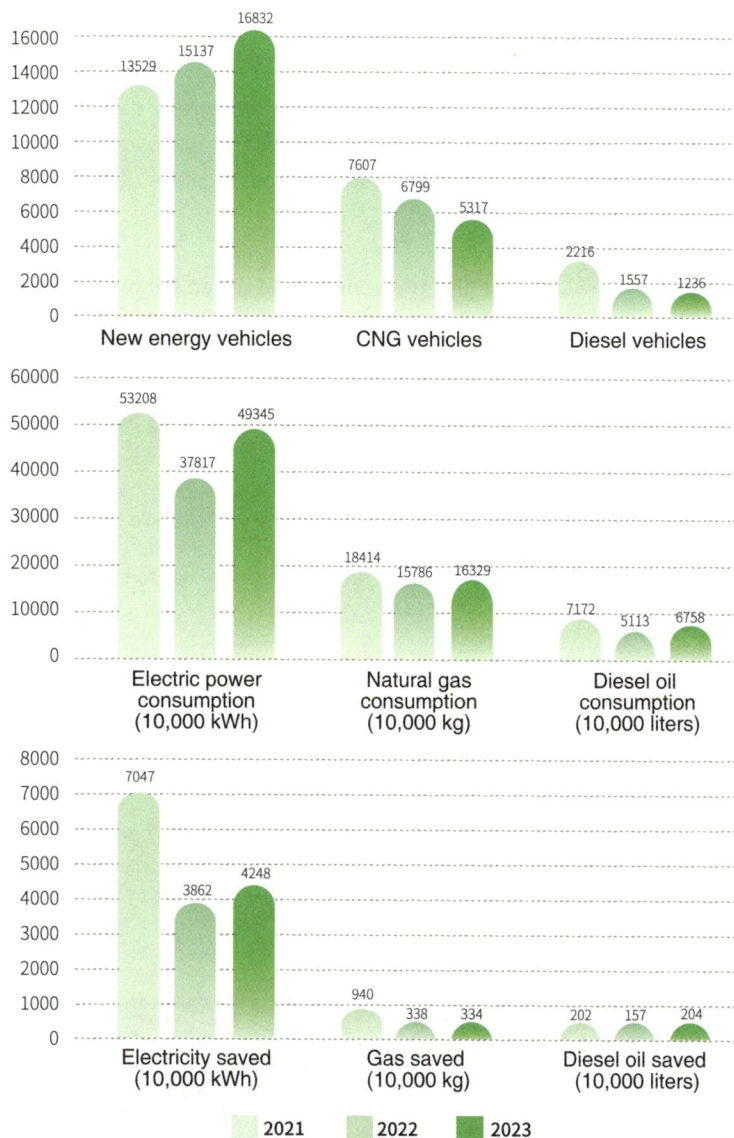

New energy vehicles: 13529, 15137, 16832
CNG vehicles: 7607, 6799, 5317
Diesel vehicles: 2216, 1557, 1236

Electric power consumption (10,000 kWh): 53208, 37817, 49345
Natural gas consumption (10,000 kg): 18414, 15786, 16329
Diesel oil consumption (10,000 liters): 7172, 5113, 6758

Electricity saved (10,000 kWh): 7047, 3862, 4248
Gas saved (10,000 kg): 940, 338, 334
Diesel oil saved (10,000 liters): 202, 157, 204

2021 / 2022 / 2023

Keeping the city and sky clear

We actively implement China's 30·60 Decarbonization Goal and firmly embrace the management concept of energy conservation as our own responsibility and a driver for development. To this end, we have scientifically formulated energy consumption plans. By harnessing data, we improve energy utilization efficiency and enhance environmental pollution monitoring. Daily management of energy conservation and emission reduction as well as the training and education on these topics are also tightened. Through a multi-dimensional and multi-channel approach, we have reduced energy consumption and pollution, ultimately contributing to a bluer sky for our city.

Statistics of Discharge of Emissions (2021 – 2023)

Index(unit)	2021	2022	2023
Carbon emissions(tonnes)	288,376	246,261	280,353
CO_2 emissions(tonnes)	1,057,378	902,957	1,027,962
NO_x emissions reduction (tonnes)	123.41	57.05	236.86
Particulate emissions reduction (tonnes)	0.17	0.13	0.20
Hydrocarbon emissions reduction (tonnes)	80.78	30.72	60.21

Low-carbon travel to embrace a green future

Engaging in the low-carbon travel service sector, we proactively develop new strengths in green travel, and meet the demand for eco-friendly travel. Guided by the principles of low-carbon development and environmental protection, we implement a variety of environmental initiatives to promote a culture of low-carbon travel throughout society and encourage green travel as a trend.

— **Advocating the concepts of green living** —

Promoting green office practices

We strive to reduce pollution emissions during our production and operations, while also increasing the coverage of green office areas.

Implementing waste sorting

We have improved the standardization of household waste sorting and transportation, implemented special actions to address mixed loading and transportation issues, and conducted various forms of publicity and training on waste sorting.

Conducting bus depot cleaning

To advance patriotic health campaigns, we regularly conduct environmental cleaning activities at our bus depots to ensure a clean environment and clean office areas of our subsidiaries.

Promoting green awareness

Through activities such as World Car Free Day publicity, pamphlet distribution, and order maintenance at key intersections and bus stops, we encourage responsible riding and green travel practices.

2023

53,589
Participants in environmental training

100%
Employees engaged in the activity of waste sorting in depots

170
Trash cans with technological facilities installed

Green Travel Month campaign

Unleashing Full Potential of Employees

The employees and the Corporation, with shared growth and mutual success, form the bedrock of the stable and sustainable corporate development. We regard our employees as the most valuable asset of our company and the inexhaustible momentum for sustainable development. So we commit to creating an environment for our employees characterized by trust, inclusion, and incentives. It enables each individual to excel in their role and align their personal aspirations with corporate development.

Protecting employee rights on all fronts

We always believe that employees are the driving force behind corporate development, and fully respect and protect the rights and interests of our employees. Strictly adhering to the *Labor Law of the People's Republic of China* and other related laws and regulations, we try our best to create a fair and inclusive workplace and continually unblock channels to voice the concerns and aspirations of our staff. Furthermore, we aim to attract and retain top talent through a competitive salary system and diverse benefits.

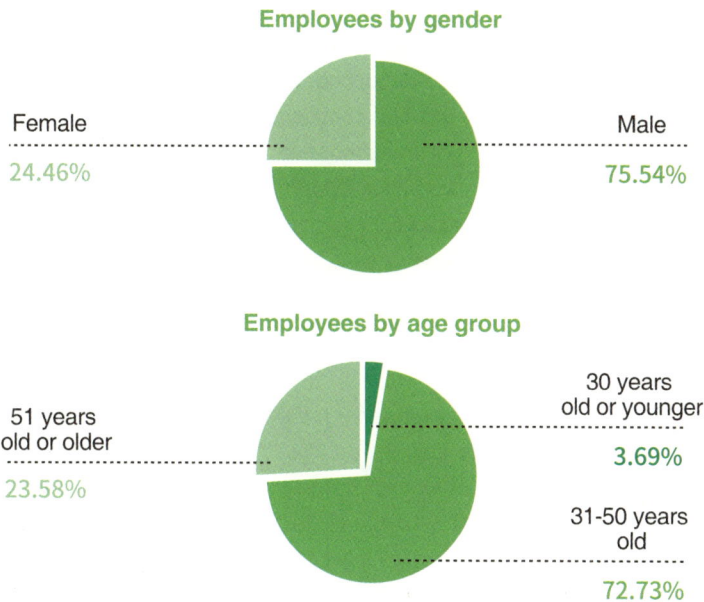

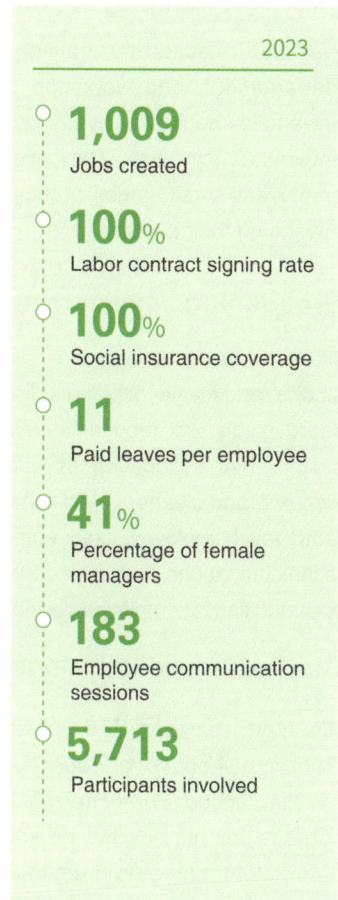

Employees by gender

Female 24.46%
Male 75.54%

Employees by age group

51 years old or older 23.58%
30 years old or younger 3.69%
31-50 years old 72.73%

2023

1,009 Jobs created

100% Labor contract signing rate

100% Social insurance coverage

11 Paid leaves per employee

41% Percentage of female managers

183 Employee communication sessions

5,713 Participants involved

■ Building a fair and respectful workplace

Committed to open recruitment and fair development, we strictly prohibit forced labor and child labor in any form. We have enforced the *BPTC Management Measures on Anti-violence, Discrimination, and Sexual Harassment in the Workplaces* and other regulations, to provide employees with equal development opportunities and create an open and inclusive working environment.

■ Improving the compensation and benefits system

We provide five insurances (basic pension insurance, basic medical insurance, unemployment insurance, work injury insurance, and maternity insurance) and housing provident fund on time and in full for employees. We continue to optimize the compensation and incentive policies and deepen the income distribution reform to share development results with them.

■ Promoting democratic management

We have held the sixth and seventh sessions, as well as the second joint meeting of the third worker representative congress. Besides, we regularly engage in various activities such as employee representative seminars, specialized inspections, and excellent proposal collections to motivate employees to participate in enterprise management.

Unlocking employee value

The development of an enterprise is attributed to the hard work and dedication of each and every employee. We prioritize the long-term development of our employees by encouraging skills training, and improve our labor skills competitions to empower them to learn and grow. Additionally, we foster innovation by providing a targeted platform to showcase their creativity and create an environment where everyone has the opportunity to succeed and demonstrate their full potential.

Improving employee training

We have released the training polices on skill recognition, online learning platform management, and workshop development. Our ongoing training programs cover pre-employment, adaptive, vocational, and professional skills, constantly improving the employees expertise. They offer a range of learning opportunities and resources for employees at all stages of their career and personal development to support them in advancing their careers.

Broadening development paths

We continue to develop exemplary employees, and keep building employee innovation studios, and master of skills studios, with the regulations on innovation studios introduced. To improve the skill recognition system, we have developed a five-tier job classification system that includes roles such as drivers, conductors, dispatchers, maintenance workers, and cleaners. Additionally, we work to establish an eight-tier promotion system (entry-level employee, junior employee, intermediate employee, senior employee, assistant technician, technician, senior technician, and special technician), allowing for ample opportunities for employee development.

Cultivating skilled talents

We have released and implemented the *BPTC Overall Plan for Deepening the Reform of Vocational Education System and Mechanisms,* and the *Cultivation Plan for the Skilled Personnel (2023-2025).* Furthermore, we have developed training courses for high-skilled personnel and facilitated the launch of the highly-skilled personnel training program in 2023 by all passenger transport branches to leverage their skills and advocate the spirit of craftsmanship.

2023

1
New technical expert in the national transportation industry receiving a special allowance from the State Council

150,000
Employees trained

1,576,688+
Training hours

77,879
Active users of "BPTC Online Class" App in total

899
Exams organized in total

5,462,641
Exam-takers in total

1,931
Drivers trained as apprentices in the new-type corporate apprenticeship training

2023 Beijing Employee Vocational Skills Competition

Employee Innovation Studio

Case: BPTC turns career dreams into reality with innovations in public transport industry

In January 2023, the 2nd BPTC Employee Innovation Competition was launched, attracting 922 innovative projects. This competition successfully encouraged the application and transformation of employee innovation results by showcasing the practical value and usage of various innovations. It also fostered an innovative atmosphere within and beyond the competition, providing a broader platform for employees to thrive, succeed, and innovate.

Finals and Award Ceremony of the 2nd BPTC Employee Innovation Competition

Case: Beijing Public Transportation Technician College has been officially approved for establishment

On September 5, 2023, BPTC established the Beijing Public Transportation Technician College based on the Beijing Public Transport Senior Technical School, filling the gap in technician education in the field of urban public transportation in Beijing. Since the establishment of the college, BPTC has actively developed the "two campuses and one base" of Changyang Campus, Qinghe Campus, and Wangzuo Training Base. With full preparation, its infrastructure has been significantly improved, leading to a higher professional training capacity and a better structure. The college introduced 3 high-skilled personnel training programs in areas such as automobile driving, transportation passenger service, and automobile maintenance, with an annual average of more than 20,000 trainees and over 3,000 students enrolled.

Beijing Public Transportation Technician College

Delivering employee care

We value the work and life quality of every employee and have implemented an employee health care plan. We continue to organize various employee care activities, such as providing comprehensive health services and diverse cultural and sports events, to deliver our care and ensure that they can maintain a happy work-life balance and lead healthy lives.

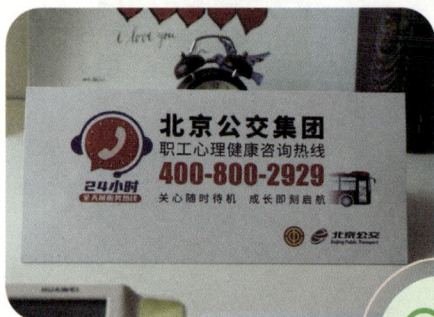

Employee mental health counseling hotline

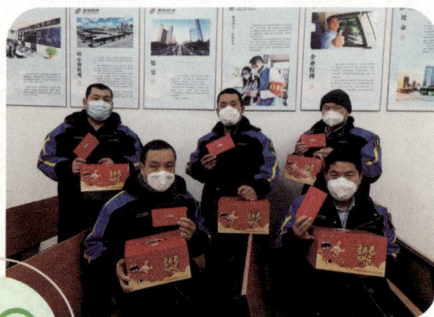

Visiting employees during Spring Festival

Reading session

The 8th employee brisk walk activity

2023

100%
Physical examination coverage for employees

75
Trainees for the second EAP specialist training

829
Total employees served in the 24/7 service of employee mental health counseling hotline

38,494
Drivers participating in the annual psychological assessment

RMB
4,851,200
Funds to assist employees in need

1,702
Employees in need assisted

Case: Building a mother's room for the well-being of female employees

On the 33rd National Breastfeeding Awareness Day, the ninth fleet of the BPTC Trolley Bus Branch officially opened a mother's room. The room is thoughtfully designed to maximize functionality, with attention to detail and a warm atmosphere, providing comfortable decoration, soothing music, convenient facilities, and standardized rules for female employees. As a spotlight of the fleet, the mother's room serves as a haven within the workplace, embodying our commitment to nurturing a supportive and caring corporate culture and demonstrating our ongoing dedication to the well-being of our employees.

The mother's room of the ninth fleet

♡ The voice of BPTC employees

Safeguarding passengers and amplifying their voices

———He Shaohua, driver of Trolley Bus Branch

In 2023, He Shaohua, a driver on the BRT2 line of Trolley Bus Branch, was elected as a deputy to the National People's Congress. Donning her public transport uniform, she represented the majority of frontline employees and walked into the Great Hall of the People, carrying the hopes and expectations of the public. Throughout her career in BPTC, whether as a station attendant or driver, she has dedicated herself fully to her role, serving Beijing's public transport system whole heartedly and accompanying the passengers on every journey.

As a station attendant, she developed a work method that includes responsibility, inclusion, compassion, sincerity, love, and keeps diligence with her brain, eyes, mouth, hands, and legs. In 2015, she transitioned from a station attendant to a driver, bringing her method to the carriage. She diligently studied driving skills and ingeniously developed her own work method from four principles: take it slow, prioritize stability, stop for passengers, and follow the laws, making the passengers safe in every trip. Thanks to her attentive care, passengers not only experience a safe journey, but also enjoy considerate amenities such as cool seat covers in the summer and warm cushions in the winter. Many passengers have become her fans and warmly greet her on their commutes.

He Shaohua, a driver of Trolley Bus Branch and a deputy to the National People's Congress

"Every passenger can voice their concerns. As a deputy to the National People's Congress, I am not only responsible for ensuring that passengers reach their destinations safely but also for listening to their concerns and opinions", said He Shaohua, who felt a greater sense of responsibility after being elected.

One morning, during peak hours, a passenger spoke in a difficult-to-understand dialect, leaving He Shaohua momentarily perplexed. She vividly remembered the helpless look on the passenger's face as he got off the bus. This incident sparked a thought: how can the needs of passengers be better met? She brought this consideration to the National People's Congress. In the past, bus drivers had to manually announce each stop, but now, buses are equipped with automatic stop reporting systems. This innovation got He thinking: why not have a smart system on every bus that can efficiently and accurately answer passengers' questions? This idea led her to advocate for the incorporation of new productivity tools in public transport sector, giving frontline drivers access to more intelligent vehicles. She put forward specific suggestions, such as having each stop announcement provide information about important nearby landmarks and the closest metro stations. She also recommended promoting intelligent travel Apps so that passengers could access personalized information independently, thus bringing the convenience of digital bus stops to the general public.

As a driver, gripping the steering wheel means guaranteeing the safety of her passengers. As a deputy to the National People's Congress, it means representing the voice of the people and shouldering the responsibility of serving the public. "The journey may have a destination, but the duty to serve is never-ending. As a representative of the people, I will always remain connected to them", He Shaohua always reminds herself.

Strengthening Bonds with Communities

Improving people's quality of life should be our top priority. With a keen awareness of social issues, we focus on key areas of social responsibility and work with our passengers to forge responsible travel and support urban renewal. In partnership with our suppliers, we strive to establish a sustainable supply chain. Furthermore, we actively encourage and support our employees to participate in various volunteer activities, fostering a sense of goodwill within the community and promoting positive development. Our ongoing efforts aim to contribute to the betterment of society and the well-being of all.

Setting role models during responsible travel

As the guardian and leader of urban travel, we are dedicated to promoting a new standard of responsible travel as our top priority. We partner with government agencies to organize "responsible travel for passenger safety" activities, conduct intersection volunteer activities, and regularly promote the initiative of stopping at a zebra crossing and maintain the order at bus stops, etc. Our aim is to ensure that every passenger practices responsible travel, thereby nurturing a strong awareness of "life first in responsible travel" among all people.

Popularization activities on responsible travel

Publicity campaign on responsible travel

Case: Responsible travel for passenger safety

To promote core socialist values, raise public awareness of traffic safety, and create a safe traffic environment, the Eighth Passenger Transport Branch organized a traffic safety awareness raising activity on the first day of the new school year. In alignment with the guiding principles of the 20th CPC National Congress, the activity aimed to promote responsible behaviors at crosswalks and set a new standard for safe travel. BPTC employees held up "waiting at the zebra crossing" signs to remind drivers to slow down, distributed traffic safety leaflets to pedestrians, and patiently explained the importance of safe travel. They also assisted in directing traffic at intersections to discourage unsafe driving behaviors. Through these actions, they helped promote responsible travel behaviors and instilled the concept of responsible travel in the public's consciousness.

Traffic safety publicity activity

Crafting a new lifestyle in urban renewal

The vitality and renewal of a city are what bring it to life. Renewal is the permanent theme of a city. Targeting Beijing's urban renewal projects, we focus on projects that aim to improve the lives of residents and the environment. We have conducted in-depth research on how to integrate the renovation of old bus depots and stations with urban renewal regulations and policies. We have established a series of "1921 city smart space" clusters with high standards. Additionally, together with local government departments, we have explored small-scale, progressive, and sustainable urban renewal paths that will ultimately enhance people's well-being.

- The first pilot projects in Huayuan Hutong and Nanlishi Road have been running well, with occupancy rates remaining stable at over 85 %.

- The renovation of Ganlu Park project has entered the bidding stage, and the pre-investment process has accelerated. It is expected that the occupancy rate would exceed 10 % by the end of the year.

- The Xinfeng Street project was selected as the "Key Digital Economic Industrial Park in Xicheng District". It is scheduled to be completed and delivered in July 2024 according to the established plan.

Steady progress in key urban renewal projects

- The mapping surveys and other preliminary work of the Hetao Park project were completed. The site clearance, design plan review, and other preparations were launched, and it is expected to begin the renovation in the second quarter of 2024.

- For the East Yongdingmen project, the renewal process of contracts for resident enterprises was accelerated. We work with relevant departments of Dongcheng District to attract high-quality resident enterprises.

- For the Fuchengmen project, we provided part of the space to support Xicheng District's local education operation while ensuring our utilization demand.

"1921 city smart space" clusters

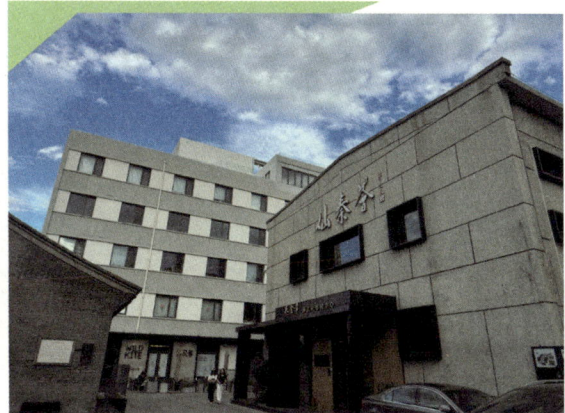

Huayuan Hutong project

Building a sustainable value chain together

Upholding the concept of responsible and sustainable development, we collaborate with our suppliers to establish a clean, transparent, and sustainable supply chain. We continue to enhance supplier CSR management, create a more open, transparent, and fair centralized procurement platform, and conduct thorough compliance management in our procurement processes. Our goal is to encourage our suppliers to raise CSR awareness and build a sustainable supply chain.

2023

100%
Supplier audit coverage

4
CSR training sessions held for suppliers

Supplier access and exit

- Strict criteria are established to select suppliers through public bidding, including the business capability of their service team, product quality assurance system, and logistics.
- After the completion of the entrusted procurement project, suppliers will exit from our pool based on their contract performance period. Anyone who violates laws and regulations as well as our supplier assessment management policies will be removed.

Dynamic supplier management

- A strict supplier assessment system is established, which includes graded evaluation and dynamic management. We stringently restrain supplier procurement practices and conduct regular evaluations by applying measures such as interviews, penalty based on assessment result, suspension of qualifications and disqualification according to the nature of problems occurred, in a bid to ensure lawful and compliant procurement.

Supplier empowerment

- We offer irregular business and special training for our suppliers. The demand side is asked to score suppliers who have undergone procurement operations for them.

Volunteering with heart and soul

No matter how small the action may be, every good deed can make a difference. Adhering to our commitment to public welfare, we actively engage in community service. We widely launch volunteer services such as learning from the model soldier Lei Feng and volunteer services for safe travel during holidays. Besides those regular services, we continue to explore new forms of volunteer services. In collaboration with volunteers, we have carried out various activities, including "23·7" super large flood rescue, and volunteer services at the Chairman Mao Memorial Hall, the Third Belt and Road Forum for International Cooperation, and services during the Spring Festival travel rush. These initiatives not only empower volunteers but also inspire others to contribute to the community.

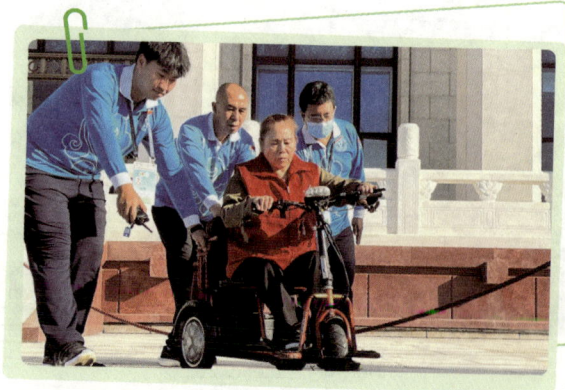

Volunteer service at Chairman Mao Memorial Hall

Volunteer service at bus stops

Cleaning bus stop facilities

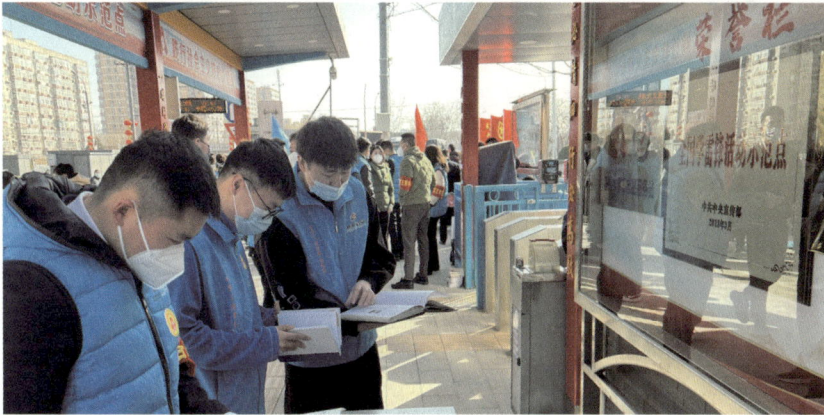

"Learning from the model soldier Lei Feng" volunteer service activity

2023

16,000+
Registered volunteers

200,000+
Volunteers on duty

49,000
Volunteer services

680,000
Cumulative volunteer service hours

■ BPTC was awarded the "Outstanding Company" for its contributions to the Chairman Mao Memorial Hall Volunteer Service Program on the 10th anniversary of the program.

Case: "Learning from the model soldier Lei Feng" volunteer service activity

On the occasion of "Lei Feng Day", BPTC organized a joint activity involving employees and local residents to learn from Lei Feng. As a part of the activity, bus staff educated residents about proper waste sorting, and used hands-on examples to help them understand and correctly dispose of different types of waste. By displaying the works of re-creation using recyclable waste, they called on the general residents to join in the action of waste sorting. In addition, they assisted residents in cleaning and organizing debris and garbage in the community, and wiping and disinfecting public areas, extending their warm-hearted service from the buses to the local community.

Bus staff helps residents clean up their neighborhoods

Taking Actions to Support Rural Vitalization

Donation ceremony for official vehicles and office equipment

Always bearing in mind its responsibility as a state-owned enterprise, BPTC has joined hands with all parties to promoting rural prosperity for realizing a blue print of common prosperity. We take measures to vitalize rural areas with a focus on the collaboration between Beijing and Inner Mongolia as well as key tasks to support economically vulnerable villages. We also facilitate travel for villagers as a part of our "Village Transport" project and collaborate with the Beijing Branch of China Post Group Co., Ltd to develop cooperative delivery services in rural areas. With concrete actions, we aim to bring vibrant growth to rural communities and contribute to a more prosperous and beautiful countryside with better well-being.

2023

○ RMB
1 million
Rural vitalization funds donated to Lhasa Communications Industry Group Co., Ltd.

○ RMB
800,000
Rural vitalization funds donated to Baarin Left Banner, Chifeng, Inner Mongolia

○ RMB
8.32 million
Worth of agricultural and sideline products procured from assistance areas

137
New employees from areas lifted out of poverty

223
Jobs created for rural migrant workers in Beijing

Aiding key areas by targeted assistance

Leveraging our resources endowment and advantages features, we continue to strengthen labor cooperation between the East and West. We have enhanced support in the targeted region, completed the annual task of supporting 3 economically vulnerable villages, and supported rural residents in education, transportation, and village environment improvement on all fronts. Our aim is to make the countryside a better home for local residents.

━ Rural vitalization initiatives ━

Paired assistance	We donated materials to key counties to receive assistance in pursuing rural vitalization and improved production and living facilities at bus depots and stations. We also donated books worth approximately RMB 23,000 to the Hotan Prefecture in Xinjiang.
Industrial development	We assisted various villages in Zhaitang Town, Mentougou District, Beijing, including Gaopu Village, Huanglingxi Village, and Facheng Village, to achieve collective economic growth.
Consumption support	We deepened the "procurement for support" consumption assistance program to encourage our employees to actively purchase agricultural and sideline products from assistance areas.
Employment promotion	We promoted stable employment for rural residents in areas lifted out of poverty through job provision, training, and support for stable jobs and hired five university graduates from paired assistance areas.
Educational improvement	Our technical school admitted 74 new students from rural areas in Western regions and sent Meng Qingke, a teacher from the Department of Automotive Technology of the school, to provide educational aid in Xinjiang.

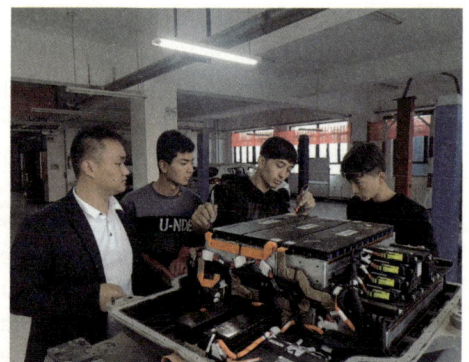

Meng Qingke, a teacher from Beijing Public Transportation Technician College, provides educational aids in Xinjiang

Unblocking rural logistics by integrating transport and postal services

Together with the Beijing Branch of China Post Group Co., Ltd, we uphold the shared mission of "Accompany You All The Way, Serve You Heart and Soul" and "Reaching Everyone Everywhere". We work to explore cooperation in traffic and postal transportation, making use of existing suburban routes to ensure that deliveries are delivered to the targeted post office on time by bus. This has not only improved the efficiency of rural logistics, but also facilitated smoother service for the people. By meeting the travel and postal needs of suburban residents, we are jointly creating a new development model that integrates public transport and postal resources.

Rural delivery service

We are committed to enhancing the convenience of bus travel and solving the challenge of the last mile in logistics. To meet the delivery needs of residents in remote mountain areas in Beijing, we planned the design and operation of delivery routes of BPTC and Beijing Branch of China Post Group Co., Ltd, and increased the frequency of bus services to shorten the delivery time, thus improving the postal service for people living in these areas.

2023

6
Cooperative delivery routes launched by integrating transport and postal services

100
Transportation for deliveries

Nearly
3,000
Deliveries

The cooperative delivery routes in operation

Rural industrial vitalization

We have successfully extended our cooperative shuttle services to rural areas, allowing for the efficient delivery of agricultural products such as mushrooms, grains, vegetables, and fruits to urban areas. This has activated the rural economy by addressing the challenges of selling and delivering agricultural products in mountainous areas, ultimately contributing to increased incomes for local farmers and the overall growth of the local economy.

"The cooperative delivery routes launched by the BPTC and Beijing Branch of China Post Group Co., Ltd is an innovative initiative to support rural vitalization and fulfill our public service mission. This partnership not only improves the efficiency of bus routes but also expands the potential for public transport development and the range of services available to the public. We seize the opportunity presented by the integration of transport and postal services, and leverage our respective service strengths, to enhance the effectiveness of bus services. We are working to deliver better travel services for our passengers."

—Li Peng, Manager of Operation Management, Sixth Passenger Transport Branch

"Building on the foundation of addressing the challenges of the last mile in travel and logistics faced by local villagers, BPTC and Beijing Branch of China Post Group Co., Ltd have leveraged their respective advantages to integrate local culture, geography, regional characteristics, and functional positioning into the service routes. This approach highlights the systematic and innovative nature of our comprehensive support for rural vitalization in Beijing. We continue to enhance the impact of our cultural services, provide spiritual enrichment while delivering high-quality travel and postal services to rural communities."

— Cong Shuwen, General Manager of Marketing, Beijing Branch of China Post Group Co., Ltd

Together for
a Promising Future

Contribution to UN SDGs

Those who work will succeed, and those who walk will arrive at their destination. BPTC remains committed to its founding missions, continues to implement the development plan set for the 14th Five-Year Plan period (2021-2025) with concrete actions, and demonstrates the profound responsibility of a leading nation's public transport enterprise with impressive achievements. From pioneering automated driving bus services to pooling the wisdom and strength of postdoctoral talents, BPTC forge ahead with relentless determination and innovation, so as to work closely with partners to"deliver better public transport services to more people" for a bright future.

Strategic Guidance to Forge Ahead with Hard Work

The future is already unfolding. The blueprint for the sustainable public transport is taking shape, with tangible results emerging from its implementation. At this critical junction in the 14th Five-Year Plan period, BPTC strives to keep pace with the times,vigorously embraces changes, and learns from the past to shape the future. By doing so, we step up efforts to work with more stakeholders to draw up a new blueprint for enhanced mobility and pioneer a new journey of sustainable urban public transport.

Blueprints in Hand, Hard Work Bringing Fruitful Results

In the backdrop of rapid changes in the development of the country and public transport industry, we strive to meet the ever-growing transport needs of passengers for better mobility, remain committed to the positioning of "building a modern comprehensive service provider of urban public transport", and focus on high-quality development and high-quality services, and efficient governance of public transport, achieving remarkable results during the first half of the 14th Five-Year Plan period.

Progress and effectiveness of the major objectives and tasks of the 14th Five-Year Plan

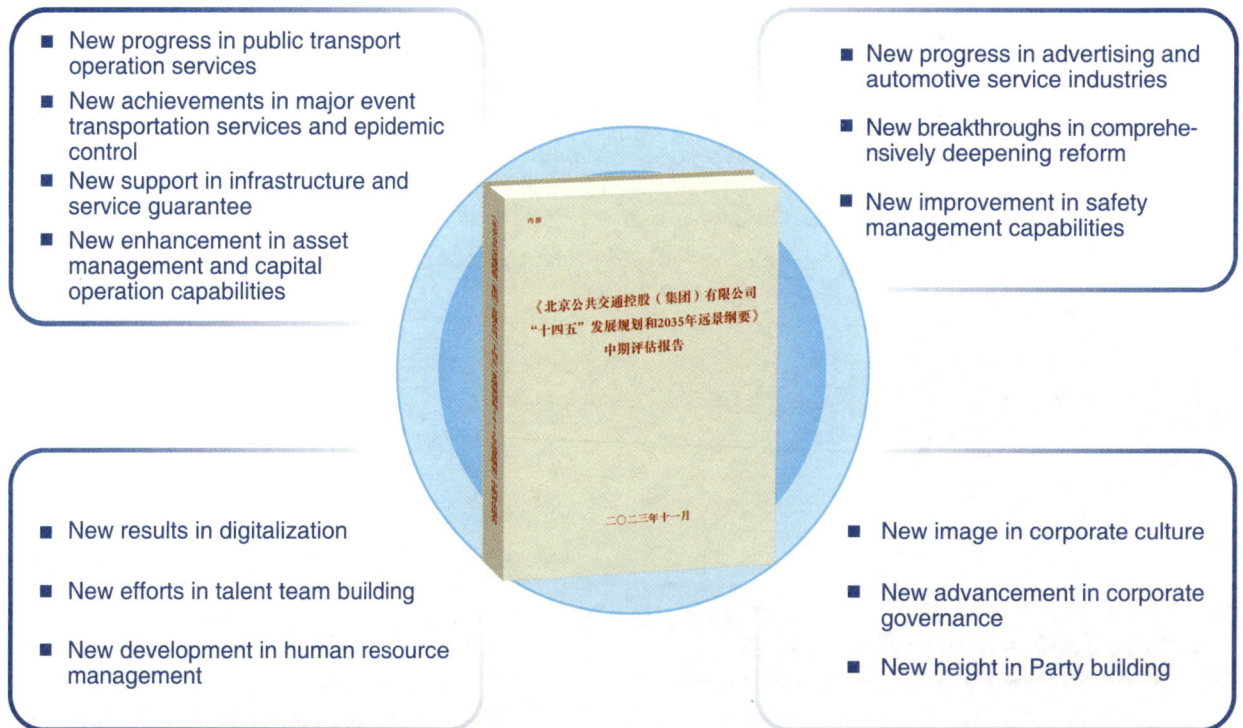

- New progress in public transport operation services
- New achievements in major event transportation services and epidemic control
- New support in infrastructure and service guarantee
- New enhancement in asset management and capital operation capabilities

- New progress in advertising and automotive service industries
- New breakthroughs in comprehensively deepening reform
- New improvement in safety management capabilities

《北京公共交通控股（集团）有限公司
"十四五"发展规划和2035年远景纲要》
中期评估报告

二〇二三年十一月

- New results in digitalization
- New efforts in talent team building
- New development in human resource management

- New image in corporate culture
- New advancement in corporate governance
- New height in Party building

Completion of targets in the mid-stage evaluation of the 14th Five-Year Plan

▶ **80.41**%   **Total assets completed**

▶ **86.71**%   **Owner's equity completed**

▶ **86.16**%   **Owner's equity attributable to the shareholders of Parent company completed**

▶ **99.54**%   **Growth rate of state-owned capital preservation completed**

▶ **105.28**%   **Route and network optimization completed**

BPTC's briefing meeting on the mid-stage evaluation of the 14th Five-Year Plan

Serve the Goals, Setting Sail Toward Success

BPTC goes with the flow to face the changes with flexible strategies and measures. Heading into the second half of the 14th Five-Year Plan, we stay committed to its strategic targets and tasks, objectively analyze external and internal environment, and accurately identify opportunities and challenges. This enables us to stay attuned to the trends of the times, constantly adjust our strategies and policies in accordance with changing circumstances, and strives to usher in a new era of public transport reform and development in the capital of a major nation, charting the course for the industry's future.

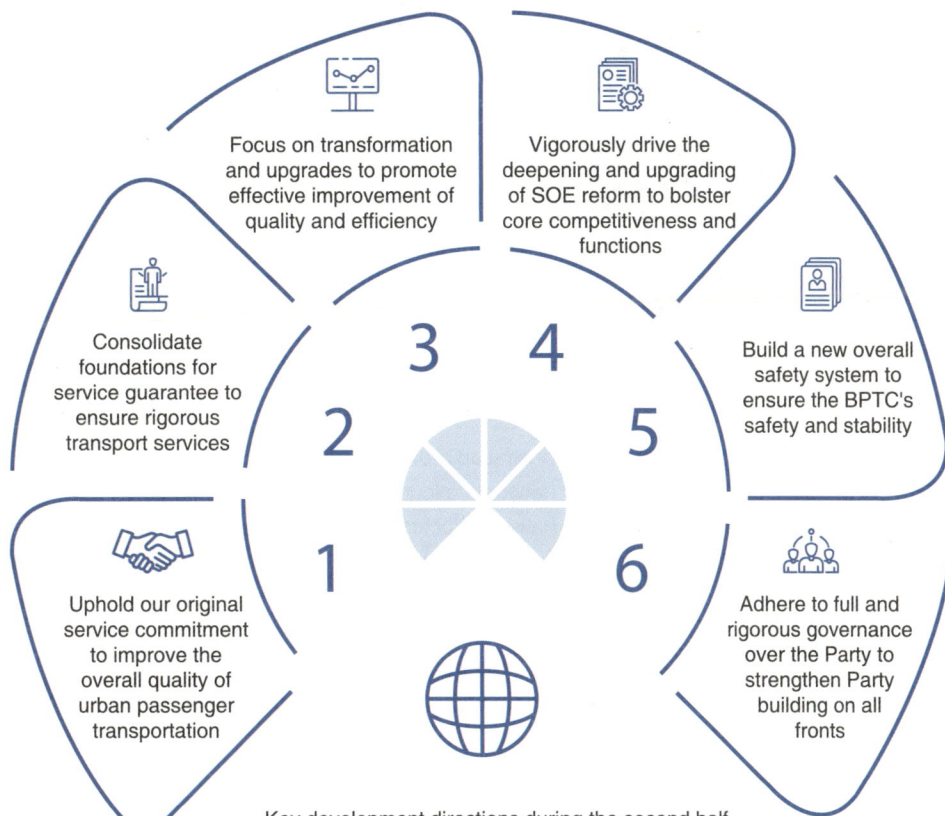

3 — Focus on transformation and upgrades to promote effective improvement of quality and efficiency

4 — Vigorously drive the deepening and upgrading of SOE reform to bolster core competitiveness and functions

2 — Consolidate foundations for service guarantee to ensure rigorous transport services

5 — Build a new overall safety system to ensure the BPTC's safety and stability

1 — Uphold our original service commitment to improve the overall quality of urban passenger transportation

6 — Adhere to full and rigorous governance over the Party to strengthen Party building on all fronts

Key development directions during the second half of the 14th Five-Year Plan period

Automated Driving to Set the Industry Benchmark for New Quality Productive Forces

The automated driving bus represents a successful exploration and innovative application of new business forms, models and technologies. It also serves as a prime example of how to actively integrate into smart cities. Embracing innovation and creativity, BPTC has gone to great length to make automated driving bus services from story-telling concept into a tangible reality in Beijing. We enhanced upstream and downstream resource integration, and deepen the synergy between innovation, industry and talent, so as to advance automated driving bus services with high quality.

Clockwise circular automated driving route for public road test

On-site inspection of road conditions around the automated driving route

BPTC's automated driving test vehicle for Bus Route 1

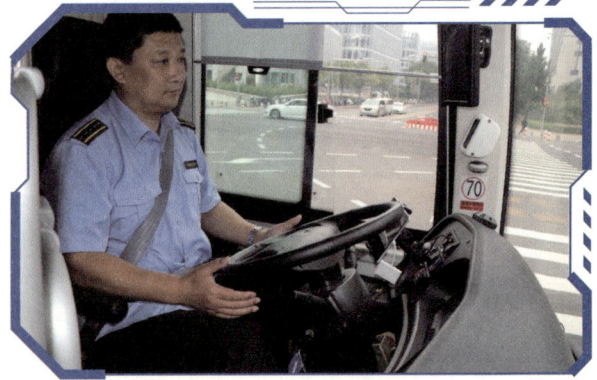
Automated driving safety supervisor monitors vehicle operation in real time

In the process of advancing the automated driving demonstration project, we effectively integrated the various elements in bus operation, such as "people, vehicles, depots, routes, networks, clouds, and data". This facilitates the steady progress and gradual realization of automated driving operations. We have conducted comprehensive research and site visits to domestic and overseas automated driving industry chains, including vehicle manufacturers, autonomous driving technology providers, communications and high-precision map companies. This allows us to gain a deep understanding of the automated driving industry's current situation, experiences and challenges. In September 2023, with the joint efforts of all parties, we put the first two 8.5-meter autonomous buses for regular testing on the urban public roads for the first time after a series of preparations, including perception system calibration, wire control adaptation, control optimization, closed field testing, expert reviews, emergency drills, and license application.

Leads The Future

数字经济
引领未来

"New quality productive forces represent a departure from the traditional economic growth mode and productivity development paths, driven by disruptive breakthroughs in technology, innovative allocation of production factors and the profound industry transformation and upgrading. It is fundamentally characterized by the leap in workers, means of labor, labor objects and their optimized combination, with a significant increase in total factor productivity as the core indicator. The innovation is its feature, with the quality as the key and the advanced productivity as its essence. Under this context, the public transport industry is an important scenario for developing new quality productive forces. New and higher requirements are put forward for workers, means of labor, and labor objects for a traditional labor-intensive enterprise like BPTC. We actively develop automated driving buses, effectively promoting the transformation, upgrading and high-quality development of traditional enterprises with new quality productive forces."

——Mr. Xu Zhengxiang, Secretary General of the High-Level Autonomous Driving Demonstration Zone Special Working Group of BPTC

August 16, 2022
The *Cooperation Agreement of BPTC Autonomous Driving Demonstration Operation Project* officially signed

March-May 2023
Preliminary testing of automated driving vehicles

August 24, 2023
Expert review completed

September 13, 2023
The first automated driving road test license for ordinary large buses obtained

January 3, 2024
Two automated driving buses entered the simulated load testing stage

November 22-23, 2022
4 safety supervisor shortlisted for automated driving bus services

July 7, 2023
Two automated driving buses successfully passed the closed field test

Early September, 2023
Two automated driving buses carried out emergency drill

September 22, 2023
Two automated driving buses started no-load testing

Case: BPTC obtained the first automated driving road test license for ordinary large buses

In September 2023, BPTC as the leading company, along with the consortium consisting of BPTC Yizhuang Operating Company, Foton AUV, and QCraft Inc., obtained road testing licenses issued by the Beijing Traffic Management Bureau.This is the first autonomous driving road testing license for ordinary large passenger buses obtained by BPTC, signifying the transition from closed field testing to open-road testing in real-world public transport scenarios for high-level autonomous driving test vehicles.On-road testing will be conducted in the Beijing intelligent networked vehicle policy pilot zone.

京D7412试
限定在 五环外北京市智能网联汽车区域内行驶
有效期至 2023年 10月 03日

Talent Cultivation to Unleash New Innovative Vibes

Post-doctoral researchers are important national strategic talent forces. BPTC attaches great importance to the introduction and training of post-doctoral talents, and uses the post-doctoral research station as an innovation platform to cultivate interdisciplinary, strategic, and high-caliber innovators with modern urban public transport philosophy and professional practices. We work together to cultivate a new force for the innovation-driven development of public transport industry, so as to infuse the public transport business with new dynamism and vitality.

Multi-channel Support for Postdoctoral Researchers

We make all-out efforts to build a national demonstration base for industry-university-research-application collaborative innovations in the public transport industry, create favorable conditions to cultivate high-caliber talents, and continue to build a new-type public transport think tank with a global vision and competitiveness, with an aim to provide strong intelligent support and talent guarantee for building a modern public transport enterprise.

Select candidates with high standards

Recruitment information is disseminated through multiple channels. With quality-first principle, we strictly evaluate, inspect, and consider factors such as the candidate quality, professional background, and research abilities to expand the scale of the Corporation's postdoctoral station. We have recruited 1 postdoctoral researcher in 2023.

Ramp up efforts to build post-doctoral station

We have proactively communicated with universities such as Beijing Jiaotong University, University of International Business and Economics to sign joint training agreements; organized in-station post-doctoral researchers to apply for general programs, and actively participated in activities organized by the Office of the National Postdoctoral Management Committee, such as the innovation competition.

Organize the mid-term evaluation review for post-doctoral researchers

In November 2023, we invited government authorities, third-party professional research and consulting institutions, upstream and downstream enterprises along the industry chain, and industry experts and scholars to form a review team to conduct mid-term evaluation review for the first two postdoctoral researchers who were onboard in 2022.

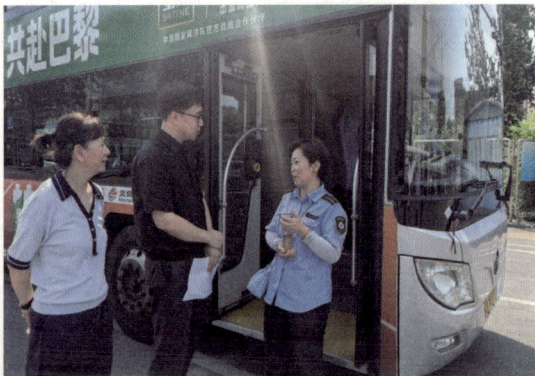

"Drivers are the core talent resources of public transport companies and industry. BPTC has accumulated rich hand-on experiences and massive data resources in the management and the training of the driver team. In the future, I will combine the hot topic of career research, sustainable career theory, with the development of the driver team, and better integrate the corporate spirit of 'putting passengers first, serving with honor' into the cultivation of the driver team."

—Wei Shilong, a postdoctoral researcher who was onboard in 2023

Giving Full Play to Post-doctoral Talents

Since the establishment of the postdoctoral research station, we have actively carried out various research projects ranging from artificial intelligence to automated driving, effectively promote the deep integration of new theories, new technologies with the development of public transport, and give full play to the innovative achievements of postdoctoral talents, thus continuously facilitating the transformation and upgrading of traditional public transport and stimulating the vitality for innovation and creativity of the public transport industry.

Mid-term evaluation review meeting for postdoctoral researchers

In-depth research

Through comprehensive research, benchmarking against best domestic and international best practices, and research on cutting-edge achievements, we have developed operational profiles of BPTC routes based on multi-source data, proposed public transport operation reliability evaluation indicators, and explored more possibilities of new operational and control strategies. We have summarized the operation features of automated driving buses, and give suggestions in terms of the ethical rules of autonomous driving buses, the legal responsibilities of automated driving, the duty of attention of automated driving bus users, and the motivation of drivers to drive. A sustainable career survey on Beijing's ground public transport drivers and a benchmarking study on "decent job" for bus drivers has been conducted, offering suggestions for driver team optimization.

Form the reports

We keep eyes on the latest trends in the development of domestic and foreign public transport industries, compile research reports including *Strategy and Inspiration on International Urban Transport Development, Research Report on BPTC's Operation Services, Research and Reflections on the Driver Management Policy of Transport for London, Analysis Report on Hong Kong Bus Driver Management Policy*, etc., learn from advanced domestic and foreign experiences, and propose corresponding suggestions.

Participate in projects

We retrieve and analyze relevant data and indicators of the public transport development of mega cities home and abroad, and participate in the compilation of *Research Report on the Establishing and Improvement of Operation Service Indicator Evaluation System of BPTC*.

Publish research papers

We publish research papers including *Construction and Application of Cloud Brain for Urban Smart Public Transport, Suggestions for Improving Beijing's Ground Public Transport Operation Services, The Era of Autonomous Driving: Challenges and Responses of Ground Public Transport and Study on Drivers' Acceptance Level of Automated Driving Buses Based on TAM.*

Partnership Building to Expand Network with Collaboration

Public transport development is a global issue. BPTC fully recognizes the importance of "making the benefits of sustainable transport better delivered to people all over the world", actively engage in international public transport exchanges to expand our network. Meanwhile, we endeavor to amplify China's voice on the global stage, and tell Chinese stories well, showcasing China's leap-frog development and achievements in public transport sector. By better integrating "bringing in" with "going global", we contribute wisdom and strength to promote the global sustainable development of transportation.

Interconnected, work together to explore transport blueprint for the future

In 2023, to expand domestic and international industry ecosystem, we participated in and attended activities such as UITP Global Public Transport Summer Summit and COTA International Conference of Transportation Professionals, to continuously expand our international network. Meanwhile, we held business discussions with the UITP headquarters and local Spanish companies, visited the Transports Metropolitans de Barcelona (TMB), Mobileye's blind spot monitoring products, and conducted online exchanges with SBS Transit Ltd. (SBST) of Singapore. We joined hands with all parties to create a new pattern of development emphasizing openness, positive interplay and close coordination of the entire passenger transport industry chain, building a new public transport ecosystem of joint contribution and shared benefits.

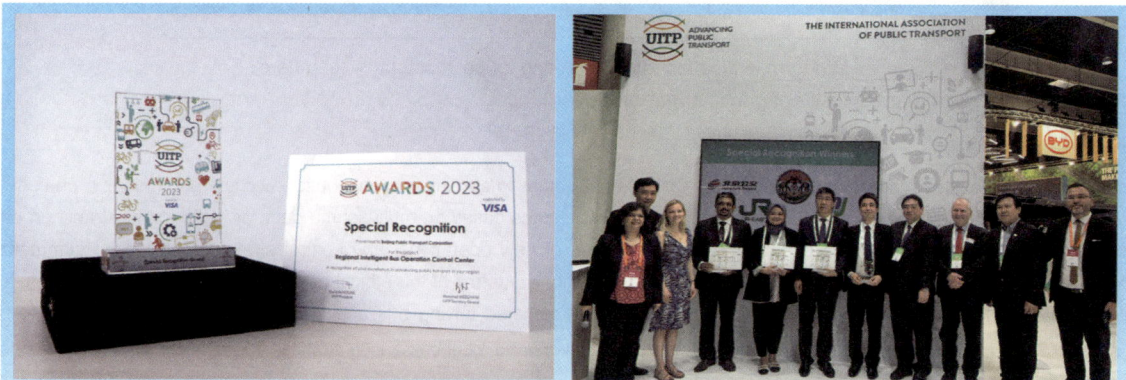

BPTC's regional integrated intelligent operation control reform project was awarded UITP Special Recognition Awards in the 2023 UITP Global Public Transport Summer Summit held by the International Association of Public Transport (UITP)

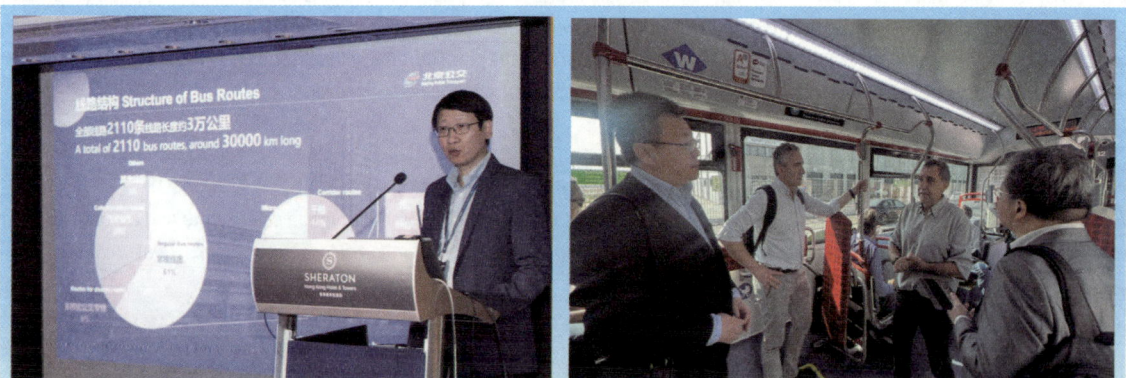

International exchange activities

Learning from international advanced ideas and experiences

We always closely track global public transport industry trends, push forward in-depth international research, and grasp the development trends of public transport industry by learning the latest research results and development dynamics in US, UK, Singapore, Japan and beyond. Meanwhile, we vigorously carry out international benchmarking analysis and research, focus on the mobility patterns, fare structures and the cost-revenue ratios of public transport operators in multiple international metropolitans, and form the analysis report on urban mobility patterns. Through intensive research and learning from international advanced experiences, we inject new vitality and impetus into the development of BPTC, comprehensively promoting the greener, more coordinated and sustainable development of public transport.

Case: Participating in the 23rd COTA International Conference of Transportation Professionals and Contributing BPTC's Solutions to Industry Development

On July 16, 2023, Mr. Xu Zhengxiang, Head of the Strategy, Reform and Development Department, attended on behalf of BPTC the Public Transport High-Quality Development Special Forum of the 23rd COTA International Conference of Transportation Professionals (CICTP 2023) and delivered a speech entitled "Promoting the Modernization of Public Transport Governance System and Capabilities in Mega Cities Under the Guidance of the *Beijing Declaration*". After expounding the background and key points of the *Beijing Declaration*, he discussed his insights on the modernization of public transport governance system and governance capacity in mega cities by combining BPTC's practical experiences, and interacted with international public transport industry scholars focusing on aspects such as "the core of public transport governance: passenger-centered", "institutional mechanism of public transport governance: high-level political leadership" and "path choices of public transport governance: technology empowerment, creating smart public transportation; low-carbon development, creating green public transport; stakeholders cooperation, jointly building a community of development for public transport", etc.

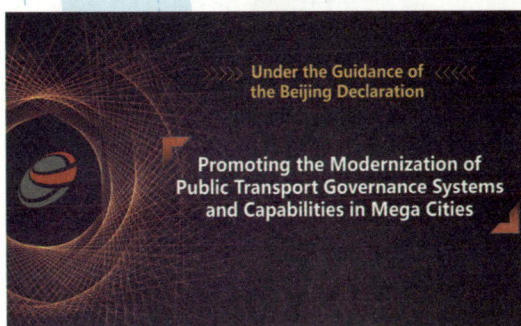

Outlook

Another new chapter is unveiled amid changing times. The year 2024 marks the 75th anniversary of the founding of the PRC. It is also a critical year for realizing the goals and tasks of China's 14th Five-Year Plan. BPTC will continue to forge forward, shoulder our mission, and serve matters of national significance. Focusing on people's needs, we will practice the value of "putting passengers first, serving with honor". Our consistent aspirations and dedication will depict an era of serving the people and shape a new-era BPTC with pioneering innovation and resilience.

We will embrace "Mobility as Life" and practice "Mobility as Service".

Committed to providing better public transport services for more people, we will concentrate on people's growing demand for high-quality, personalized, and intelligent travel, shore up weaknesses, and highlight connection and network optimization to improve efficiency. We will strengthen the integration of the bus and rail transit and optimize network layouts to create a clear-structured ground public transport network with clear functions. Serving the new pattern of the capital's urban development, we will comply with the highest standards to build a new-era system of public transport services compatible with the capital's urban development and the diverse travel expectations of the public. In response to the development of capital functions, we will transform and upgrade our bus depots, fill up the gap in service facilities, and explore more possibilities for providing urban public services. We will continue to promote Beijing-Tianjin-Hebei integrated transport and set the stage for the tenth anniversary of the coordinated development of the Beijing-Tianjin-Hebei region.

We will deepen green development and safeguard a better environment.

Guided by Xi Jinping's Thought on Ecological Civilization, we will stick to the path of eco-prioritized, green, and low-carbon development and contribute to a beautiful China and a beautiful Beijing. As China pushes forward the carbon peaking and carbon neutrality action, we will put into use more new energy vehicles and optimize the energy mix of vehicles. To build a green transport system, we will tap into the potential of green transport and improve the coverage and accessibility of public-transport-first and green travel services to make green travel a trend. We will expand the application of new energy facilities such as supercharging stations and shared charging stations and establish a new energy battery maintenance, recycling, and dismantling industry that is suitable for multi-level battery recycling. In addition, we will fulfill the responsibility of carbon emission control and engage in carbon trading to contribute to better air quality, biodiversity protection, and a beautiful environment in the capital of a great nation.

We will strengthen technology empowerment to create "intelligent public transport 3.0".

We will maximize the value of sci-tech innovation in seeking the best solution, implement the "cloud digital empowerment" and "digital +" actions, and amplify the effects of digitalization in production, operations, management, service, etc. These efforts will help us build a new system of intelligent public transport management such as intelligent operation, intelligent driving, intelligent bus depots, intelligent parks, intelligent office, and intelligent Party building. We will deepen regional intelligent operation control reform and foster "intelligent vehicles", "smart stations", "digital routes", and "dynamic networks". Seizing the opportunity of expanding the Beijing high-level autonomous driving demonstration zone 4.0, the Corporation will make greater efforts in the demonstration and application of public transport autonomous driving in multiple scenarios to set a model of BPTC's autonomous driving operation. We will nurture strong talent strength and stimulate the innovation and creativity of talent, which will lay a solid intellectual foundation for the long-term development of BPTC.

We will embrace openness and coexistence in enriching the "public transport ecosystem".

We will join hands with all stakeholders for a better future, deepen strategic cooperation and exchanges with organizations at home and abroad in more areas, and discuss new cooperation opportunities with partners to promote the healthy, sustainable, and high-quality development of the public transport industry around the world. The fruits of development will be shared with most employees so that bus drivers can have a greater sense of decency and dignity and our employees can have better satisfaction, more sustainable happiness, and greater security. We will consolidate the results of poverty alleviation, serve rural vitalization, and strengthen industrial support for remote areas in the West China and paired assistance areas. We will deepen transport-postal collaboration and cross-sector industrial integration under the framework of "inclusive transport" and make public services equally accessible in urban and rural areas. We will advocate responsible travel and build a favorable environment to help the whole society develop a good pattern of co-building, co-governance, and sharing.

Through a century of trials and tribulations, the great journey continues, and like a mighty roc soaring high, we are now set to reach new heights. As the tide of our times is surging forward, BPTC employees in the new era will remain committed to our dreams fearlessly and keep our actions to create happier and better travel services for people sincerely. With relentless efforts, we will offer public transport service with the highest standards and strong support that satisfy passengers, to write a magnificent chapter on developing public transport in the capital of a great country in the new era.

Key Performance

	Indicators(unit)	2021	2022	2023
Economic Performance	Revenue (RMB billion)	8.191	6.861	8.847
	Total assets (RMB billion)	64.521	64.327	66.577
	Net assets (RMB billion)	42.355	44.440	45.722
	Asset-liability ratio (%)	32.08	30.92	31.32
	Total tax payment (RMB million)	415	289	446
	Number of operating vehicles	32,896	32,783	33,133
	Number of routes in operation	1,225	1,299	1,293
	Annual distance covered by buses (billion kilometers)	1.139	0.984	1.151
	Annual passenger trips of buses (billion)	2.296	1.726	2.087
	Response rate of complaints (%)	100	100	100
	Passenger satisfaction rate (%)	93.49	93.52	94.04
	Supplier audit coverage during the reporting period (%)	100	100	100
	Number of potential suppliers declined due to CSR non-compliance	1	0	0
	Number of suppliers terminated due to CSR non-compliance	1	0	0
	Number of CSR training sessions for suppliers	3	1	4

	Indicators(unit)	2021	2022	2023
Social Performance	Number of employees	89,014	84,211	78,936
	Labor contract rate (%)	100	100	100
	Social insurance coverage (%)	100	100	100
	Percentage of female employees (%)	26.49	25.43	24.46
	Percentage of female management (%)	39.30	40.54	41
	Number of annual paid leaves per capita per annum (days)	10	11	11
	Employee body-check coverage (%)	100	100	100
	Employee turnover (%)	1.73	1.86	1.87

Indicators(unit)	2021	2022	2023
Workplace safety input (RMB billion)	2.408	2.164	2.298
Safety training coverage (%)	100	100	100
Safety drill coverage (%)	100	100	100
Traffic violation rate (%)	0.33	0.27	0.24
Party A's liability accident death rate (passenger/million vehicle km)	0.00307	0.0005	0.0026
Cumulative volunteer service hours (10,000 hours)	99	73	68
Funds to assist employees in need (RMB 10,000)	209	303.15	485.12
Number of employees in need assisted	1,090	860	1,702

Social Performance

Indicators(unit)	2021	2022	2023
Number of obsolete vehicles	1,071	1,619	1,642
Carbon emissions (tonnes)	288,376	246,261	280,353
CO_2 emissions (tonnes)	1,057,378	902,957	1,027,962
Percentage of non-fossil fuel energy (%)	14.40	15.92	17.40
Percentage of buses using new energy and clean energy (%)	91.06	94.27	94.70
Gross annual energy consumption (tce)	495,424	418,298	453,639
Energy consumption per unit of gross output value (tce/RMB 10,000)	0.24	0.20	0.22
Natural gas consumption (10,000 kg)	18,414	15,786	16,329
Electric power consumption (10,000 kWh)	53,208	37,817	49,345
Diesel oil consumption (10,000 liters)	7,172	5,113	6,758
Annual drinking water consumption (10,000m³)	263	208	223.7
NOx emissions reduction (tonnes)	123.41	57.05	236.86
Particulate emissions reduction (tonnes)	0.17	0.13	0.20
Hydrocarbon emissions reduction (tonnes)	80.78	30.72	60.21

Environmental Performance

Report Content Indicators

Contents		CASS-CSR 4.0 on Public Transport Industry		GRI Standards	Page number
Cover Story					P1
Preface					P4-P5
Message From the Senior Management		P2.1 P2.2 G3.1 G6.2		2-14 2-16 2-17 2-22	P6-P7
About BPTC	Corporate Profile	P4.1 P4.3 P4.4		2-1 2-6 2-7	P8
	Corporate Culture	P4.1 G1.1		2-6	P9
	Organization Structure	P4.2		2-9	P10-11
	Corporate Governance	M1.1 M1.3 M1.4 M2.6 M3.1 M3.5 M3.6 S1.1 S1.2 S1.4		2-13 2-16 2-27	P12-15
CSR Management	CSR Philosophy	G1.2		2-22	P16
	Management Approach	G2.1 G2.2 G2.3 G3.1 G3.2 G3.3 G4.1		2-12 2-13	P16
	CSR Communication	G6.1 G6.2 G6.3 M3.4 M3.6		2-16 2-29 3-1 3-2 3-3	P17-19
	Highlights in 2023	P3.1		2-16	P20-21
	CSR Honors	A3			P22-23
Unchanged Aspiration and New Glories		M2.1 M2.4 M3.6 S4.1		203-1 413-1 413-2	P24-43
EnjoyableTravel: Offering More Options	Easy Travel in a Prosperous City	M2.1 M2.2 M2.3 M2.4 M2.5		2-6 203-1 413-1 413-2	P46-49
	Responsiveness to Passengers' Needs	M2.1 M2.2 M2.14 M2.16 M2.18 M3.1		203-1 413-1	P50-53
	Digital Empowerment for Intelligent Travel	M2.1 M2.4 M2.5 M2.7 M3.6		2-6	P54-55
	Safety Regarded as our Priority	S3.1 S3.2 S3.3 S3.4 S3.5 S3.6		403-2 403-7 403-10 416-1 416-2	P56-59
	Coordinated Beijing-Tianjin-Hebei Development In the Last Decade	M2.1 M2.2 M2.4 M3.6 S1.4		2-24	P60-61
Mission Delivery: Going Through Thick and Thin Together	No Fear of Challenges and Devotion to Guard	S4.6 S4.8 S4.10		413-1	P64-67
	Exceptional Services for Grand Events	M2.1 S1.4 S4.6 S4.8 S4.10		2-6 2-24 413-1	P68-69
Shared Journey: Creating a Brighter Future	Enjoying the Beautiful Scenery on the Eco-friendly Trip	E1.3 E1.5 E1.6 E1.7 E1.9 E1.10 E1.11 E2.1 E2.2 E2.3 E2.4 E2.5 E2.6 E2.8 E2.9 E2.11 E2.12 E2.15 E2.21 E2.22 E2.24 E3.1 E3.2 E3.6		301-2 301-3 302-1 302-3 302-4 302-5 305-1 305-7 306-2	P72-74
	Unleashing Full Potential of Employees	S2.1 S2.2 S2.3 S2.4 S2.5 S2.7 S2.8 S2.9 S2.10 S2.11 S2.12 S2.13 S2.14 S2.15 S2.16 S2.17 S2.18 S2.20		2-7 2-19 401-1 401-2 403-1 403-2 403-3 403-5 403-6 403-7 404-2 405-1 407-1	P75-79
	Strengthening Bonds with Community	M3.8 S4.1 S4.2 S4.3 S4.4 S4.6 S4.8 S4.10 S4.11		203-1 413-1 413-2 414-1	P80-83
	Taking Actions to Support Rural Vitalization	S4.5 S4.6 S4.8 S4.12 S4.13 S4.14		203-1 413-1	P84-85
Together for a Promising Future	Strategic Guidance to Forge Ahead with Hard Work		G1.1 M3.4 M3.6	2-22 2-23 2-24	P88-89
	Automated Driving to Set the Industry Benchmark for New Quality Productive Forces		M2.1 M2.4 M2.5 M2.7 M3.6	2-16	P90-91
	Talent Cultivation to Unleash New Innovative Vibes		M2.4 S2.14 S2.16	404-2	P92-93
	Partnership Building to Expand Network with Collaboration		M3.4 M3.6	2-6	P94-95
Outlook		M2.1 M2.4 M3.6 S2.16 E1.7 A1		2-6 2-16	P96-97
Key Performance		M2.18 M3.9 M3.13 S2.1 S2.3 S2.5 S2.9 S2.15 S2.18 S2.20 S3.4 S3.5 S3.6 E2.4 E2.5 E2.9 E2.25 A2		2-7 201-1 302-1 302-3 302-4 302-5 303-5 305-1 403-5 405-1	P98-99
Report Content Indicators		A5			P100
About This Report		P1.1 P1.2 P1.3 A6		2-3 2-4	P101

About This Report

This is the 11th CSR report issued by Beijing Public Transport Corporation. We hope to disclose the Corporation's ideas, actions, and achievements in sustainable development to stakeholders and make it a tool for deeper stakeholder communication and collaboration, and eventually facilitate the sustainable development of the Corporation and society.

New contents

This report has added a new chapter entitled "Unchanged Aspiration: Earning New Glories", which focuses on the innovation and reform of BPTC in delivering our aspirations and serving the people. It highlights the vivid practices of BPTC in deepening the service concept, perfecting services, and expanding the service scope in 2023.

Reporting period

The report covers information about BPTC from January 1 to December 31, 2023. To enhance comparability of the data and continuity of the content, and the time effectiveness of publicity, some parts may cover information beyond the aforementioned scope.

Reporting scope

This report mainly discloses Beijing Public Transport Corporation's willingness, actions and performance in practicing sustainable development and fulfilling social responsibilities. For better expression and readability, Beijing Public Transport Corporation is also referred to as "BPTC" and "We".

Data source

All data used in the report is from the BPTC's official documents and statistical reports. The quoted data is the finalized statistics. In case of any inconsistency between the financial data and those in the annual audit report, the annual audit report shall prevail. We guarantee that all data and contents have been reviewed by BPTC's management prior to the release of this report. We pledge that the report is free of false records, misleading statements or major omissions in the report, and we are responsible for the objectivity and authenticity of the data related to BPTC in this report.

Reference

The report is prepared in accordance with Guidance on Social Responsibility (ISO 26000:2010) issued by International Organization for Standardization (ISO), GRI Sustainability Reporting Standards (GRI Standards) issued by Global Sustainability Standards Board (GSSB), The 2030 Agenda for Sustainable Development of United Nations, Chinese national social responsibility standard, Guidance on Corporate Social Responsibility Reporting (GB/T 36001-2015), Guidelines on Corporate Social Responsibility Reporting for Chinese Enterprises (CASS-CSR 4.0) on Public Transport Industry issued by Chinese Academy of Social Sciences, The Stock Exchange of Hong Kong Environmental, Social and Governance Reporting Guidelines (HK-ESG),which balance both national standards and international regulations.

Preparation process

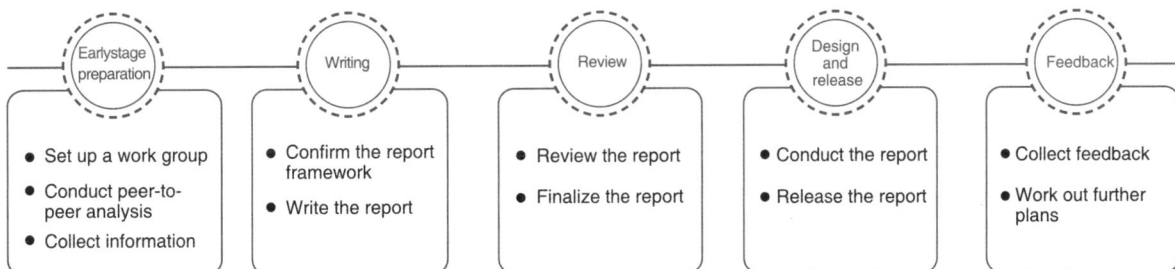

Earlystage preparation	Writing	Review	Design and release	Feedback
• Set up a work group • Conduct peer-to-peer analysis • Collect information	• Confirm the report framework • Write the report	• Review the report • Finalize the report	• Conduct the report • Release the report	• Collect feedback • Work out further plans

Access to the report

This report is available in both Chinese and English versions. We provide printed forms, and you can purchase it online to get more information about our social responsibility performance.

Address: No. 29, Lianhuachi Xili, Fengtai District, Beijing.

Contact: Lan Yifan

Postal code: 100161

Tel: 0086-10-63960088

Scan the QR code and share your feedback with us

SDG Solutions
国际SDG的中国行动

SDG GOOD PRACTICES

金钥匙·SDG领跑企业
GoldenKey·SDG Forerunner

北京公共交通控股（集团）有限公司

可持续发展是破解全球性问题的"金钥匙"。贵公司积极行动，精准识别问题症结，以创新的解决方案突破问题难点，为实现联合国2030年可持续发展目标贡献力量，入选"金钥匙·SDG领跑企业"。

Sustainable development is the "golden key" to solve global problems. The company has been selected as "Golden Key-SDG Forerunner" for its proactive actions to accurately identify the problems and provide with innovative solutions to contribute to the achievement of the UN 2030 Sustainable Development Goals.

可持续发展 经济导刊
CHINA SUSTAINABILITY TRIBUNE

图书在版编目（CIP）数据

北京公交社会责任报告. 2023 / 北京公共交通控股（集团）有限公司编著. -- 北京 ：经济管理出版社，2024. -- ISBN 978-7-5243-0130-1

Ⅰ. F512.71

中国国家版本馆CIP数据核字第2025HN2648号

责任编辑：张莉琼
责任印制：许　艳

出版发行：经济管理出版社
（北京市海淀区北蜂窝 8 号中雅大厦 A 座 11 层　100038）
网　　址：www.E-mp.com.cn
电　　话：（010）51915602
印　　刷：唐山玺诚印务有限公司
经　　销：新华书店
开　　本：889mm×1194mm/16
印　　张：13.25
字　　数：382 千字
版　　次：2024 年 12 月第 1 版　2024 年 12 月第 1 次印刷
书　　号：ISBN 978-7-5243-0130-1
定　　价：138.00 元（全二册）

联系地址：北京市海淀区北蜂窝 8 号中雅大厦 11 层
电话：（010）68022974　　邮编：100038